Library of Congress Cataloging in Publication Data

Bretón, Marcos.
    Away games : the life and times of a Latin
baseball player / Marcos Bretón and José Luis Villegas.
            p.   cm.
Originally published:
New York : Simon & Schuster, c1999
Includes bibliographical references and index.
        ISBN 0-8263-2232-8 (pbk.)
1. Tejada, Miguel, 1976–   .
2. Baseball players—Dominican Republic—Biography.
3. Oakland Athletics (Baseball team).
I. Villegas, José Luis.
II. Title.

GV865.T35 B74 2000
        99-048734

All photos appear courtesy of José Luis Villegas

ACKNOWLEDGMENTS

THIS BOOK would not have been possible without the love and support of our families. Thank you to our fathers, Reynaldo Bretón and Manuel Villegas, two immigrants from Mexico who worked hard, raised two families, taught us to be proud of who we were, to hold on to our Spanish, and to love baseball. *Gracias,* Papis! Love also to two little miracles—Jacqueline and Jeraline Villegas—for all the joy and pride they've brought their parents. To Rodrigo and Nina Bretón for all their love and support. The Villegas siblings: Connie, Carmen, Janie, Gloria, Mary, Manuel, and Lorenzo. Allen and Mamie Wong. Erwin and Lisa Wong. To our friends who have become family, we thank Aaron Walter Crowe, for his undying friendship and assistance in the research of this book. Josh du Lac, Maria Camposeco, Doug Moran, Ken Chavez, and John Trotter, for caring so much. We owe a large debt of gratitude to everyone at the Alicia Patterson Foundation, especially to Margaret Engel, for her guidance and compassion. Thanks also to our agent, Peter Sawyer of the Fifi Oscard Agency, for believing. To our editors at Simon & Schuster, Dan Lane and Jeff Neuman, for taking a chance. Many, many thanks to our editors at the *Sacramento Bee*, especially Gregory Favre, for being so supportive. To Rick Rodriguez, for being a wonderful role model. And Mark Morris, for helping us in so many ways. Thanks also to Peter Bhatia, Emmett Jordan, Merrill Oliver, Mort Saltzman, Tom Negrete, Ken Cody, Dan McGrath, Genaro Molina, R. B. Brenner, Mack Lundstrom, Mariann Barsolo, Frank Scatoni, Randy Hagihara, Sam Abell of *National Geographic*, and Art Carey and his red pencil. There were many people whose time and assistance were invaluable, including Enrique Soto, the Tejada family, and the people of Bani, in the Dominican Republic; Simon Baigelman of the Windemere Hotel in New York City; James Lloyd Gates, Jr., Tim Wiles, Bruce Markusen, and Scot Mondore of the National Baseball Hall of Fame and Library; Mr. and Mrs. Carlos Madé of New York City; Vidal Maldonado of the Pedrin Zorilla League; Mito Rivera; Sandy Alderson, Raymond Abreu, Mike Quade, Luis Martinez, Tomas Silverio, Ron Plaza, and Eric Carrington of the Oakland Athletics; the 1996 West Michigan Whitecaps; Pedro Gomez; Luis Rodriguez Mayoral; and all the current and former players who shared their time and stories with us between 1993 and 1997. *Gracias a todos!*

To our beautiful wives, Jeannie Wong and Ruth Villegas, for their love, their friendship, their devotion, and their inspiration.

And to the memories of our mothers, Consuelo Villegas and Elodia Bretón. They will always be in our hearts.

IN MEMORY OF

Justo Bretón y Alejandrina Turnbull de Bretón
Anacleto Martinez y Hermila Garcia de Martinez
Mora Tejada
Nazario Velasquez y Rosario Lopez de Velasquez
Basilio Villegas y Eduarda Najera de Villegas

CONTENTS

Introduction

THE DREAM

A RHYTHMIC CHANT, a joyous noise drawn from the soul of Africa rang through the barrio of *Los Barrancones* in the Dominican Republic. The skies overhead—brilliant blue one moment, dark and foreboding the next—were opening up, dropping a warm, stinging rain on faded, pastel-colored dwellings, on pigs and dogs fighting for scraps of food, grizzled men in baseball caps, youths swilling cheap rum, and naked children playing next to girls dressed in pink satin party dresses. It was a Sunday morning, a special day of belated commemoration for the loss of a woman, both wife and mother, heart and soul, to one destitute family in this Caribbean nation—an island where natives and African slaves were dominated first by Spanish conquistadors and then, in this century, by U.S. Marines and the long arm of American culture.

It was February 1997. Miguel Tejada was twenty years old. And he was joining relatives and friends as they chanted and prayed for the memory of his mother, who had died in 1989. As his entire barrio worshiped amid the squalor they have always known, Tejada knew he was at a crossroads in his young life: While still rooted in a level of Third World poverty that has no equal in the United States, Tejada had nonetheless become a vessel of hope for the hopeless gathered before him in their Sunday best. He was the baseball star, the five-foot-ten-inch marvel who could play shortstop like a wizard, run with explosive speed, throw with power and accuracy, and launch towering, majestic home runs. A former shoeshine boy who used to beg for spare change in his bare feet, whose only real education was an education of hunger, Tejada's baseball skills had moved him within a heartbeat of buying his family out of economic misery. If Tejada reached his goal and made it to the major leagues as national publications and baseball scouts predicted, he would carry on a legacy begun in 1902—a full forty-five years before Jackie Robinson was credited with breaking the color barrier.

Making the majors would also mean Tejada would have achieved the Dominican dream—a passion shared by the thousands of impoverished boys who stake their lives on a deeper, more poignant version of the American dream where baseball is their only hope. A dream that is bittersweet because it is so ironic.

For Miguel Tejada, making it would mean succeeding in a country that has invaded the Dominican Republic twice this century, that controls the Dominican economy and the hearts and ambitions of all young Dominicans who either have traveled to the United States, want to live there, or have family and friends there. For Tejada, it would also mean excelling where he isn't understood, far from all he has ever known, around average Americans who, to him, seem like millionaires, and in a game where he is an outsider.

Though shared by other Spanish-speaking nations and territories of the Caribbean, this passion is not felt as deeply as it is in the Dominican—the poorest country in baseball's Spanish-speaking world. Not coincidentally, this island of 8 million people sends the most Latin players to the major leagues.

Tejada was the latest street kid turned hot prospect—and everyone around him knew it.

Indeed, gathered in eager anticipation were distant cousins and suddenly solicitous neighbors, old friends, new acquaintances, and people who could barely clothe their children. Spurred by love and desperation, good intentions and barely concealed opportunism, all wanted a piece of Tejada, the very first from *Los Barrancones* to ever have a chance at getting out.

Tejada prepared himself for this day as best he could, but it wasn't long before he retreated to the stone-floored hut he shared with his father and six other family members. Cloistered inside, his privacy protected only by the stained bedsheet that passes for his bedroom door, Tejada hardly looked like the future millionaire that everyone from *USA Today* to *The Sporting News* and the Oakland Athletics predicted he would become.

Tejada's high cheekbones and bright, dark eyes projected a look of serenity that masked the emotions churning inside him. On this day, his beaming smile was nowhere to be found. A sweaty mass of humanity was gathering before a makeshift shrine to his mother, which had been set up on a frayed mahogany table in the Tejada family home. On the table were a blue wooden crucifix and oil paintings of the savior, Jesus Christ, an invading Spanish soldier trampling a dark-skinned peasant while riding a charging white steed, and a bearded Moses proclaiming the Ten Commandments. They danced before these symbols, chanting and singing, as, outside, six young men pounded hand-carved wooden drums that had been heated at an open fire to bring out a fuller, richer sound. The drummers' shouts and hollers grew louder and louder, piercing the prayers led by an elderly shaman, who struggled to keep her composure as she read from the Gospel, burned a sweet, smoky incense, and blessed all in the house with holy water contained in a Mickey Mouse glass.

While the shaman sprayed the water around the room with a ginger leaf, Tejada's eldest half-sister, Augustina, a heavy-set woman of forty, bolted to her feet, stormed outside and berated the drummers. "Shut up!" came her muffled shout. "This is a holy day. We can hear all of you in there." With that, the men scattered in different directions, all bearing looks of anger and fear, like little boys chastised by their mothers. They waited anxiously for a time, but before the shaman had completed her mass, they took the drums and stormed the house. Beginning slowly until all could get the rhythm, the music built methodically, and once all had locked in on the beat, the chant took off like a bird in flight. Children and adults were drawn to the Tejada home by the wondrous sound from within. Soon, fifty people crammed into a space where fifteen would have been crowded. Outside, young and old peered through wooden window slats and moved along with the music.

It was a beat that soared higher and higher on the single spiritual chant of "Gloria . . . Gloria . . . Gloria . . . Gloria." Finally, Tejada came out from his hiding place and began making his way toward the memorial for his mother. No one, not even Tejada's father, knew for sure what had killed her. They thought it might have been pneumonia. Their poverty had prevented them not only from getting her adequate medical care, but also from getting definitive answers on the cause of her death. All the family could do was accept the end when the end came.

On this day, resplendent in a silver necklace with an eagle-shaped pendant, Tejada felt strong, and he was greeted like a young monarch about to ascend the throne. Sitting down among friends, neighbors and family, old men sipping rum knelt at Tejada's feet in unvarnished adoration. Women brought their children before him, as if asking Tejada to bless them. At one point, a distant aunt grabbed her seven-year-old by the arm and, dripping with disgust, said, "Look, Miguel. He's afraid of the ball." The mother then gazed upon her son as if he were useless. Miguel looked at the boy with a pained expression. With his eyes he seemed to be asking, "What do you want me to do about it?"

It's not that Tejada wasn't happy to be among his people. He was. But the pressure was clearly taking its toll. After the season Tejada had in 1996, this was understandable. As a shortstop with the Class A Modesto Athletics of the California League, regarded as one of the toughest minor league circuits, Tejada played the American game with such flair and abandon that he could make even calloused baseball veterans giggle.

Named to the California League's All-Star team, Tejada hit 20 home runs for the season. That is a remarkable feat for a shortstop, the hardest position in the game and one where weak-hitting little guys with a flair for glove work still far outnumber the special players like Tejada—those who can make the great plays while striking fear into the hearts of pitchers. Tejada likely would have led his team with 30 home runs or more had he not missed nearly a month of the season with a hairline fracture in his left thumb.

After the season, he was named the most exciting player of

the California League and its top prospect. *USA Today* wrote that he was the most gifted shortstop in the minor leagues. *The Sporting News* picked him as one of five "can't miss" players on the rise. (A testament to the growing power of Latin talent in baseball, four of these five players picked by *The Sporting News* that year were Dominican.) In those moments between the lines, it was as if Tejada had taken all the hunger, all the fear, all the sorrow, and all the longing of his young life and used it as a warrior would use a weapon. And it was then, during the game, that his spirit overcame his poverty, his instincts overcame his lack of education, and his dreams overcame his reality. If he played well in 1997, it was almost assured he would reach the major leagues. Until then, however, Tejada was dancing on a string, living an existence where he only truly came to life when he was on the field—a life where the miserable reality of his barrio was only a shattered knee or a broken limb away. All of this was on his mind as he was led into his house for a final blessing for his mother.

The music and the chanting subsided, leaving a roomful of limp, sweating family members, squinting from the burning of incense and the powerful afternoon sun now burning high in suddenly clear skies. Miguel held hands with his family as a holy woman read from the Bible. Then his sister Augustina walked up to him, looked deep into his eyes, and with tears streaming down her cheeks, haltingly spoke for her family:

"When Miguel was a little boy, he was so good to our mother, so sweet. And from the time he was little, his brother would say that he was good at baseball, that he was good enough to be a major leaguer. Miguel would come home from playing, and he would take our mother by the hand and say, 'Mama, someday I'm going to reach the major leagues. Some day, I'm going to make a lot of money and I promise you, I'll buy you a house. Some day that's going to happen.' "

Pausing for a moment, she continued, "Mama, you didn't live long enough to see that day. So now we ask of you Lord, to please bless Miguel as he goes to America. He's so close to reaching that goal. Please give him the strength to make it, Lord. Give him the strength to make his wish for our mother come true."

Tejada stood impassively as his sister spoke. He almost

seemed embarrassed. When she finished, he embraced her. He then embraced his father and other members of the family. And as the drummers began playing again, Tejada moved toward the door, a distant look in his eyes. In three days' time, he was scheduled to fly on a first-class ticket from the Dominican capital to Phoenix for the annual rite of spring training. For the first time, he was going with the major league players, booked in a first-rate hotel and set to earn major league expense money. If he excelled during the exhibition season, there were whispers that Tejada could be the starting shortstop for the Athletics on Opening Day, 1997.

That would be quite an accomplishment for a young man whose exceptional services were acquired by the Athletics for only two thousand dollars—a tiny fraction of what American players of lesser talent can command. When the offer came in 1993, Tejada was seventeen and earning poverty wages by working in a garment factory, ironing shirts, pressing pants, growing used to his sweat smelling like bleach. No one from his barrio had ever finished school or become any more than what he already was—dirt poor—so Tejada took the money and gave it to his father. He didn't have college offers to use as leverage against his meager bonus, or agents who could protect his interests, or parents who could help him maneuver through the land mines of modern-day major league sports. He was just a kid with precious few English skills and no other compelling options in his life but to play baseball.

The way major league baseball saw it, they were doing Tejada a favor—giving him a big opportunity. That's what the Athletics told Tejada when they signed him, and, in one sense, they were right: He had nothing else going for him. But the Athletics also were getting something special, a potential multi-million-dollar talent for the bargain price of what one major league player gets for a couple of weeks' meal money. In this sense, Tejada is connected to almost every Latin who has ever played major league baseball. Latins have always been attractive to major league scouts because they could be signed for less than American players, providing cheap labor, like so many other Latin immigrants in other walks of life.

In his barrio, surrounded by his people and filled with the memory of his mother, none of this seemed to matter to Tejada.

"I just want to get there," he said of his pending journey to Phoenix and his chance to play alongside superstars like Jose Canseco and Mark McGwire. "I want to show what I have, to prove what I can do."

He couldn't know then that fate was conspiring against him, that his journey would be even more treacherous than he had imagined. Tejada had already traveled a hard road just to get where he was on that day of his mother's memorial. Indeed, her death was not even the most difficult obstacle he would have to overcome. *"Solo dios sabe que me espera en la vida,"* said Tejada.

Only God knows what life has in store for me.

Try as he might, Tejada could find no more certainties as darkness fell on the Dominican and he headed for a nightclub where he could listen to music among friends. As he sat quietly amid the laughter and strains of Dominican songs of longing, loneliness, and desire, Tejada suddenly said to no one in particular, "I know I'm going to make it."

When no one responded, he spoke again the ambition of millions of young men like him, "I know I'm going to be the one."

1

MIGUEL TEJADA

As HE WOULD BE for most of his early life, Miguel Odalis Tejada was malnourished on the day of his birth—May 25, 1976. His mother couldn't afford to see a doctor while she carried Miguel in her womb, nor could she afford to stop working until just before Miguel was born.

"My father didn't want any more kids, but my mother did," Miguel says today. "I was a surprise. And when I was born I was ugly, ugly, ugly." He scrunches up his face as he says this, imitating the frowning baby his family says he was—a scowling infant with unattractive blotches on his dark skin. "My father said they thought I was going to die, that I looked like I was sick."

Miguel was the eighth child born to a family living in a shantytown outside the city of Bani, which sits forty miles southwest of Santo Domingo, the Dominican capital. His parents, Daniel and Mora Tejada, already had two sons together— Juansito and Denio. In addition, Mora had four girls with another man, while Daniel had another son.

By the time Miguel was born, most of the older children were already working.

Miguel would work as well, first earning money at the same age American kids are usually starting kindergarten.

In Miguel's family, the boys shined shoes or helped their father work piecemeal construction jobs, moving earth, stacking concrete blocks, or mixing mortar that would stick to their fingers and legs long after they had given up trying to wash it off. The girls in Miguel's family cleaned and cooked for others as their mother did.

As a toddler, little Miguel was like other dark-skinned babies at the bottom of the Dominican's socioeconomic scale. He would ramble around a dirt road in front of his family's dwelling completely naked, unprotected from the filth of farm animals roaming freely amid raw sewage. Today, it is still very common to see impoverished babies completely nude in the barrios and shanties of the Dominican.

To the unaccustomed, the scene is at first reminiscent of something out of a *National Geographic* special—like a scene out of an African village.

The difference between the Dominican and Africa is that in the barrios of Miguel's youth, squalor commingled with television antennas and constant reminders of the United States. All around, Miguel's neighbors stored their water in empty Clorox bottles while wearing clothes donated by U.S. Catholic charities—making it very common to see rail-thin, barefoot Dominican kids wearing faded T-shirts from some Elks Lodge in Ohio or a bowling shirt from a company team in Pennsylvania. Seemingly everyone wore a frayed baseball cap or owned a beat-up Zenith television set or dreamed of owning a fancy American car.

Miguel's brothers were like any other Dominican boys. They played baseball day and night. Miguel's older brother Juansito, hobbled since childhood by a poorly healed broken right leg, played with verve and skill—deftly fielding balls fashioned from balled-up rags and running aggressively on calloused feet hardened by countless hours of playing on jagged rocks and pebbles. Miguel's other brother Denio was also very good.

His father, Daniel, had been a ballplayer as well, but in his day the game was just a diversion for the impoverished, nothing more. In fact, the Tejada boys had no real thoughts of being major leaguers. They were so poor and their lives so remote, it would have been ludicrous to dream of such a thing. Boys like them had become big leaguers with some regularity since the very first Dominican—Ozzie Virgil—suited up for the New York Giants in 1956. But after an initial burst in the late 1950s that produced future Hall of Famer Juan Marichal and the three Alou brothers—Felipe, Matty, and Jesus, all of the San Francisco Giants—the presence of Dominicans in major league baseball could hardly be described as a force. Not until the mid-to-late 1980s would Dominicans explode on the major league scene, fueled by the realization of baseball men that, with the proper work, large numbers of players could be produced for very little money. That explosion would come too late for Juansito and Denio Tejada. Instead, their lives would be marked by two disasters, the first of which came on a Friday, August 31, in 1979.

Hurricane David was the most powerful weather system to strike the Dominican in the twentieth century, leveling city and countryside and 90 percent of the nation's crops and pounding the island with thirty-foot waves that kept coming for five days, spurred on by a tropical storm that moved in after the eye of David careened northward toward the Florida Keys.

Satellite photos taken at the time show the Caribbean as a black background with the outline of neighboring Cuba spared by a confluence of killer clouds swallowing up the Dominican. To look at the photos, it's as if the entire island had been erased.

When the rain and 150-mph winds finally stopped, David had caused $1 billion in damage while killing thousands and leaving one hundred thousand Dominicans homeless—including the Tejadas.

To this day, Miguel doesn't remember much of the storm or its aftermath, but his family does—they lost everything. Which is to say, they lost what little they had. All their clothing, their beat-up stove, an antiquated radio, their food, and what few family mementos they had.

All that survives are memories of displacement and a desperate trek into Bani, searching for survival. Like most refugees, the Tejadas were not accepted with open arms and joined a substantial homeless population still in shock from the ferocity of David and the devastation it had wrought. It would be roughly two weeks before they found a spot in a refugee camp where more than two hundred people lived on top of each other.

• • •

NECESSITY DROVE Miguel to build a little box and hustle shoeshines from men working or gathering in Bani's main plaza, a tree-lined square like thousands of others in Latin America. Miguel would hoard whatever coins he could get and share them with his brothers, who would use the money to buy bread or fruit. During this time, Miguel's mother was often away in Santo Domingo, cleaning houses and working in a bakery. On the weekends, Miguel would eagerly await her arrival and the anticipated dispersal of crumbling pieces of week-old breads and pastries. He had begun going to school by this point, but his attendance was sporadic. In a sense, these years were like a blur of hunger, a time without roots or a sense of stability that made an indelible mark and colored his every move years later.

For five years, Miguel lived this way. When he was eight, his family relocated to a slum in Bani dubbed *Los Barrancones*. In the Spanish language, the word *barrancon* means an obstacle of great danger, and is often used to describe a ravine or a gorge. In some dictionaries, the word is illustrated with a saying: *salir del barranco,* to get out with great difficulty.

With this identity firmly in place, Miguel turned to baseball. He had nothing else; playing the game was the first thing that made him feel whole, made him feel free, made him feel strong.

So he began thinking as the other boys did, of baseball as his one outlet of aggression, his only means of entertainment and form of expression. Kids like Miguel had little chance at an education, but most could run. And when they ran they could begin to dream, to escape, to test themselves, their strength, their intelligence, and their instincts every time they swung a stick or tree branch fashioned in the shape of a bat.

After being taught the game by his brothers, Miguel spent almost all his time running the dirt streets of *Los Barrancones,* to a dilapidated sandlot where burros were known to feed on the dried grass of right field.

Miguel was short and squat, thin through his shoulders but powerful in his legs, and it wasn't long before baseball was causing him to miss school, something he would do often— especially if he happened to be walking to school with other boys his age.

By the age of eleven, Miguel had stopped going altogether. Instead, he worked at a garment factory in Bani, washing clothes and ironing pants and shirts by the dozen, pressing garments until he grew woozy from the smell of starch and steam. During this period, Miguel would rise early in the morning, work, and then return to playing baseball by the afternoon, never missing a chance to take a few swings.

The contrast in his life was already established by the time he was eleven. There was the Miguel who played baseball and the Miguel who was living the rest of his life. That meant working, earning, and worrying about hunger—a hunger hardly satisfied by the steady diet of cornmeal mixed with pieces of salami or eggs that he and his brothers ate. They also ate a lot of bananas, papaya, yucca, sweet potatoes, and, when they were lucky, pork.

By the age of twelve, he spent nearly all of his time hovering around the sandlots where boys could be discovered, signed to professional contracts, and sent to the United States in search of millions.

So he set out to be different, to be noticed, to be better—a child's goal and an unrealistic one at that, considering it came from a kid who wasn't even the best player in his family, let alone the best in his barrio. Around Bani alone, there were dozens of Miguel Tejadas. Miguel would see them every day at the baseball park in Bani, shagging flies in the hard, patchy outfield grass.

Bani's park is about a three-mile walk from *Los Barrancones,* its peach and yellow exterior a magnet drawing most of Bani to come and watch even the most meaningless practices as if they were major league playoff games. Spectators sit on concrete stands built in a horseshoe shape, which overlook a barren field with no infield grass and enough rocks and potholes to make any player worry about taking an errant grounder in the face. The outfield grass is a shade somewhere between green and yellow and the outfield wall is made of concrete with no padding to protect a daring player.

The sun beats down on the park each day with a relentless mixture of heat and humidity, usually chasing spectators to the upper rows of the stands where the most shade can be found. Along with church, this is the place where Bani's residents come together in common interest—a ballpark that is both an entertainment center and a proving ground for young boys.

Half-drunk, unemployed men watch from the stands, their potbellies and dirty hair a testament to their failed lives. Still, these men laugh and brag and criticize as if they were baseball stars, sometimes nearly coming to blows over arguments as stupid as who the best player is. On any given day, twenty, thirty, or more men will gather, yesterday's prospects or men too lazy or too shiftless to have taken their own shot. They shout vulgarities to each other. They crack up in unison. They brag about how good they once were. They hover around promising young players. And they come back the next day and do it again.

In this place, Miguel learned how to play baseball.

As a boy, he began to develop a talent for hitting the ball, striking it flush so it made the distinctive crack that every hitter aims for every time he steps to the plate.

Even though he was thin and small, Miguel could follow the ball with his eyes and whip the bat fast enough to make contact. When he was in the field, he mostly played catcher and made a habit of diving, sliding, and lunging for every ball—even if it was far out of his reach. By thirteen, he was starting to make a habit of playing with much older boys and men. He found not only that he could hold his own with them but that he was getting faster, his strength concentrated in legs that a baseball scout would later say reminded him of football's Hall of Fame running back Walter Payton.

He would continue playing endlessly, barely noticing the arrival of Christmas in 1989.

There was little warning of what was coming.

Miguel barely remembers his mother being sick. She had seemed fine in the months leading up to the holidays. Though she was often away working, Miguel had been close to his mother. And she babied Miguel, encouraged him, loved him, and helped him define a sense of purpose for himself. Miguel would vow to his mother that his baseball skill would one day take her away from Los Barrancones to a much better place.

Though hardly an innocent, Miguel had an inner sweetness that came from his mother. She would always tell him to be a good person, that being a good person was more important than being a great ballplayer. Those gentle pleadings didn't make much sense to Miguel until after, until she was already gone from his life.

Mora Tejada died on December 21 at the age of forty-nine, passing away in her sleep. Miguel has very few recollections of those days, except praying on his knees to her every night before he went to sleep. For a time, he went back to the way he was as a child refugee—he simply lived, existed. His life had no direction and was filled with only the obligation to make money—a feeling heightened by the fact his father left to look for work in another town. So did Juansito, who was five years older than Miguel.

Other family members had scattered as well, leaving thirteen-year-old Miguel and sixteen-year-old Denio to fend for themselves. Often, the Tejada boys would rely on neighbors to eat.

Of all the hardships Miguel had endured, this was the worst. He readily admits now that he all but gave up once she was gone. He stopped playing baseball for a short time. He and Denio grew even closer as the dull ache of hunger came back. Miguel had stopped caring about most things and seemed oblivious to the perilous life that awaited him.

Again, it was baseball that saved him.

He still looked like any other boy out there, but he didn't play like one. At least Enrique Soto didn't think so.

A failed minor league prospect with the San Francisco Giants, Soto was twenty-seven in the spring of 1990 and was doing some scouting work with the Oakland Athletics. Soto also ran baseball clinics for Bani's youth in an effort to get a scouting career off the ground. He was desperate to find some recruits he could recommend to the Athletics. If they thought his boys could play, Soto believed he might be able to get a full-time job with the Athletics.

About five feet ten inches tall, Soto was of average build and slightly plump around the waist. His skin was olive, the product of a racially mixed heritage. His hair was straight but it was rapidly thinning on top, making him look older than he really was. When he smiled, his narrow face flashed a knowing, slightly wicked look that seemed to say, "You can't fool me." But behind this suspicious demeanor and cynical façade was an older version of Miguel, a man as dependent as Miguel on baseball as a way out.

Soto had the intellect and baseball skills to make a great baseball coach or manager. But he had neither the language skills nor the connections with a major league club. He was sick of working as a laborer, so scouting was his great hope. By the time Soto met Miguel, he was desperate.

And he had an idea. He knew major league baseball was starting to recruit heavily in the Dominican, and he knew that Dominicans of his generation had failed in large numbers because they lacked fundamentals. So with some of his own money and some help from the Athletics, he drilled kids all day, every day, before they developed too many bad habits. For those who showed promise, he lured them to his camp with a tempting promise: "I can refine your talent and I can teach you something even more important—discipline. Without discipline, the Americans will never give you a chance. I can give that to you and if you have the ability, you can become a star."

Equal parts entrepreneur and romantic, what Soto really had going for him when he crossed paths with Miguel was that he could connect with the kids. Every day, in the same floppy blue sweat pants, Soto would stand surrounded by fifty or more young recruits and not only succeed in holding their attention but make sure they all knew they had better listen to him.

"Don't listen to me!" he would scream at a boy defying his orders. *"Go ahead. But you know what you have waiting for you?"* Soto would then pause, before booming *"Miseria,"* the Spanish word for misery—in this case a reminder of the poverty all his recruits lived in.

There were no rich baseball players in Soto's training camp, or any other in the Dominican for that matter. There is a saying in the country that goes, "The rich kids don't have to play baseball. They can rely on their daddies. Only the poor depend on the game."

Though he knew baseball, Soto viewed himself as a failure in the game.

Like Miguel, he had played baseball since he was a young boy and showed promise as a shortstop, signing a contract with the Giants as a teenager in 1980. After training for a time in the Dominican, the Giants sent Soto to the United States in 1981— to their rookie league team in Montana. "If they were interested in me they didn't show it," said Soto of the months he spent alone as the only Hispanic on his team. Soto recalls it all now with the acrid memories of an outsider, forced to learn the game on his own without the benefit of instruction, which American players got routinely.

At the end of his lone season, Soto decided never to go back. He drifted out of baseball for several years. Later, he made some acquaintances in the Oakland organization and began to coach kids and recommend the best ones.

As for Miguel, there was no reason for Soto to pay any attention to him early on—he was simply too small, and it was impossible to tell whether his little body would ever develop. But when Miguel turned fourteen, Soto noticed he had an aura that made him stand out from the other boys, a power in his compact body that flashed like a bolt of lightning every time he swung the bat. Soto asked Miguel to stay after practice one day in the summer of 1990.

"Do you want to be a professional?" Soto asked Miguel. "Do you want to practice with me?" The answer came back quickly, and soon Miguel was one of Soto's recruits—part of a group of about fifty boys who had been working out with him since 1990.

Of that group, Soto would only recommend a handful to be signed to professional contracts. He had had a hunch Miguel would be one of those boys, but at first he couldn't be sure. By the looks of his tattered clothes, his skinny ribs, and his wild demeanor, Soto could tell that Miguel was poor—even by Dominican standards. And he knew that such poverty comes with overwhelming limitations that many boys simply can never overcome.

Could Miguel, a boy growing up with no rules, conform to a game made of rules? Could he show the discipline to practice? Could he go beyond his sandlot instincts and physical ability and learn to play the American game—a tactical game of concentration, restrained reaction, and calculation? And most of all, could Miguel stay out of trouble, away from alcohol and the growing drug trade in the Dominican?

Today, Soto says, "Once I asked him to join me, I never had any doubts about his baseball talent. But I did have doubts about him."

Indeed, under Soto's strict, drill-sergeant regimen, Miguel

began to chafe and rebel. He showed up late for practice. He talked back to Soto. He goofed around with the other boys.

Before his mother's death, Miguel understood this sort of behavior could derail his career before it even started. But after her death, it was as if he completely lost his bearings. Ironically, Miguel chose to rebel against the one thing that could save him.

After a few weeks of screaming and cajoling, of small punishments and silent treatments, Soto had had enough: He threw Miguel off his practice squad. With tears streaming down his cheeks, Miguel left while Soto privately lamented the victory of limitation over potential—a way of life in the Dominican. In a country with so many natural resources, there was so much poverty. And in a boy with so much baseball talent, there were so many obstacles he apparently couldn't overcome.

Miguel says he remembers crying that night, feeling a sense of desperation, of hopelessness.

But the next day he was back, pleading his case.

Soto was surprised to see him and at first resisted Miguel's conciliatory words. But Soto took him back. And before long, he would take him back again. And again. And again.

Both lost track how often Miguel was thrown off Soto's teams. What ultimately saved him was not his childish pleadings or his melodramatic declaration, "Soto, kill me but don't throw me off the team." What saved Miguel was his situation, his life, his struggle.

As he did with other boys, Soto would drive Miguel home after practice. But once there, he discovered that Miguel's problems were rooted in his abandonment at home. "I remember one time I went looking for him and his brother Denio told me that he was inside, in his room, and that I should go in. I did, but when I peered into his room I didn't see anyone. I was annoyed and I went out and told Denio that Miguel wasn't there.

"He sent me in again and told me to go all the way in the room—that I would find him in there. I did and Denio was right. He was in there. But the reason I didn't see him was that he was completely submerged in this big hole in his mattress. The hole just swallowed him up and from outside the room you couldn't tell that there was anybody in there. He was just inside that hole, asleep. I woke him up and said, 'Come on, let's go get something to eat.' "

Soto took Miguel to his home that afternoon and his wife cooked for him. At that moment, Miguel's vulnerability, a child-like softness that was as much a part of him as anything else, touched Soto in a way he never expected. As Miguel sat there at his table, eating his food clumsily, Soto found himself talking with Miguel as if he were talking to his own child.

In a manner devoid of the cunning, deliberate ways he had learned as a boy, Miguel told Soto that "he didn't know things. That he wasn't trying to do the wrong thing in practice but that he simply didn't know what the right thing was." Soto decided that afternoon that he would give Miguel the best he could. At this point, there was no reason to believe this would lead to anything.

Moreover, Soto knew well the cruelties of baseball for Dominicans—how injury or lack of interest from Americans could mean the end of a dream and a life sentence to poverty. All Soto had to do was recall his own experiences with the Giants.

By the time Miguel was fifteen and approaching sixteen, the Athletics had begun signing a handful of players from Bani to professional contracts and training them with the idea of sending the best of them to the United States. The great Juan Marichal, the only Dominican elected to the baseball Hall of Fame, was the director of scouting for the Athletics in the Dominican and was doling out tiny bonuses of up to five thousand dollars for the young boys Soto and others recommended to the organization.

A regal presence in his country, Marichal was fighting an uphill battle in the recruitment wars against richer, better-staffed teams like the Los Angeles Dodgers and Toronto Blue Jays. In fact, Marichal knew full well that the first recruits he recommended to the Athletics in the early 1980s had no business playing professional baseball.

The purpose they served was to fill out minor league rosters and thereby help train other, more talented players. Hamstrung by tighter budgets than more prosperous teams, the Athletics were looking for bargains—cheap talent they could develop at a very low cost. This was the atmosphere that existed as Miguel turned sixteen and began to close in on the promise that Soto saw in him—promise that stood in stark contrast to Miguel's life away from the field.

"They were abandoned," Soto says. "They didn't have anything, no one was around to help them." By this point, Soto was slipping money to Miguel and his brother so they could eat. Meantime, the prospect of signing a professional contract grew with each day in Miguel's mind. After two years of working with Soto, it had become clear to him that baseball was his only way out. All around him, boys he had grown up with in *Los Barrancones* were dropping like flies.

So he clung to the game and to Soto.

And Soto clung to him.

In May of 1993, Miguel turned seventeen—the age when Dominican players become eligible to sign professional baseball contracts. Soto felt that Miguel was ready to be signed and mentioned him to some of Marichal's assistants with the Athletics. But they didn't react one way or the other.

Miguel had finally reached the age he had looked forward to for years, the age where he could begin to prove himself, but no one was interested in him. No one from *Los Barrancones* had ever been recruited to be a professional ballplayer up to that point, and for a time it seemed Miguel would be no different from the forgotten boys of his youth, the same boys who played alongside him and his brothers, the ones who now carried pistols in their pants pockets, were unemployed, or had gone to New York as illegal immigrants.

Miguel learned to play the position of shortstop with these boys, the position of choice for young Latin men aspiring to be professional ballplayers. This was because over the years, Latins had experienced the most success at a spot where smaller, quicker bodies were preferred. Shortstop was where Alfredo Griffin played for the Toronto Blue Jays, Oakland Athletics, and Los Angeles Dodgers. Griffin, a Dominican, was Miguel's hero. Griffin had grown up poor just like Miguel, but by the early 1980s, he had become a millionaire, an All-Star, and a hero in his own country. In 1988, Griffin helped lead the Dodgers to a World Championship. Miguel was twelve that year and decided he wanted to switch from catcher to shortstop. He wanted to be like Griffin.

Taking the field on his first day at shortstop, Miguel was feeling cocky, feeling he could handle any line drive hit in his direction. And in the very first inning, Miguel got his first test. A teenager from the neighborhood hit a hard grounder that took one, a second, and then a third bounce before reaching him. Steadying his feet, Miguel planted himself and—following the ball with his eyes—positioned his hands at chest level.

But on that last bounce, the ball jumped hard off a rock and shot straight up, crashing into his lips and front teeth and spilling blood all over his shirt. Laughter rang out across the diamond as Miguel fell backward and rolled over, clutching his mouth with his hands.

With tears in his eyes and blood on his hands, Miguel picked up the ball, but it was far too late to get the runner at first. Miguel was disoriented, and he felt his face throbbing as his lips swelled and the blood dried on the front of his shirt. But the game kept going and more balls came at him, bouncing off his chest, his arms, his shins.

He was all alone out there between second and third base, chasing the ball again and again, lunging, diving, snaring it in his glove, and throwing wildly to first base. In a sense, playing shortstop was fitting for Miguel, because it is the hardest position in the game, a spot where most everything hit at you is out of reach or requires a superhuman effort. And there is always the possibility of getting hit in the mouth. The position was a mirror of Miguel's life.

On that first day, Miguel was oblivious to his pain and to everything around him, playing hard until darkness fell on *Los Barrancones*. Once the game was over, some of the boys stopped to talk, to horse around, or to posture for one another as boys do. But not Miguel.

Barefoot and still hurting from his first taste as a shortstop, Miguel turned away from the others and did what he often did after a game. He ran toward home wondering what he was going to eat that night, wondering whether he would ever escape *Los Barrancones*.

For weeks after his seventeenth birthday, when no professional team showed a real interest in him, Miguel felt as he had on that first day he played shortstop.

He felt totally and completely alone.

2

"A BOATLOAD MENTALITY"

MIGUEL TEJADA is unlike any American-born player in the game of baseball today. Simply put, no American player will ever have to escape from the Third World, from a place like *Los Barrancones,* from a mindset of poverty, and then have to compete at the highest level of professional sports while learning a foreign language.

But he is not unique.

Virtually every Dominican in the major leagues has lived in circumstances very similar to Miguel's. The details and experiences may differ, some may have had it a bit easier, others even harder, but the essence of their lives is the same.

The immigrant athlete, equal on the field but distant and apart away from it, is a player who will star between the lines and then slip between news columns, rendered mute by a Spanish-speaking tongue in an English-speaking country obsessed with hot quotations and clubhouse characters. This distinction doesn't stop with Dominicans. Cubans, Puerto Ricans, Venezuelans, Mexicans, Panamanians, and Colombians round out this new wave, a presence the American sports fan didn't truly begin to notice until the 1997 World Series. But over one week that October, Spanish-speaking players for the Florida

Marlins and the Cleveland Indians—with names like Livan Hernandez and Omar Vizquel— dominated games and suddenly ESPN and *The New York Times* were breathlessly reporting the obvious: that Latin players were becoming a force like never before in baseball history.

After all, no fewer than fifteen Latins had been selected to play in 1997's All-Star game, a contest that became a showcase for Latin talent.

Sandy Alomar, Jr., of Puerto Rico and the Cleveland Indians, was selected MVP of the game. Jose Rosado, of Puerto Rico and the Kansas City Royals, was the winning pitcher. Mariano Rivera, of Panama and the New York Yankees, saved the game. And two homers were hit by Puerto Ricans: Alomar and Javy Lopez of the Atlanta Braves. A third was hit by Edgar Martinez, who was born in New York City, but is of Puerto Rican descent.

But what was and continues to be missing is the very heart of the Latin story, the story of young men like Miguel Tejada, men whose lives are often framed by the narrow vision of Latin America in the United States—a vision constricted by stereotypes of the funny-sounding Latino from a banana republic. *Baseball has been bery, bery good to me.*

In 1998, on his way to a historic season, Sammy Sosa—a Dominican and Chicago Cub—mouthed those words often, using them to his advantage as a way of endearing himself to the media and sports fans while he and Mark McGwire shattered baseball's hallowed single-season home-run record. As smart as he is talented, Sosa knew the words would make Americans laugh because, until recently, they were about all Americans knew about Latin players—that they talked funny.

But Sosa also knew the hard truths beyond the words. He had been a shoeshine boy just like Miguel Tejada.

Indeed, the history beyond the stereotypes of his and Miguel's lives—the history of how Latins are brought into America's game—is a story of capitalism and cutthroat competition. It is a story in which opportunity is held out like a lottery ticket that most impoverished Latin kids will never cash in. The business of recruiting young men like Miguel Tejada is carried out in barrios and barren valleys, bursting coastal cities and desolate mountain villages of the Dominican Republic—the primary laboratory for baseball's talent expeditions into the Third

World. Most important in these transactions is that the market is—as former Oakland Athletics General Manager Sandy Alderson once said— "favorable to entrepreneurs."[1]

In the context of major league baseball, being an "entrepreneur" in Latin America means scouring the islands and territories of the Caribbean basin for skinny kids who will do anything to latch on to a major league team. This strategy has paid big dividends for major league owners. By 1998, Latin America produced roughly 25 percent of the players on major league rosters, half of which came from the Dominican.[2]

This has occurred because the island creates players born with the perfect combination of qualities desired by the major league scout—baseball knowhow and a sense of desperation born in poverty horrific even by Latin American standards.

If it sounds a bit like a meat market that's because it is. It's a hunt that begins the moment scouts start assessing young bodies still thin from malnutrition, trying to imagine whether— with the proper nourishment—those bodies can develop into major league stock. Mario Soto—a Dominican and former All-Star pitcher for the Cincinnati Reds—scouted for a time with the San Diego Padres and took that principle one step further. He said he and other scouts would get into the habit of meeting the parents of prospective players to check out their bone structure and builds, looking them up and down for defects, for height, for muscle tone, and for weight.[3]

In this way, a good scout can begin to assess whether a boy has potential to grow beyond what he was as a child. This is ground zero for the talent sweepstakes in Latin America, and always a consideration in the assessment of Latin talent. While how fast a young man is, or how strong he is, has always been at the heart of all professional sports, the evaluation of young Latinos for major league baseball has far more profound implications.

Simply stated, if an American athlete—no matter how disadvantaged—fails in his quest to become a highly-paid professional, that athlete is still an American and has a far greater chance at making a decent living than a Dominican. Failure for him means becoming an undocumented immigrant in the United States or returning to a place like *Los Barrancones*.

There simply is no comparison.

Miguel only began to get noticed for anything in his life when his baseball talent began to flower as a teenager, a god-given ability exploding from his legs, torso and eye-hand coordination that clicked to an elevated level after years of swinging tree branches, sticks, and old baseball bats. For Miguel's friends born without his ability or resolve, for the countless thousands of Dominicans lacking baseball talent, there isn't much hope left when the realization hits that a baseball career won't happen.

Some end up as pathetic men screaming at kids practicing for the future, like those who watched Miguel as he grew up. Many work hard as laborers, construction workers, or sugar cane cutters, or toil in such industries as the textile mills of Bani. Thousands emigrate to the United States, both legally and illegally and often find themselves surviving in the barrios of New York City. And even those players with real baseball talent must first overcome their humble beginnings in the eyes of American scouts, who often discard Latin players for the way they look or carry themselves.

The Athletics had a chance to sign Raul Mondesi—the Dodgers All-Star right fielder—when he was a teenager, but thought he was too small and too skinny and passed on him.[4] Mondesi would have gladly signed with the Athletics for only a few thousand dollars, but the A's decided that was too high a price for a kid under six feet and thin as a rail. Soon thereafter, in 1987, the Dodgers signed him and began working with him. He was sent to the United States, began eating balanced meals, developed the upper body of a football player and became a star.

Mondesi is not alone. George Bell—the 1987 American League MVP—was signed for thirty-five hundred dollars by the Philadelphia Phillies, left unprotected, and snatched up for practically nothing by the Toronto Blue Jays.[5] By the late 1980s, Bell—a Dominican—had become one of the most feared hitters in the American League. Julio Franco—the 1991 American League batting champion—was signed at sixteen for four thousand dollars by the Phillies, who then traded him to the Cleveland Indians after he batted .300 or better for four straight seasons in the minor leagues.[6] Pedro Guerrero—multiple All-Star and co-MVP of the 1981 World Series—was signed at sixteen for twenty-five hundred dollars by the Cleveland Indians, who gave up on him when he was still only seventeen, trading him to the Los Angeles Dodgers for someone named Bruce Ellingsen. Guerrero went on to a lifetime batting average of .305, hit 100 RBIs three times and was the 1987 Comeback Player of the Year.[7] And Sosa, who had one of the greatest offensive seasons of any player in baseball history in 1998, was signed for only thirty-five hundred dollars by the Texas Rangers.[8]

All of these players lived a time-honored tradition for Latins in major league baseball—being released, traded, or passed over.

"It happens to all of us," said Tony Oliva, a Cuban and the American League batting champion in 1964, 1965, and 1971. "We all get released. . . . To the Americans, we are like some stray dog, like a rudderless ship at sea."[9]

Reflecting the philosophy of big league teams, Sandy Alderson said, "If properly done, one can get an advantage in a place like the Dominican Republic. The advantage one can gain might seem minimal but a minimal advantage can have a tremendous long-term consequence.

"For example, if you are developing two or three players a year in your farm system from traditional domestic sources of talent and you can add just one more player to that resource pool every year, then, in effect, you've increased your productivity by 33 percent."[10]

So looking for that "one" player becomes a search among hundreds and hundreds of kids like Miguel Tejada. Dick Balderson—vice-president of the Colorado Rockies—is blunt but honest in describing this philosophy.

He calls it "a boatload mentality."[11]

This mentality is rooted in being able to sign large numbers of players for very little money. So if only a handful of those kids ever make it to the big leagues, teams still come out ahead. "Instead of signing four [American] guys at twenty-five thousand dollars each, you sign twenty [Dominican] guys for five thousand dollars each," Balderson said. Each year, every major league team has anywhere between a handful and a hundred young Latin prospects training in camps. The State Department restricts the yearly number of foreign players each team can bring to its minor league operations to thirty. With thirty teams all recruiting in Latin America, that works out to anywhere between five hundred and seven hundred Latin players being brought to the United States to play in the minor leagues each year.[12]

This explosion didn't happen by accident.

It started slowly, after the momentous year of 1976—when players won the crucial right of "free agency," allowing veterans to jump to whichever team paid them the most money once their contracts had expired. The effect on baseball was profound: Average salaries jumped from $52,300 to $146,500 by 1980. By 1991, they were at $845,383, and by 1998, $1.3 million. At the same time, the amount of money teams paid to sign promising American players shot up as well—to an average of $50,000, with the more talented players routinely garnering six figures and now, upward of $1 million, $2 million and beyond.[13]

The chasm between American players and Latin players is embodied in Alex Rodriguez, the star shortstop with the Seattle Mariners who, in 1996, had one of the greatest years any player has ever had. In his first full year as a pro, Rodriguez won the American League batting title by hitting .358, slugging 36 home runs, driving in 123 runs, and leading the American League in doubles, runs, and total bases. Three years earlier, in 1993, Rodriguez signed with the Mariners for $1.3 million, even though his roots are Dominican. The reason he was able to do this is simple: Rodriquez was born and raised in the United States, his family having emigrated shortly before his birth in 1975.

So as the top prep player in the nation and the first player selected in the 1993 amateur draft, Rodriguez had clout and used it: When the Mariners balked at paying him what he wanted, he threatened to go to the University of Miami. The Mariners paid and Rodriguez has no illusions why.

"I'm really grateful I was born and raised in the U.S." If he had been born in the Dominican, he said, "I'm sure I would have been a top prospect but maybe I would have gotten $5,000 or $10,000. Or maybe $4,000. . . . The point is, it would have been a much tougher road.[14]

"You have to pay for talent. . . . You should not treat someone unfairly because they don't have the leverage some of these high-school kids have here. Just because they don't have the opportunity to go to Stanford or the University of Miami." That is, however, precisely what attracted baseball people to the Caribbean when they needed a solution to exploding costs in the 1970s and 1980s.

Major league owners had recruited in the Caribbean since the turn of the century, attracted by cheaper players then just as they are today. But what triggered the present onslaught was different, more serious, more calculated, and completely unprecedented in modern American sports.

In fact, some baseball veterans say Latins could have been a force in the game long before the 1990s, but scouting directors were either too racist or too short-sighted to fully develop what was there.

In 1981, before the boom, Dominican and Montreal Expos Manager Felipe Alou put those feelings into words: "It's like they throw a net in the ocean, hoping that maybe they'll get a big fish. The problem is, if they don't get a big fish, they'll throw all the smaller ones back."[15] Alou and others say hundreds of young Latinos, some as young as fifteen, were wasted and never properly developed. The results were obvious: By 1977, Latins made up 11.6 percent of all player rosters, a number that barely rose to 12.6 percent by 1987.[16]

But with their hand forced by increasingly powerful American players, general managers of the 1970s and 1980s began realizing there was money to be made off those "little fish."

And they would find that there was more talent in the Caribbean than they ever imagined. The Dominican became the top exporter of baseball's Spanish-speaking world for several reasons. In the 1970s, Cuban players were still sealed off from the major leagues by a U.S. embargo now approaching its fortieth year. In addition, Dominicans are easier to sign in larger numbers than Puerto Ricans, who, as American citizens, became part of the annual amateur draft in 1989.[17]

With teams restricted to only those players they can draft, the best prospects can leverage negotiations as Rodriguez did. If a player doesn't come to terms, a team squanders a draft choice. This made Dominicans even more appealing, because as with Venezuelans, Panamanians, and Colombians, teams can sign as many as they please.

Unlike the Dominican, Panama and Colombia only produce a handful of players. Venezuela didn't become a hot destination for baseball until the late 1980s and 1990s—after its oil-dependent economy crumbled and desperation made baseball all the more appealing.[18] And Mexicans are recruited in smaller numbers because Mexican officials insist on market value for their players, killing the interest of many big league executives.[19]

With those realities firmly in place, the Toronto Blue Jays and the Los Angeles Dodgers, two teams lucky enough to employ scouts who knew the country and how to mine it for talent, moved in to become the leaders in the Dominican bonanza. By the early 1980s, both teams had built baseball "academies" in the Dominican, glorified dormitories surrounded by practice fields where young men would be drilled in baseball fundamentals, with the best players being sent to the United States.

The two leading scouts in this competition—Epy Guerrero of the Blue Jays and Rafael Avila of the Dodgers—both realized that by the late 1970s, Dominicans and other Latins needed more help if recruiting in Latin America were to become profitable.

Work on the fundamentals of baseball, of course, was what they had in mind. But what became equally important was feeding the young boys they were recruiting. Avila, a Cuban, and Guerrero, a Dominican, intimately knew the backgrounds of the boys available in the Dominican, and both realized that with a little nourishment, those boys could begin to compete in the United States. Avila, in particular, had long thought that Latin America could be a major baseball-producing region. So by the mid to late 1970s, he was lobbying his bosses to put up a little money for food and shelter so the boys could mature and grow.

The Dodgers resisted at first, unconvinced that any formalized recruiting could take place in a country like the Dominican. So Avila and his assistant Elvio Jimenez improvised. "We built two rooms in Elvio's backyard and we put eight beds in each room, and Elvio's wife would feed them. If she spent $150 on food, we'd pay her back. Now, we get results."[20]

By the early 1980s, it was becoming clear to the Dodgers that Avila knew what he was doing, so the team went about scouting for a site to build an academy. Again, economics were the key when former Dodger owner Peter O'Malley traveled to the Dominican Republic himself to oversee the acquisition of property.

Spurred by the Blue Jays, who were spending one hundred thousand dollars and were beginning to advance Latin players in the minor leagues, the Dodgers sensed they could secure a substantial piece of the ground floor in Latin America if they moved quickly.

Just as the Spaniards had cut up Dominican land centuries before to harvest sugar, the Dodgers began plowing amid the island's sugar-cane plantations, replacing its yield stock with baseball diamonds, batting cages, and pitcher's mounds—the new growth industry of Latin America.

Avila likes to recount how the Dodgers found their baseball academy.

"When we got [to where the academy is now] we saw the For Sale sign on the property across the street. . . . We looked at the property for sale, and [O'Malley] said, "I don't like this place at all, but that one over there, I like." It was a hill! There were cows and horses all over the place. It looked like a jungle. . . . If you realize that we spent approximately four hundred thousand dollars for the land, the construction of the entire camp, baseball fields, leveling of the hill, equipment, the bus, you see how far money goes, and what a good deal it was for the Dodgers. Imagine what that would cost in the United States!"[21]

Opened in 1987, the Dodgers' Campo Las Palmas spread across fifty Dominican acres and soon was churning out major league players like Mariano Duncan, Ramon Martinez, Raul Mondesi, and Juan Guzman.

The Blue Jays also were getting results, sending Manny Lee, and Tony Fernandez to the majors while developing George Bell into one of the dominant hitters of the late 1980s. They also virtually stole Alfredo Griffin from the Cleveland Indians and gave him a chance to play, for which the Jays were rewarded when Griffin was named cowinner of the American League Rookie of the Year award in 1979.

By the early 1980s, the American pastime began feeling the impact of Latin America.

In 1983, Dominican Tony Pena of the Pittsburgh Pirates won the first of four Gold Gloves that would distinguish a career enduring into his early forties. Beginning in 1980, Cincinnati Reds pitcher Mario Soto, who is from Bani like Miguel Tejada, started a five-year stretch where he was one of the most feared pitchers in the National League. In 1981, Mexican pitcher Fernando Valenzuela became a sensation with the Los Angeles Dodgers. Venezuelan Ozzie Guillen of the Chicago White Sox was voted the American League Rookie of the Year in 1985 and won a Gold Glove for his shortstop play in 1990.

Puerto Rican catcher Benito Santiago of the San Diego Padres won three consecutive Gold Glove awards between 1988 and 1990. Dominican shortstop Tony Fernandez of the Blue Jays won four consecutive Gold Glove awards between 1986 and 1989. And in fact, at least two Latins have been awarded Gold Glove awards every year since 1988—a departure from the late 1970s and early 1980s, when, if it weren't for Venezuelan shortstop Dave Concepcion of the Cincinnati Reds, Latin players often wouldn't have won any. Indeed, in 1978, and 1980, no Latin-born players were singled out for excellence in the field—omissions that are unlikely to ever happen again.

George Bell of the Blue Jays won the American League MVP in 1987, Cuban-born and American-raised Jose Canseco of the Oakland Athletics won it in 1988. And Puerto Rican pitcher Willie Hernandez of the Detroit Tigers won the American League Cy Young Award and the MVP in 1984. With the success of these players, other teams began swarming Latin America and the Dominican in particular—driven by the competitive nature of sports and the even stronger drive to profit. In fact, while the 1980s and the success of Latinos in that decade whetted the appetite of major league baseball, the true measure of the Latin influence in baseball didn't begin to be felt until the mid-1990s.

By then, virtually every team in baseball had at least one scout in the Dominican, particularly smaller-market organizations without the cash to vie for big-money free agents—such organizations as the Oakland Athletics, the Montreal Expos, the Pittsburgh Pirates, and the Milwaukee Brewers. Today, these teams are loaded with Spanish surnames, trying to find an edge against clubs with much more money to spend. Other teams, such as the Houston Astros, feared they had arrived too late in the Dominican and instead focused more energy on Venezuela.

While competitive into the 1980s, scout Epy Guerrero had a falling out with the Blue Jays and left while the team scaled back its interests in the Dominican. Every other team developed players in small numbers. But none has been as successful as the Dodgers, who by 1997 had nine Latins on its major league roster, also the most of any organization. What the Dodgers have had over other teams is Avila and the desire to spend money.

In fact, many teams have let the Dodgers develop players for them. The Expos traded for Pedro Martinez in 1993 after he had come up through the ranks in the Dodgers organization. In 1997, Martinez won the National League Cy Young Award and then became the highest-paid player in baseball for the Boston Red Sox. Henry Rodriguez—another Dodger castoff—became a name player in Montreal, as did pitcher Juan Guzman for the Blue Jays and Mariano Duncan for the Reds and Yankees.

Some teams have only done well because they had the right scout working for them, like Avila of the Dodgers. It was Avila and his staff who spotted Duncan, Ramon Martinez, Pedro Martinez, Pedro Astacio, Raul Mondesi, Wilton Guerrero, Guzman, and Jose Offerman. Blanketing the island, Avila—a plump, bespectacled man with snow-white hair shooting out from under his Dodgers hat—used the Dodgers' perfectly manicured baseball academy as incentive to lure Dominican prospects. Once inside, he would employ a mixture of paternal love and authoritative fear to get the most from his players.

With his knowhow and the Dodgers' money behind him, Avila was able to hold off other challengers in the Dominican. But other teams were able to make inroads with the help of Avila's fiercest rivals in the Caribbean. Indeed, at one time in the early 1980s, the San Diego Padres were signing some of the most talented players in the Caribbean because of one man: Luis Rosa.

A Puerto Rican Vietnam veteran, a former banker who gave up a lucrative career to haunt rickety baseball diamonds in the Caribbean, Rosa was a dynamo, a charismatic charmer who would woo Latin kids with promises of fame and money while assuring their parents that they would be protected. When he went to work for the Padres in the late 1970s, Rosa had a passion for baseball and a friendly relationship with Jack McKeon, then the Padres' Vice President of Baseball Operations.

But within a few years, he was cornering the market on

Latin America—particularly Puerto Rico, before the island became subject to the amateur draft in 1989. Back then, Puerto
Rico was as wide open as the Dominican is today and was a
place other teams could still fight with success against the
Dodgers. Once with the Padres, Rosa signed Benito Santiago,
Carlos Baerga, Robby Alomar, and Sandy Alomar, Jr. He also
signed Ozzie Guillen of Venezuela. All have been All-Stars,
Gold Glove winners, and, particularly the Alomars, have become superstars with other teams. But all were either traded
away or lost to free agency during Padres management shake-
ups that saw Rosa leave for the Texas Rangers.

Once there, he signed Juan Gonzalez and Ivan Rodriguez—
respectively, the 1996 and 1998 American League MVP and the
perennial Gold Glove catcher considered the best in the game
today. A tireless worker who often outlasted his competitors,
Rosa was the flashy lone wolf, where Avila was the solid company man. While Avila is both respected and feared in the Dominican, Rosa made himself a family friend to the boys he was
courting. "One of the first things you have to do here in Latin
America is getting to know who is going to be the boss when it
comes time to signing a contract. And who do you have influence over. And the two persons I have always influenced are the
mother and the son."[22]

"Like with Juan Gonzalez's father, his dad shoved the contract in my face when I wanted to sign him. And to myself I
thought, 'Tough luck, I already have him.' And so I got up from
the table like I was leaving and Juan said, 'Where are you
going?' I said, 'Your dad doesn't want me to sign you.' He said,
'You just sit right down.' And he went and talked to his mother.
And when they came back I knew I had won the war. The
mother liked me. And so his father gave me this mean look and
said, 'He wants to sign. What can I do?' "

Being the product of an American territory, Gonzalez was
able to pry seventy-five thousand dollars out of the Rangers,
just as many Puerto Rican blue-chip players are able to sign for
more money than prospects from poorer Latin countries, such
as the Dominican.[23] Still, those bonuses fall short when compared to those of top-level American players from the contigu-
ous United States. As for Rosa, he eventually became the
director of Latin American scouting for the San Francisco Gi-

ants—that is, until 1997, when he was arrested in the Dominican Republic for allegedly sexually harassing young Dominican boys. According to Dominican authorities, Rosa threatened fifteen young baseball prospects with termination of their contracts unless they had sex with him.[24]

The scandal rocked the Dominican and made front-page news in every daily newspaper on the island, as it did in *The New York Times*. In a deeply Catholic country, a country where baseball is the bedrock of national identity, the allegations against Rosa shook Dominicans in a profound way. There is no greater pride among Dominicans than their baseball stars. So the thought that fifteen *"innocentes,"* innocents, as Dominicans called them, might have been violated by one of the most successful baseball scouts in history was simply too much to take. Rosa's career was ruined, his contract with the Giants terminated, his reputation tarnished forever.

As he sat in a Dominican jail, he continued to plead his innocence while the business of signing players was carried on by his competitors. And in terms of business, if history is any judge, the Giants would not recruit as many good players without the man who understood Latin America so well. Every time Rosa had left a team before, his departure meant a decline in the quality of recruiting in the Caribbean. In fact, aside from the Dodgers, Athletics, and a few others, most clubs have seen their Latin scouting personnel turn over repeatedly—making for wild fluctuations in the fortunes of some teams, such as the Padres.

Unlike the situation in the United States, where bunches of scouts vie for territories made up of American players in either high school or college, scouts like Avila and Rosa can operate as if they were in the wild west. Both have strong instincts and know when to use guile and bravado.

That sort of pioneer freedom has been marked by other allegations of wrongdoing, of teams' stealing players away from each other.

In the United States, once a player is drafted, no other team can approach him, but in the Dominican, scouts routinely swarm all over players and consider them fair game until they have signed a contract. So, many teams, once they decide they like a promising player, will stash him in their baseball camps until they have him signed. In 1986, Papi Bisono—former commissioner of Dominican baseball—told a story of a frantic Dominican mother whose son had disappeared for days. She pleaded for Bisono's help, and he found the boy with a major league team. "She'd heard that her son had been taken away by a baseball scout and asked me if I could help find him. And this was one of the many complaints I'd received from these camps. The scouts who ran them kept the kids hidden: That is the real truth. These camps were hideouts because the scouts didn't want their kids seen by other scouts. It almost seemed like they were concentration camps."[25]

But these stories and the success of Latin players in the major leagues completely obscure the true underside of this talent search, the fact that hundreds of young Latinos are routinely discarded every year. According to statistics kept by major league baseball, between 90 and 95 percent of foreign-born players are released at the minor league level.[26] What often happens to those castoffs is a tragic last chapter in the mad dash to develop players. Signing a child of fifteen or sixteen would, more often than not, result in the release of a child at eighteen or nineteen—the age when most American players are just starting their professional careers.

So in 1984, it was decided that the minimum age of Latin prospects would be seventeen. Still, the "boatload mentality" ruled the day. Reflecting a widely held view in baseball, Alderson says, "To put it not callously but directly, [Latin players] are higher maintenance."[27]

Or, as Billy Harford, formerly director of minor league operations for the Chicago Cubs, says, "Some of these kids come from backgrounds where they don't even know how to use a toilet."[28]

Miguel Tejada was one of those kids.

And like so many other prospects, he could also scarcely read or write in his own language, let alone in English. To compensate, several teams began offering rudimentary English classes to their prospects while teaching them lessons in hygiene. "Every time they sign a Dominican they tell him, 'OK, we're giving you an opportunity.' Like they're giving them this big chance. They never tell the kid how talented he is or how good he's going to be. They always talk to him in a way to make the boy beholden to them," Enrique Soto says.[29]

But with so many Latin players now becoming legitimate stars, stars who are recruited with obvious talent, the question is: Would it be tolerated if underprivileged Americans were treated by major league baseball the way Latinos are? Or does the fact that they are immigrants—mostly black immigrants—make it acceptable?

People in major league baseball certainly think so.

"In the Dominican you have guys coming out of the woodwork to play baseball. . . . So to call it exploitation, that's a pretty harsh word. These (players) are getting opportunities they wouldn't otherwise get," says Dick Balderson of the Colorado Rockies.[30]

When assessing the story of Latinos in baseball, it is this rationalization that has blurred a separate and unique experience in the American game.

Their story has never come close to making a dent in baseball lore or the American consciousness as has, for example, the story of Jackie Robinson and other pioneering African-Americans. It remains reported without context, fueled by the feeling that Bell, Franco, Mondesi, and others should feel fortunate just to be in the United States, no matter what the circumstances. And in fact they are grateful, while thousands of Latinos would give anything to be like them.

So the hot prospects and also-rans keep eagerly coming by the hundreds with nothing to illuminate their experiences.

"Why does this happen?" Felipe Alou asks. "Because of our Latin American roots. . . . Baseball is a 100 percent capitalist business, and as with all businesses, when there is room for exploitation there will be exploitation."[31]

In the modern lexicon of the Latin player, there is a poignant saying that embodies their competition against Americans for the precious spots on big league rosters: *Quitando les la comida.*

Taking away their food.

Hence, when a Latin beats out an American for a roster spot, the Latin sees the victory on the very basic level of having just won another man's meal money. "Americans grow up eating cheeseburgers, but it's not that way for us. So once you start eating that good food you don't want to lose that good food. That is not an exaggeration. It's reality. It's a reality of baseball in our country," explains Mario Soto.[32]

It is unlikely that an American player would ever choose to explain the situation with such a metaphor, but this is how Latins see it—no matter how rich they get. Even after Pedro Martinez won his Cy Young Award and a $12-million-a-year contract with the Red Sox, he spoke of being embarrassed—because of where he was from. "I've seen great poverty," he said.[33] Other Dominicans would understand him. It's not false modesty. It comes from the same place—*Quitando les la comida.*

THAT SAYING has never been reported in the sports pages of American newspapers, which have also missed the larger story of the Dominican and how it came to be what it is today. And like all stories with fuzzy endings, the beginning—how the country was first opened up to baseball—has been lost in the translation from Spanish to English.

It is a story of one gentle man who was the grandfather of all Dominican shortstops, but who was never allowed to play in the major leagues because he was black. His name was Horacio Martinez, a defensive wizard whose dazzling prime was in the 1930s and 1940s—before Jackie Robinson broke baseball's color barrier in 1947. Though Martinez is largely forgotten among modern Dominicans, he was a bright light of a generation of black, Latin players kept out of the major leagues by baseball's racist policies.

But his legacy goes beyond what he did on the field. Martinez is also credited with discovering future Dominican Hall of Famer Juan Marichal and Felipe Alou in the 1950s—recommending them to the San Francisco Giants.

Those simple acts, transacted through old-fashioned handshake deals, blazed the Dominican trail that would be fully developed by Avila, the Dodgers, and the rest of baseball in the 1980s.

But the way Martinez was rewarded and remembered for his accomplishments is symbolic of the Latin story in American baseball. In the 1950s, Martinez was athletic director at the University of Santo Domingo and had become a venerated figure in his country while taking it upon himself to mentor young men, to prime them for chances he was denied.

"He was an exemplary man," Felipe Alou says today.[34] "He was honest. He was a great shortstop, a great citizen."

To earn some extra money in the mid-1950s, Martinez agreed to do some scouting for the New York Giants. With Jackie Robinson having opened the door for black players in the major leagues, the Giants were suddenly interested in the talent of the Dominican. So Martinez was recommended to the Giants by his old boss from his days in the Negro Leagues, by a man named Alex Pompez, who owned the Cuban Stars, a Negro League team in the mid-1940s. And in 1956, Martinez informed Pompez that Felipe Alou had major league ability. Coincidentally, that same year, Ozzie Virgil, Sr., suited up for the Giants and was credited with becoming the first Dominican in the major leagues. (Although he was born in the Dominican, Virgil grew up and went to high school in the Bronx.)

If the Giants approved of Alou, he would become the first player to travel from the island to the big show. They did, and by doing so an eighteen-year major league playing career and a distinguished run as the only Latin-born manager in baseball in the 1990s was started. Meanwhile, baseball was altered forever. The Dominican was on the baseball map. "They signed me for two hundred dollars," Alou said.

The next year, Martinez recommended another Dominican kid to the Giants—future Hall of Famer Juan Marichal. Both Alou and Marichal had been wooed by other teams and could have easily gone elsewhere. But Martinez wanted to honor his deal with Pompez so he steered his young men to the Giants. While both got the chance of their dreams, the Giants profited as well.

Carl Hubbell, the Hall of Fame pitcher, was working in the Giants' front office in 1958. He knew what he had in Marichal when he signed him for five hundred dollars. But as would become typical, Hubbell's excitement was not conveyed to Marichal. "When I got to the States [in 1958] all the young people had somebody to help them out, someone to counsel them," said Marichal years later. "Everyone, that is, except me. That made me feel bad, made me think they were discriminating against me, but what happened is that Carl Hubbell told all the instructors not to come anywhere near me. That I was a natural and that he didn't want anyone to change that. But I didn't know that at the time."[35]

In his first year in the minor leagues in 1958, Marichal won

21 games. The next year, he won 18 and was promoted to San Francisco, where he would post six 20-win seasons, never receive a single vote for the Cy Young Award, and become the first living Latino to be enshrined in the Hall of Fame. (Two other Latinos, including the great Roberto Clemente, had been inducted posthumously before Marichal was inducted in 1983.) "For three years, that five hundred dollars was my economy. I lived off it and when I got to the major leagues I got thirty-five hundred dollars. I thought I was rich."

Horacio Martinez himself had been barred from playing in the major leagues because of his skin color. In his prime, while playing for the New York Cubans of the Negro Leagues, Martinez was so fast, his teammates called him "rabbit." And in the early 1940s—when the talent level in the Negro Leagues reached its zenith—Martinez stood out, selected to the league's All-Star game in 1940, 1941, 1943, 1944, and 1945.[36] In those now legendary games, Martinez played alongside a Who's Who of African-American players. In those days, the very best Negro League players of teams from the eastern and western halves of the United States would showcase their skills, playing at a level that often exceeded that of major league baseball. Indeed, playing with Martinez on the "East" All-Stars were the likes of Buck Leonard, Roy Campanella, Monte Irvin, James "Cool Papa" Bell, and Josh Gibson—all now enshrined in baseball's Hall of Fame. And playing against him on "West" teams were Hall of Famers Satchel Paige and Jackie Robinson himself.

In every All-Star game but one, Martinez got at least one hit, and in the 1945 game, he went 2 for 2 with 3 RBI in a 9-6 loss to the West team. For the record, Robinson went 0-5 that day.[37] When Robinson integrated baseball two years later, Martinez was thirty-three and starting to slow. He finished his playing career as a star in his native Dominican and in Cuba before retiring to become a manager in the Dominican league and a scout for the Giants.

"There are American black players who have been elevated to the Hall of Fame, who have been recovered from the forgotten, and that work has been done by Americans. But we don't have and will never have that kind of representation to promote a Horacio Martinez," Alou says. "He wasn't just some scout. He was a great athlete and he spoke a great deal to me before I left to play in the United States. This was back in the 1950s when there was so much racism in the United States, but I came here aware of all those things because I had a great teacher. I was his first player signed to make it to the big leagues and for me, it was like I was on a mission."[38]

Meanwhile Martinez continued working and recommending many players after Alou and ended up fighting an uphill battle with an uninterested team. By the mid to late 1960s, the Giants had traded all of their Dominican players except for Marichal and forfeited their dominance in the region to other teams. Later, Martinez didn't fare very well either.

"When other scouts were earning twenty-five thousand and thirty-thousand dollars a year, Horacio was only earning nine thousand dollars," Marichal said. "So when the Giants were looking to liquidate some of their scouting positions, they were going to retire Horacio at half his salary. I was out of the organization but the Giants asked my opinion and I told them they should retire Horacio at his full salary because he didn't even earn a third of what other scouts were earning.[39] And so they did, but [before that] when the Giants offered me a job [in the late 1970s] they were going to release him but I didn't permit that. For me, Horacio was like a father and I wasn't going to take his job away from him. He was the best scout they ever had." Martinez eventually drifted out of baseball, an old man afflicted with Parkinson's Disease, while Marichal went to work for the Oakland Athletics.

By 1992, when he was seventy-eight, Horacio Martinez could barely speak and was confined to a wheelchair, his eyes glistening with frustration at his inability to articulate himself.

Miguel Tejada was sixteen that year. He was playing baseball in the sandlots of Bani, a year away from making a run at a dream made possible by Horacio Martinez. Sadly, Tejada didn't know who Martinez was. Neither do many others. His is just one of many stories known only in Spanish amid the palm trees and the baseball diamonds of the Caribbean.

A story that grew even fainter that year when Horacio Martinez died.

3

THE HAITIAN BUS

ON MAY 25, 1993, Miguel Tejada turned seventeen—the age Dominican boys fantasize about from the time they are very young. At seventeen, they are old enough to become professional baseball players. For three years, Miguel had been working out with Enrique Soto, practicing endlessly at the ballpark in Bani, painstakingly honing his swing, his fielding, his throwing, and his baserunning day after day, week after week, with no other purpose in his life and no other goal to shoot for. Miguel's practices were intense and physically challenging. Every day, Soto pushed Miguel and groups of other boys like a charismatic military leader trying to make a ragtag army believe in itself.

The principal motivation driving Miguel's workouts was fear of failure, a stinging, demoralizing, emasculating brand of failure burned into Enrique Soto in the heartland of America, on the back roads of Iowa and Michigan, Montana and Illinois in the year 1981, when Soto played in the minor leagues in the San Francisco Giants organization. A star in Bani as a young man, Soto soon learned that such a distinction means nothing in the north, where Dominican immigrants go—hat in hand—to find a living somehow, some way. All Soto found were coaches who couldn't care less, instructions that made no sense, and people who viewed him as he had never viewed himself: as an immigrant whose intelligence level was automatically downgraded the very first time he opened his mouth to speak.

In the bitter cold of April and the lonely, unforgiving solitude of summer and fall, Soto encountered an attitude that shaped the rest of his life: Most Americans thought Latin players were dumb and slow. That feeling came out in practices, when Soto would look his coaches straight in the eye and not know what the devil they were talking about. He would stare hard into their faces, trying to grasp any word, any phrase he could process and use. More often than not, there was no explanation, no clarification, no understanding.

He would find himself sitting at the end of the dugout, alone, detached—his talent not enough to smooth over who he was. He was without allies, without the camaraderie or the kind of familiarity that clears a path for opportunity in American life. "I was like a servant or a shoeshine boy. A common Latino. It's like I wasn't there. . . . In reality, the only opportunity they gave me was to go back home."

His final numbers from an aborted season of Rookie League ball in Great Falls, Montana: a 0.81 batting average and 11 errors in 15 games at shortstop.

So when Soto saw Miguel's talent, he knew it was equal to that of any American. But he also knew that talent wasn't enough. Miguel lacked a foundation of discipline, a familiarity with rules, an understanding of how things work outside his barrio—simple things like showing up on time or taking instruction. These were things that had scarcely been part of Miguel's life in *Los Barrancones*.

Miguel, for all his talent and all his bravado, was still terrified beneath the surface. Without the regular influence of his parents, Miguel was like a blank slate. From a coach's perspective, this had its advantages. Soto found Miguel easier to dominate, to bully, and to baby because Miguel didn't have the confidence in himself, the independence that other boys who had the benefit of being raised by two parents had.

Soto would stare into Miguel's eyes and Miguel would look down or look away, faithfully submitting to Soto's will. Life on the streets had taught Miguel a great deal, and he was no fool. Soto had earned his trust, so he curbed his undisciplined impulses. Soto knew things he didn't know. Soto could take him where he wanted to go. So he listened. "In a sense, I became like his mother, his father, his coach, his uncle, and his brother. I think anyone from the outside would have thought I didn't like him or was cruel to him. But I behaved that way because that's what Miguel needed. He needed me to be hard, so I was hard."

During practices, Soto would scream at Miguel when his attention flagged, he would bellow if he didn't hustle. And he would always remind him what the stakes were. *"You know where you are from, Miguel!"* Soto would scream. *"Do you ever want to get out?"* As he got older, Miguel would listen more intently. And every day he would show up for practice. Once there, Miguel and about fifty other boys would run laps, all of them dressed in a confused rainbow of colors, wearing whatever they owned, whether it matched or not. Some boys would show up with the hat of the Philadelphia Phillies over the jersey of the Athletics—creating an odd mixture of red, green, and gold. Some of those same boys would then strap on blue shoes, or different-colored socks. If they were lucky, they would wear worn cleats that Soto got for them from the Athletics. He would pass them out after practice, pulling them out of the trunk of his car and handing them to a kid who showed promise.

For a time, baseball clothes were all that Miguel owned, and he could be seen after practice walking around Bani in his cleats and baseball pants, a street urchin dressed like a ballplayer. And then it would be back to work the next day, often wearing the same clothes to take infield practice from Soto, who would hit yellowing balls with frayed seams at Miguel as if neither one of them would ever get tired. All the while, Soto would be working with groups of other boys positioned in the outfield, assisted only by two coaches yet keeping his eye on everyone. Leaving Miguel for a moment, Soto would break groups into hitting and fielding, with some taking hacks in a makeshift batting cage and others learning how to run backward on a fly ball. Picking up a bat, Soto would launch balls to outfielders and watch in exasperation when novices turned the wrong way before making the catch. Much profanity would follow, with boys standing in place, cowed, embarrassed, and too meek to answer.

A gregarious, outspoken man, Soto is known by virtually

everyone in Bani. Young people in particular flock around him because he has a connection with major league clubs. To Soto, preparing Dominican kids for life in the United States was personal, but not entirely because of his failed attempt at a professional career. He was truly bothered by the way his country was dominated by the United States and the way its best young people left the island strong and proud, only to become immigrants on the lowest rung of America's social ladder. "I like Americans, I like the United States. It's a great country and baseball gives our youth a lot of opportunities. But Americans get a lot out of it too. They take our young people, they take our very best. They take and take and take and still want more. That's what I don't like. We are a country also. We're underdeveloped, we have a lot of problems but there are good people here. They don't deserve to be treated like common trash."

In the Caribbean, and particularly in the Dominican, Americans are considered invaders, the powerful ones, the people who effectively toppled a Dominican president and inserted another one more palatable to U.S. interests. Americans are the ones who own many of the sugar companies in the Dominican, the ones who have controlled the country to such a degree that scholars have called it "a company state." Meanwhile, combined unemployment and underemployment in the country has run up to 80 percent.

An avid reader, Soto is very aware of his country's history. His love of baseball has become a way for him to make a career for himself and at the same time prepare destitute boys like Miguel for the challenges they will face in the United States. That motivation is what drives him to rise at dawn, get dressed, and pick up packs of kids in his car for a day's practice. While Miguel and other young boys stared out the window or laughed and joked among themselves, Soto constantly hammered his points home: discipline, practice, control, intelligence, sincerity. Cars, women, gold chains, and other trappings of success would only unravel a career if a player wasn't mentally prepared, he would say—over and over again.

Once on the field, Soto's demeanor could turn menacing. While he cared for all the kids, he and Miguel had a special chemistry. Miguel had come to rely on Soto for all things and would confide in him feelings he wouldn't share with anyone else: how he felt about his family situation, the death of his mother, the way his father would leave the house for long stretches of time, leaving him virtually orphaned and left to his own devices. Soto recognized that Miguel yearned for family.

"It hurts him to talk about it," Soto would say. "Because when he talks about it he has to say things that don't make his family look good, and he doesn't like to do that. He doesn't want to say hurtful things about them."

So Soto would tell him to forget it. What was happening to him was a reality, a fact of life—he would try to tell Miguel not to tear himself apart because of the failings of others. And then, whether at practice or afterward, he would tell him that he was special, that he had a talent he should be focusing on. "If you make it to the major leagues, you can provide what your family didn't provide," Soto told Miguel.

By the time he was seventeen, Miguel was convinced of his special ability. What excited Soto the most was how Miguel made contact at the plate. Miguel was still a small boy but he had a natural aggression. This was no ordinary kid, Soto would say to himself. Still, Miguel was wild, especially with his throws from shortstop to first base. On the field, Miguel was all emotion, sometimes raw, sometimes beautiful, sometimes disastrous. Playing freely at an early age creates a style that professionals like Raul Mondesi of the Los Angeles Dodgers never lose—a wild abandon epitomized by Mondesi's overaggressive baserunning and his utter disdain for hitting the cutoff man. Time and again, instead of throwing to an infielder waving his arms frantically at him, Mondesi will—from the warning track in right field—launch bomblike throws toward second or third base.

This was the way Mondesi learned to play as a boy in his hometown of San Cristobal, just down the road from Bani. To his way of thinking, God himself gave him a powerful right arm, and it would be a sin not to use it. In America, that sort of play is often seen by coaches as "hot-dogging." Miguel played the same way. Despite taking a grounder to the face the first time he played the position, Miguel gravitated toward shortstop because he knew he could make the plays. He reveled in racing deep in the hole between second and third, snaring a grounder, and hurling it toward first base. He got a charge every time he drew a reaction from the other boys, from the men in the stands, and from Soto. The concept of holding on to the ball, of not attempting an improbable throw, simply never entered his mind. If it was hit near him, he was going to go after it. If it was hit over his head toward the outfield, and he had even the slightest chance of making the play, he was going to go after it. So what Soto tried to do was harness that talent, to refine it by teaching Miguel discipline.

By the spring of 1993, the Athletics had signed Soto as a scout and were giving him balls and bats for his baseball camps.

Boys were repeatedly getting tossed out of Soto's practices for insubordination or for simply not being serious enough. "What do you think would happen if you took that attitude to the United States? What do you think Mr. Gringo is going to say to that?"

Sometimes, he would get an unenthusiastic shrug of the shoulders, which he would follow with: To hell with you. I'll see you out begging on the street.

But while his drills on the diamond were crucial, Soto developed a training program he felt was just as important—a regimen designed to prepare his players' minds. He would drill Miguel and the rest of the players over and over again, repeating instructions in a boisterous monotone until they trained their minds to listen and react.

Baseball in America, he would say, is not the game it is in the Dominican Republic. On the island, it's a game of instincts. But in America, it's a game of instructions. One of Soto's drills would have Miguel and other boys squatting at the bottom of the stadium's concrete stands—a pavilion that runs straight up twelve rows, a steep climb. Soto would have the boys, poised like frogs, jump up to a higher step on his command.

"Arriba!" he would scream for up. "Abajo!" he would yell for back. In teams of four, the boys would start, leapfrogging up from a standing position. Possessed with a biting sense of mischief, Soto would mix up his cadence, stutter slightly, start to bark one word, then scream another—losing his temper when boys jumped the wrong way or jumped before his command.

Watching Soto's practices, the object of this drill was obvious. Boys like Miguel would shine on the field, showing off their natural ability with ease. But they could be easily drawn off, foiled by a lack of concentration. Usually, by the time the boys reached this drill, they had been practicing for three hours or more and were drenched in sweat, tiring from fatigue and the ever-present humidity. But fatigue brought about vulnerability, Soto would say, a vulnerability that was the enemy of every Dominican trying to make it in America's game.

"Are you a man?" he would yell at Miguel. Often, Miguel would not utter a sound. Other times he would say yes very quietly. "Are there men here?" he would yell to the others. "Men listen, they pay attention. They understand." Hearing this, Miguel would throw himself into a workout, intent on proving he was indeed a man. Meanwhile, every time Miguel or some other player was fooled by Soto's commands, a hail of laughter and catcalls would come from the spectators. Miguel would try not to pay attention.

But Soto would. "You're a man, right?" Soto would scream at no one in particular. He would then do a mime of a drunk opening a beer bottle and drinking it. "A real man, right?" he would yell. "Yeah, I know what kind of man you are."

This was Miguel's world, and his life was marked by how well he did, how hard he focused, and how much he learned. At the end of each practice, Soto would have Miguel and his other recruits practice signing their names, telling them that they would need to know that skill when it came to signing contracts and autographs in the United States. So there Miguel would sit, cross-legged, working a pen over paper signing his name in tiny letters while the other kids next to him signed their names as well. Soto would also make them memorize their parents' full names, their birth dates, and other vital information.

But weeks after Miguel's seventeenth birthday, all this training was getting him nowhere. Not a single team was showing any real interest in him, and even the scouts Soto knew with the Oakland Athletics were less than enthusiastic.

There were several reasons for this, some that had to do with Miguel, others he couldn't control. By 1993, the Athletics had been recruiting in the Dominican for roughly a decade. But they didn't really begin signing Dominican players in earnest until late 1987, making them latecomers to a market already owned by the Los Angeles Dodgers. The Athletics ventured into the Dominican with the approval of Sandy Alderson and on the advice of Juan Marichal. In and out of baseball following his retirement as a player in 1974, Marichal convinced the Athletics he could find quality Dominican players for them, so they began investing modestly in player development. Unlike the Dodgers and Blue Jays, the A's were little guys in the Latin market, and Marichal worked without the benefit of an academy where players could live and be supervised around the clock.

Instead, the Athletics' Latin prospects trained at a rusted, fading old park in the capital, Santo Domingo, a place where hallways reeked of urine, where players practiced while smoke-belching trucks rumbled by, their exhaust fumes wafting over a concrete wall constructed with jagged pieces of glass at the very top to keep outsiders from climbing over. Inside, players ran laps on hard, red clay infields and lifted primitive barbells and dumbbells during conditioning drills—workouts topped off with oranges, rolls, orange juice, and bananas. The Dodgers felt that by building an academy, they could control what their players were eating and what they were doing during their off time. But during Marichal's early days, the A's ran their Latin operations on a tight budget, and players were left to find their own housing in Santo Domingo. Recruits often lived in cheap apartments in packs of four, five, and six so they could afford rent and food.

By 1993, the A's had gotten a few players to the major leagues, most notably Luis Polonia, the first Dominican the Athletics developed into a big leaguer. Brought up in 1987, what Polonia had going for him was his bat—he was hitting .321 with the Athletics' Triple A team in Tacoma when he got the call by then-Athletics manager Tony La Russa.

By the time Polonia first tried on the Athletics' green and gold, he had been a standout in the minor leagues—leading the Class A Midwest League in at-bats and hits in 1984; leading the Double A Southern League in triples in 1985; leading the Triple A Pacific Coast League in at-bats and hits in 1986, a season in which he batted .301 with 63 stolen bases. In 125 games with the Oakland Athletics in 1987, Polonia hit .287 while collecting 125 hits, 4 home runs, 49 RBIs and 29 stolen bases—a more than solid effort for a twenty-two-year-old rookie. Still, the next year Polonia began the season again in Tacoma—hitting .335 and stealing 31 bases in only 65 games. The A's promoted him again, and he hit .292 in 84 games for the Athletics. He also played in the League Championship Series, in which he collected 2 hits in 5 at-bats against the Boston Red Sox. And he played in three games of the 1988 World Series, which the Athletics lost to the Los Angeles Dodgers.

Then, on June 21, 1989, Polonia, Eric Plunk, and Greg Cadaret were dealt to the New York Yankees for Rickey Henderson. Henderson would go on to lead the A's to a World Championship that year. In baseball, business was business, and Polonia's trade was just that. Sent to New York, Polonia sadly ran afoul of the law and was busted and convicted in Milwaukee of having sex with an underaged girl. He would never quite be the same again, bouncing around the league to a number of teams. Meanwhile, the Dominicans who followed him in the Athletics system didn't exactly cover themselves with glory. Felix Jose, an outfielder and free swinger, appeared briefly in the 1988, 1989, and 1990 seasons before being traded in August 1990 to the St. Louis Cardinals.

Johnny Guzman, a left-handed pitcher, threw in five games in 1991 and two games in 1992 before being released. Catcher Henry Mercedes played briefly for the Athletics in 1992 and 1993 before being picked up by the Kansas City Royals. The Athletics had started another Dominican, Stan Javier, with success, but they didn't sign or develop him. Javier had been acquired in a trade with the New York Yankees that also brought pitcher Jose Rijo to the team in December 1984. Signed at fifteen by the Yankees in 1980, Rijo had made his major league debut in pinstripes at nineteen, pitching in 24 games in the 1984 season while going 2–8 and posting 2 saves. Rijo's arm was live, his potential limitless when, at nineteen, the Athletics acquired him. At twenty, twenty-one, and twenty-two, he pitched with moderate success for the Athletics before they traded him to the Cincinnati Reds at the end of the 1987 season. Even though the Athletics acquired powerhouse hitter Dave Parker in return, Rijo would come back to haunt them—beating them twice in the 1990 World Series while earning the Series MVP award. He would then become one of the best pitchers in the National League until arm problems ended his career.

Given this less-than-heralded history of Dominican recruitment, it was with difficulty that Soto tried to sell the Athletics on Miguel. Not having developed a lasting franchise player from the Caribbean, it was as if the Athletics still didn't know what they were looking for or what they wanted. Some coaches working the Dominican also questioned the Athletics' commitment in the Caribbean region.

The question was, why weren't Dominican players advancing in the Athletics system? By 1991, fifty out of the 170 players in their minor league system were Dominican. Between December 1987 and March 1988 alone they signed thirty Dominican players to contracts.[1]

Years later, some within the Athletics conceded that, at least at first, they viewed the Dominican not as a place to sign top talent, but as a source of cheap supplemental players whose main purpose was to fill out minor league rosters in the United States. Ron Plaza, a long-time instructor in the Athletics system who speaks Spanish fluently, was one of the point people for the Athletics in the Dominican.

Plaza remembers well why so many Dominicans weren't making it with the Athletics. "When we first went in there, we had a bunch of kids we signed that we knew weren't going to be prospects. But when you're trying to fill up a ball club, you have to sign a lot of players. . . . We did a lot of signing for numbers because we wanted to be by ourselves down there. We didn't want to have a co-op team, so you make a lot of mistakes in terms of signing people."[2]

With this atmosphere hanging in the air, Soto started badgering the Athletics about Miguel, but his efforts were getting him nowhere. Soto took Miguel to the Athletics' training camp in Santo Domingo for a tryout in the early summer of 1993. There, he played well, he hit well, he ran well. He did everything he had been taught to do and did it dressed in mud-caked white baseball pants, a torn Athletics T-shirt and a sweat-stained Athletics hat. At the end of the day, Miguel thought he'd passed the test, but the scouts were unimpressed.

They didn't see why they should pay money to sign Miguel when they already had a stable full of young kids who were better than he was. Miguel's competition were primarily other star players from Bani. Many of them were kids Miguel knew: Eddie Lara, a smooth shortstop who could hit and showed great range in the field; Freddie and José Soriano, brothers with phenomenal defensive skills and blazing speed; Arturo Paulino, from a nearby town called Palenque, who played the infield with intelligence; and Juan Polanco, another star shortstop and stolen base threat. Joining them in the Athletics camp was the player everyone thought had a great shot at the major leagues, a small, fiery shortstop named José Castro, who possessed a great arm, great speed, and great hands.

There were others, but these were the main kids occupying the minds of the Athletics scouts by June 1993. Miguel was poorer than all these boys, his life more remote. Except for Soto, no one had really seen him play. Soto thought Miguel was better than any of the other boys so he asked for another tryout. Still, no offer. Just under five-ten, Miguel showed up for the tryout dressed in ragged, ugly colors and wearing the same orange shirt and pants. He couldn't afford anything else. Miguel didn't know how silly he looked, until he was spotted by the other players already wearing Athletics uniforms.

To the other boys, Miguel was a novelty. One boy noticed that Miguel's clothes were the same colors as the buses running between Santo Domingo and neighboring Haiti—buses often carrying poor Haitians viewed by Dominicans as second-class citizens.

In the Dominican, as in Puerto Rico, the natives call their public transit by an odd-sounding name which, phonetically, is pronounced: "Wau-Wah." And so it was that from the summer of 1993 onward, the boys with the Oakland Athletics teasingly dubbed Miguel "Wau-Wah." Or, when being more formal, "La Wau-Wah Haitiana."

The Haitian bus.

The boys would laugh at Miguel when they said this, or make cracks about his cheap clothing. Miguel would try to play it off with boastful predictions that he was bound for stardom. He would say, "*Nos vemos en Tacoma,*" which means I'll see you in Tacoma, where the Athletics Triple A franchise was based in 1993. Without a leg to stand on, Miguel made his Tacoma comment to anyone who would listen, particularly the older Dominican players who hadn't yet reached Tacoma themselves.

Soon, Miguel was known as a *payaso*, or clown, a foolish loudmouth who hadn't done anything and yet was putting himself ahead of men who were establishing track records in the Athletics system while he was still an unsigned nobody. But to Miguel's way of thinking, all of the boys standing in line ahead of him could not match his abilities or desire. It was just a matter of time until he could prove it.

But weeks were slipping by and still no contract. Soto would drive him home at the end of practices, encouraging him, telling him not to give up. Miguel also took to staying in Santo Domingo during the week, rooming with other players while practicing with the Athletics. In the early mornings, he would rise and rush to the Athletics training park in Santo Domingo and work out as if he were a signed player. The atmosphere at the facility was far different from anything he had ever experienced. Santo Domingo was everything Bani wasn't. A sprawling metropolis of three million people, Santo Domingo can be an assault on the senses of the unprepared, a crazed, polluted, intimidating city where everything moves at hyper speed. The Athletics trained in an industrial area of the capital, where factory workers and other laborers toiled just outside the walls of the park called La Normal. But Dominicans rarely called La Normal or any other park by its formal name. To them, each park—whether it be Yankee Stadium or La Normal—is identified by a fusion of Spanish and baseballese: "El Play." They will say: "I'll see you at El Play." Or "At 3:00 P.M., I'll be at El Play."

And so life at El Play in Santo Domingo became a waiting game for Miguel. By July 1993, the staff of instructors evaluating the Athletics' Dominican investment were in the throes of their own competitive season: the Dominican Summer League. Set up and sanctioned by major league baseball, the league is a competition between the Latin recruits of major league teams, a proving ground where the standouts get an invitation to go to the United States. Also-rans might get asked back for a second summer, or they might not. Some are asked back for a third time, but that is all. There are no fourth summers for players in this league.

During most games, the only people in the stands are scouts and coaches, scribbling notes and assessing every move. Beginning in June, the season runs until September and is rated at the level of "rookie league." This is one of the lowest levels of the treacherous minor league system, where advancement means having to pass muster in instructional leagues, rookie leagues, Class A, Double A, and Triple A on the road to the majors.

Not all players have to prove themselves at every level: Some are shipped straight from Class A or Double A to the majors. Some never make it at all. But most Dominicans who pass the summer league test are sent either to low-level instructional leagues or rookie leagues in the United States, where they begin their climb through the organization.

For Miguel, his mission was clear. First, he had to get the Athletics to notice him somehow, to pick his face out of the dozens wearing Athletics uniforms. Then he would go head to head with the kids already in line ahead of him, performing like a demon so the evaluators would notice his ability. If he could secure a foothold, landing a spot on the Athletics summer league team, he would then have to play very well, behave very well, take instruction, and make the coaches feel he had talent.

If he ever got to the United States, he would have to shine in competition against American high-school and college kids, some of whom had signed for more money than Miguel could ever imagine. He would also have to cope with being away from the Dominican for the first time, with having his lack of education exposed for all to see day after day. If he remained healthy and played well, then maybe he would have a chance at advancing. But even if he impressed the scouts, there was also the very real chance that the Athletics would have an established big league infield, stalling him in the minor leagues unless he got lucky and was traded to a team with an opening. As luck would have it, the Athletics had solid, even potential All-Star talent in their middle infield in the summer of 1993, young players who might start for years to come.

At Miguel's shortstop position, there was Mike Bordick, a native of Marquette, Michigan, and a standout player at the University of Maine. Bordick batted .300 in 1992 for the Athletics and was considered a legitimate comer. As the 1993 season progressed, Bordick proved he was no fluke by playing flawlessly in the field, posting numbers that would eventually give him the second-best fielding percentage in the American League.

While Miguel cooled his heels at the back of the line in the Dominican, Bordick was starting a streak of 59 consecutive errorless games between July 7 and September 10. Also in 1993, the Athletics promoted a new second baseman named Brent Gates, their number-one draft pick in 1991. A former University of Minnesota All-American, his stellar credentials included being starting shortstop for Team USA in the 1989 Intercontinental Cup competition and being named Big Ten Player of the Year in 1991. Gates's ascent was so swift, his promise so great, he spent only one full year in the minor leagues. On May 5, 1993, he made his major league debut by stroking two hits at Fenway Park against the Boston Red Sox. Although Gates joined the Athletics 22 games into the 1993 season, he would lead the team in multihit games with 49 and finish second on the team in RBI with 69. He committed only 6 errors in 391 chances at second and hit a solid .290. At twenty-three, Gates was just beginning, and with Bordick coming into his own at twenty-eight, Miguel's chances seemed nonexistent, just another in a long line of Dominican rejects.

Luckily for him, he didn't know that. Yet with no contract in hand, Miguel could only watch from the sidelines because the Dominican Summer League is reserved for boys signed by major league teams. So he watched while older players competed against clubs run by the Toronto Blue Jays, New York Yankees, Philadelphia Phillies, and a host of other major league teams.

DURING THAT SUMMER every move Dominican players made was logged in scouting reports that were painstakingly filled out and forwarded to ranking scouts in the Athletics system. At this stage of the game, no players were safe from scrutiny or protected by talent or reputation. They were all starting from the same point, their bonuses meager and their obstacles daunting. Most players could be released for not paying attention, for tardiness, for talking back, or for not progressing quickly enough.

While Miguel waited, some of the older boys in camp were starting to stand out, particularly José Castro. At five feet ten inches, Castro was a switch hitter who was approaching his nineteenth birthday that summer. Signed by the Athletics in March 1993, Castro had a buzz following him, the kind of excitement generated when newfound talent inspires hope for the future.

Castro was a smartass, he had an attitude, a strut that was plainly evident every time he took the field. Castro had relatives in New York City and, in fact, had been there himself and was already saying he would live in the United States no matter what. He planned for baseball to be his ticket off the island, but his familiarity with New York was always there to fall back on in case his prospects stalled.

But that seemed unlikely in 1993. Miguel would watch Castro with a sense of awe that summer, quietly marveling at his arm strength. In fact, he was already making major league-quality plays that summer, finishing them off with fantastic throws that seemed shot out of a cannon. Castro had great hands and a beautiful way of anticipating the ball while fluidly moving his body to meet it and make the play. At that point, he had the refinement that Soto wanted for Miguel.

The Athletics could swallow Castro's smirk and his habit of talking back because his play was stellar. Miguel didn't have such luxuries. He had to be on his best behavior. "What if I don't get signed?" he would ask himself. "What will I do then?" But on July 17, 1993, he finally stopped wondering.

The Athletics offered Miguel a contract. At that point, the most they were paying was five thousand dollars and they didn't think Miguel was worth that much. So they offered him two thousand dollars—a low amount even for a Dominican player. At that moment, there was little money to be made off him, so Miguel had no agent. He didn't even know what his contract really said. Soto had taught him as much as he could, but the actual terms of Miguel's deal were out of his hands. Miguel was still alone. Negotiations would be a one-way street. His choice: Take it or leave it. This was a far cry from the treatment of the bonus babies of America with their parents, their agents, and their lawyers.

There Miguel sat, alone with "Chago" Marichal, Juan's pudgy, balding nephew. "Chago" has a plump face with a wiry mustache, gray flecks in his five-o'clock shadow, and a tough demeanor when behind closed doors with a prospect. He tends to get right to the point.

"Here are the terms, son," he will say. "The Athletics are giving you a great opportunity." When told the money he would get Miguel nodded and took pen in hand. In his tiny, barely legible script, he signed his name. Chago said, "Welcome to the Oakland Athletics, son. What you have to do is give it everything you've got." Miguel shook Chago's hand and soon had two thousand dollars to spend.

There were no wild celebrations or irresponsible spending sprees. Instead, Miguel bought furniture for his father and clothes for his siblings, spending the entire two thousand dollars within a matter of weeks.

Suddenly, friends he didn't know he had and relatives he hadn't seen in years were coming around, asking for money or whatever he could spare. Miguel was happy, he was happy as other Dominican players before him had been happy.

Although he would make millions later as an All-Star slugger, Julio Franco remembers the day he got his four-thousand-dollar signing bonus as one of the happiest of his life. Miguel was finally getting paid to play baseball, to be a professional, to be somebody. The Athletics gave him a pair of spikes, a glove, a hat, and some T-shirts. He stayed in Santo Domingo, living with the other prospects. Together, they would pool their money and buy beans, rice, and plantains.

He was now a professional, and he yearned to start playing. But with the summer league season already under way, the Athletics had other ideas. Even though they only shelled out two thousand dollars for Miguel, they didn't want that money to go to waste by having him play half a season while getting credit for playing a full year. Since there was a three-year maximum for each summer league player, the Athletics decided that Miguel would sit and watch for the rest of the season.

And so he did, playing only in simulated games after the real players had finished and gone home. In those games, with no one watching but a few coaches, Miguel started his professional career—at a salary of one hundred dollars a week, paid in cash. At the end of each practice, he helped the other boys, picking up balls, bases, and other equipment stored in the bowels of La Normal.

The next day he would be back, watching others play, dreaming of his chance to play.

4

THE WAY NORTH

THE OAKLAND ATHLETICS baseball complex sits on roughly seventy acres of farmland cut from a jungle, thirty-five miles outside the Dominican capital of Santo Domingo. One can reach the complex via a circuitous road of clogged suburban streets and desolate country roads where ox-driven carts haul produce day and night. The drive from Santo Domingo to the complex, which sits outside the small town of La Victoria, is a jarring one. "Dominican driving!" Enrique Soto announces as he skids across potholes and tears around poor, startled oxen before getting back into his lane as an exhaust-belching truck barrels past him at 80 mph. The force of the truck whips over Soto's car, causing its front tires to momentarily zig-zag. Soto seems to enjoys this. Looking over in perfect deadpan, he laughs in a mockingly sinister way.

Then he says: "You like Dominican? Right now, you got no choice, no? Heh-heh-heh-heh." In reality, it's a wonder the two-lane roadways of the Dominican don't produce massive crashes every day, considering the breakneck speeds of cars and trucks and buses hurtling back and forth, wildly passing each other while negotiating a gauntlet of burros, tractors, motor scooters, and fearless pedestrians walking the roads.

Lining the road to the complex are vast, lush fields of vegetation and underbrush stretching to the horizon. People of "el campo" dot the landscapes. Destitute locals work the land and live in shantytowns like *Los Barrancones* or worse. At night, a driver or a pedestrian must know the way by instinct because there are no street lights. Under the stars, the dense countryside provides no clues to the unfamiliar. Driving on and on and on, it sometimes seems as if the road leads to nowhere, making it difficult to imagine such an untamed, otherworldly place could be a hotbed for major league baseball. But that it is. Suddenly, after winding hard left for several miles, the road straightens and leads to a gravel pathway, bordered by brush and peppered with squatters who burn their garbage before a tiny, hand-painted, green and gold sign bearing the insignia of the Oakland Athletics. Seeing it, one can't help but wonder what corporate season ticket holders from the Oakland hills, Alameda, or San Jose would think if they saw this. Turning slowly down the gravel path, visitors are checked out by a uniformed guard with drooping pants, a slight paunch, ragged hair, and a sawed-off shotgun. The shotgun is a business decision—there are things of value inside those gates and people with nothing outside them. It's the same way at many restaurants and hotels in the Dominican, particularly those along the beautiful coastlines.

If everything checks out and clearance is granted, one takes a road stretching about a quarter mile to an enormous dormitory sitting adjacent to two perfectly manicured playing fields, a batting cage, a practice infield, and pitchers' mounds.

Inside the main, two-story building are dorm rooms filled with bunk beds where up to seventy players can live. Next door is a large recreation room where the boys congregate after practicing all day to watch bad American movies or baseball games at ear-splitting decibels. Around a pathway of Spanish tile are extra rooms for live-in staff, with the best rooms saved for visiting Athletics coaches who travel here periodically to offer instruction and assess the latest bumper crop of players. "Surveying the livestock," as prospect Arturo Paulino once put it.

Behind the complex, the Athletics have assembled a makeshift gymnasium with primitive weights and dumbbells. And around the corner from an administrative office where Raymond Abreu—a former small college football player and Price

Waterhouse executive who oversees the whole operation—sits is the most important room of all: the cafeteria. It is here, guided by the model developed by Rafael Avila and the Dodgers, that the Athletics pump proteins and carbohydrates into emaciated future stars like Miguel Tejada.

Juan Marichal had been pushing the Athletics to buy a complex for years and finally, the team relented erecting the building and laying the fields on a sprawling patch of earth fit only for cows and chickens. The cost for the land, the construction, the clearing of underbrush, and the seeding of baseball-worthy grass was roughly $1 million, or what the Athletics and other teams spend on the bonus of a single top American prospect.[1] Because of this, it's easy to see why baseball men like the Dominican so much. The Athletics acquired the property from a family who grew weary of tending it. The team had looked at about a half dozen sites before settling on a spot just outside La Victoria, but every time a deal was imminent the price would triple when it was discovered the Athletics were the buyers. "When Juan was negotiating for the land we finally took, he was going strictly on his own, he wasn't mentioning Oakland," said Athletics instructor Ron Plaza.[2] "Getting the complex was important because we never had control of these kids before. The only time we had them was on the field. Then they would go home and we'd have a lot of problems. We had a couple of kids walking around Santo Domingo one night and they ended up in jail.

"We couldn't control what they ate, how much they slept. But once we got them at the complex they were ours. They slept there. They ate there. There was no place to go."

"Campo Juan Marichal" opened in May 1994. It was an ideal site in one sense because it was safely outside the wild environs of Santo Domingo, where players were scattered all over town, most living in deplorable conditions. Antonio Santibel, for one, a tall, wiry pitcher who lived in a tiny hovel in a depressed Santo Domingo barrio, would endure long bus rides home to his family outside the coastal town of La Romana when the team had an off day. He would then make the three-hour trek back to Santo Domingo the next day for practice.

Left to his own devices, he ate mostly rice and beans with enormous amounts of salt. Santibel was from a family of sugar cane cutters. He was six feet tall and thin as a rail, with long limbs and pointed joints. By the time the complex came around it was too late for Santibel. He was released by the Athletics at the end of the 1993 summer league season. He was a sweet kid, good-natured and almost childlike, a product of a complete lack of education and a lifetime of dreaming and hoping while wielding a machete in the cane fields outside La Romana. Maybe if he'd had a stable environment, like the Athletics complex, Santibel would have had a chance. Or maybe not. Shortly after he was cut from the A's, the Baltimore Orioles gave him a look. Santibel killed his chances by being goaded into a fight with another boy.

So all Santibel had at the end was an Athletics cap and a taste for Copenhagen chewing tobacco. Juan Perez, a left-handed pitcher in the Athletics system, said Santibel went back to cutting cane in La Romana, to the same life he had before. His short time with the Athletics was merely a brief interlude in a life of poverty. While Santibel went back to piecemeal wages and back-breaking work, much luckier boys were sequestered back at the Athletics complex, living on grounds that were a virtual island in a sea of farmlands and everglades.

Miguel was thrilled when he moved into the complex and anxious to start a season he knew would be his proving ground for the big time. All that winter he had practiced hard with Soto in Bani, and he felt happy to be part of the team.

After watching other players take their chances the year before, Miguel was dying to get going. But his coaches had seen nothing to change their assessment of him. While going through various drills in practice, there was no flash of inspiration, no towering hit, no fabulous stop that led anyone to believe Miguel would be anything but a bench warmer. "He was one of the crowd," said Luis Martinez, the manager of the Athletics summer league team in 1994.[3] Making Miguel's chances seem even more remote was that the Athletics couldn't allow him to travel to the United States as he was. He had too much of *Los Barrancones* in him. He was still too thin, too small, too uneducated, too unrefined, too unfamiliar with the concept of team, too immersed in the only thing he had ever been able to count on—his sense of individuality. In the eyes of American coaches, Miguel's aggressive style would be great if channeled into a "team" concept. That's the American game. Miguel had learned baseball in *Los Barrancones,* in games that were actually more collections of boys giving everything they had every chance they got. The object was to get noticed. If you got noticed, you got signed. If you got signed, you got sent to the United States. If you got sent to the United States, you had a chance to reach the major leagues, to make the big money and reap the benefits that went with that. But Miguel was far from that goal. "Miggy was a strange kind of kid," Plaza said. "He was a little bit different. We'd be having a meeting and you'd look over and he'd be yawning. He never talked back to anyone but he wouldn't be paying attention. We would have meetings in the evening after practice and I know the kids would be tired and sometimes Miggy would sit there with an expression like: 'I don't want to be hearing this.'

"We'd be holding the meetings in Spanish, not in English, and he'd still be sitting there, just not with it. And I'd say, 'Miggy, god damn it! Tell me what I just said.' And he'd just sit there, not able to tell me.' "[4]

So starting from scratch, as if they were remaking young men, the Athletics set about shaping Miguel so he would be fit to play and survive in the United States. In a sense, Miguel was lucky he came along when he did. The Athletics were learning from their mistakes, building a more competitive program. They hired a psychologist to weed out boys unprepared for discipline—a significant issue for the Athletics in their Latin recruitment.

"There were lots of problems," said Hector Rodriguez, a Dominican psychologist the Athletics hired for a time in the early 1990s. "The players were having a difficult time adapting, they were having language problems and also there was the problem of incorporating into American culture."[5]

The Athletics had also hired Dominicans with real baseball experience to coach prospects, unlike the early days when most instructors had never played professional ball.

One of those new coaches was Luis Martinez, who had been signed as an infielder by the Athletics in 1985 and learned baseball the hard way. Totally unprepared by the Athletics, Martinez lasted four years in the minors before being released. The tone for his career was set that first spring of 1985, when he was shipped to the Athletics' Class A team in Medford, Oregon.

"We had three days in Medford before the season started. There were four of us Dominicans on the team. [After arriving] they told us that our checks hadn't come and that we were to eat at a particular restaurant and charge it to the team. But we were embarrassed because we couldn't speak English, so we didn't go. And for three days, all we ate was potato chips from vending machines that we would get by putting our coins together," Martinez said.[6]

"I've never been so hungry in my life. We did that because whenever we tried to speak English, the other players would laugh at us. That affects you. Later, the manager heard about our problem and asked this Cuban-American guy on our team to help us. He did for a while, but then he got tired of it. We were really on our own. One of the few words I knew in English back then was pancakes. So we would go to restaurants and that's all I could say. One time I tried to order an egg but when they asked me how I wanted it I didn't know how to say scrambled, so I ended up saying pancakes. That's all I ate for weeks. To this day, I will never eat another pancake again as long as I live."

The end for Martinez, as a player, came at the conclusion of the 1988 season. As a coach, he took it upon himself to make sure Miguel and other Dominicans were ready for battle. That process began in May 1994 when Miguel stepped on a scale with his Dominican coaches watching. The team wanted to establish a baseline for its players, to keep records of how much they weighed when they came in so they could track the effects of baked fish, fresh vegetables, purified water, and baked chicken with rice and beans on their players. "What we found was that once these kids started eating, some would put on as much as ten pounds in a month and gain as many as thirty pounds," Abreu said.[7] Miguel weighed roughly one hundred seventy pounds and seemed smaller and more frail than other players.

With the summer league season starting in June, the team went to work, practicing all day in a series of drills beginning at 8:00 A.M. and ending at about 4:00 P.M., with breakfast and lunch squeezed in between. Early meals would be light: fruit, hot dogs, sandwiches. Miguel and other boys were taught to re-move their caps when entering a room, to stand in line in an or-derly fashion, and to maintain decorum while eating. After practice, Miguel and his teammates were required to shower, ei-ther before they ate dinner or slightly after. Dinners were tradi-tional Dominican meals of chicken or fish, with heaping plates of white rice, beans, and vegetables. Miguel would eat quickly, shoving large pieces of chicken into his mouth and chewing feverishly, often leaving his slightly greasy fingertips adorned with tiny grains of rice. On some nights, down time would mean watching television or hanging out on the expansive grounds that were fenced off by sturdy chainlink fences and ringed by wild underbrush and hundreds of palm trees.

Miguel had been lonely the year before in Santo Domingo, but the isolation of the camp exacerbated those feelings. Miguel and the other boys would listen to merengue at night, lying on their bunks in their underwear, laughing and hooting and hol-lering. Often Miguel's mind and thoughts would drift away, to dreams still unfulfilled. The next day it was back to practice and the social skills the Athletics wanted him to learn. English was hardest of all. Taught by instructors transported into the camp for lessons, Miguel would take his place at tables with his team-mates—pencil in hand—and begin his class.

The boys would recite the alphabet, earnestly butchering the simplest exercise while having a particularly hard time bending their mouths to pronounce a W, which came out sounding like "dole-you." The lessons were held three times a week for roughly an hour. Boys were broken into groups accord-ing to how much education they had. Some, like Miguel, had al-most none and started out by playing games of "Simon Says."

Despite his lack of education, Miguel began to set himself apart. After some early scoldings from Plaza and others, a pat-tern started to develop. Miguel stood out by outworking every-one else. He wanted to learn English because he wanted to express himself when he made his run at the majors.

So he applied himself when learning the difference between a brother-in-law and a sister-in-law. He would repeat over and over: "The English word for *hermano* is 'brother.' " It was all very regimented, down to regulations requiring players to make their beds every morning, to wear sandals in the shower to guard against athlete's foot, to brush their teeth, to comb their hair, to respect their coaches, and to think of themselves as part of something. "Part of the psychology of poverty, the culture of poverty, is a lack of discipline," Rodriguez said. "So we try to establish a mindset of professionalism, to strive for excellence. . . . In baseball there is a hierarchy. There is a manager, there are coaches, trainers, and for those people you have to have respect. But if a player is coming from a home where there is no order in that player's house then it's going to be difficult to work in an organizational structure."[8]

Rodriguez could easily have been describing Miguel's life. Based on those generalizations, Miguel would have been high on the list of potential troublemakers. But he wasn't. In fact, something began happening in practices, too—something that developed over time as the days approached for the start of the 1994 summer league season. "He was inexhaustible," said the Athletics' Dominican batting coach Tomas Silverio.[9] "He would cut in line for batting practice and if he had twenty swings coming, he would want twenty more. Then he would get his glove and go out to infield practice and take grounder after grounder, working harder and harder with each day. I'll never forget it as long as I live. He would take opportunities away from other players."

In baseball, first impressions—those magical moments when a coach or scout first lays eyes on a "phenom"—are legendary. But in Miguel's case, these coaches were being slowly won over. "My first impression was that his physical conditioning wasn't that impressive," Silverio said. "He was very small. . . . We would do a sixty-yard drill and we would look for them to do it in about 4.7 seconds, but he didn't reach that. And I noticed that he breathed like a bull, through his nose. When he ran he would make that sound, 'whooh, whoooh, whooh, whooh.' You could hear it. You could hear that breathing. You could tell he was looking for that little extra.

"He said he wanted to work, but I have to tell you he didn't have the tools to make you notice him. He had to come back because they didn't want to sign him." And even though Miguel was earning points for his work ethic, he had no game experience to set himself apart. So the evaluation went on, with the emphasis on other players. The Athletics had sent Jose Castro

to the United States that spring but there were other players getting far more attention than Miguel.

Eddie Lara had played in the summer league season in
1993 and had batted .343. The coaches liked the way he played
shortstop, though they were concerned about his commitment,
fretting that he was too flighty and undisciplined for the United
States. Because of this, they held on to him for another year to
see how he did in '94. Lara was from Bani, like Miguel, and was
one of those kids pegged as having exciting physical skills but a
questionable head—a very serious concern for an organization
still struggling to establish itself in the Dominican.

Lara is a small kid with a round head, chubby cheeks, an
overbite and a nervous twitch in his eyes that makes him blink
repeatedly. His voice is permanently hoarse for some reason
and sometimes when he talks, little formations of spit accumu-
late at his mouth corners. Like Miguel, Lara was the hope of his
family, particularly since he had never known his father—his
parents separated when he was very young and his father left
the family to live with another woman in Santo Domingo.
Though Lara was normally sweet-tempered and wanted to play
professional ball very badly, he was not doing well in the American baseball system. He had a tendency to talk back, to bristle
at the hard orders he was taking and the regimented schedule
he was living. And he would confound his coaches by following
a brilliant play at short with a bonehead lapse of concentration,
letting a ball roll right through his legs, forgetting to tag out a
runner, moving slowly toward a ball and letting it go past him
when he had the speed to reach it. "I made Lara run lots of
laps," Silverio said. "He was running a lot that summer." [10]

Also rated above Miguel was Arturo Paulino, who was
known to everyone as "Tabacco." Like Lara, Tabacco had
played in the summer league in 1993, batting .285 and playing
solid infield. But unlike Lara, he had been sent to Arizona the
spring of '94. Tabacco was a sensitive kid, a brooding, pes-
simistic young man who played with emotion. Tabacco had
dark skin, deep, inset eyes, and a protruding brow that got noticed in the United States. In 1996, while playing for a Class A
team in western Michigan, some of Tabacco's American teammates derisively dubbed him "ET."

Also returning to the summer league team for the '94 season was Juan Polanco. He had batted .262 the year before but was showing some pop in his bat and was beginning to put on bulk to go with his speed and fielding ability. Polanco was also from Bani and had been signed by Soto. That summer he seemed poised to break through. In the week leading up to the first game of the season, Martinez and his coaching staff decided to start Lara at short and Polanco at second, while Miguel rode the bench. The team wanted to start older players. In those practices in late May '94, the coaches worked with an added purpose—now in their new complex, the entire organization felt enhanced pressure to produce. So they drilled the boys over and over on fundamentals. Players were being taught in English, with outfielders learning to scream "I got it!" when calling off another player. Pitchers and catchers repeatedly practiced a drill in which the ball would get behind the catcher and the pitcher would yell, "To the left. To the left. To the left," or right, depending on which way the ball went. Miguel took turns in infield practice behind Lara and Polanco, who were looking much better to the coaches than he was.

"Lara was better than Tejada in batting, he could hit to the opposite field, and [Miguel] didn't have the physical conditioning that Lara had," Silverio said.[11]

On top of that, while Miguel's intensity impressed his coaches, it sometimes concerned them as well. Especially in batting practice, Miguel would be so pumped up, he would lunge at pitches, literally jerking his body upward while flailing at the ball. So as batting coach, Silverio worked hard at making him plant his feet, keeping his head down and his body centered as he drove through the ball. By the eve of the first game, Silverio had made good progress, keeping Miguel's feet planted more and more each day. The ball was beginning to jump off Miguel's bat with a pop that surprised his coaches.

He had hit the ball hard on the sandlots of Bani, but this place was different. He wasn't being pitched to by barrio burnouts or lifeless kids, but by real prospects with live arms who were throwing hard. Meanwhile, coaches with minor league experience were giving him his first taste of serious curveballs. And he had other lessons to learn, lessons that—in the long run—were every bit as important to him as what he was learning on the field. Miguel was part of an investment by the Athletics and, in a larger sense, an investment by major league baseball in Latin America.

As part of that investment, Miguel's attitude, like the attitudes of other boys, was under constant scrutiny because it was believed that substandard attitudes were helping derail many Dominican players, not only in the Athletics system, but throughout baseball. Not only Dominican players, but all Latins were suspect in this sense. So Miguel's coaches were on the lookout and, being only eighteen, it wasn't long before Miguel ran headlong into American-style discipline. In his dormitory after a practice, Miguel was standing completely nude before taking a shower and was horsing around with some of the other boys. Silverio happened to be standing in the dorm as well and when their eyes met, Miguel took his genitals in his right hand and said: "Tomas, I have something here for you." It was meant as a joke, but Silverio was stunned. He immediately dressed Miguel down in front of his friends and told him there would be a punishment waiting for him the next day.

Being a veteran baseball man, Silverio knew that coaching a team required different methods for different players. When Eddie Lara, with his lazy streak, mouthed off, his punishment was running laps around the outfield. Lots of laps. But what do you do to a kid who never tires of working and, in fact, only seems whole, happy, and secure when sweat is pouring off his forehead, when he is taking batting practice for so long his arms go numb, when he is fielding so many grounders he wears out his coach before he gets tired?

To punish that kid, you sit him down. You make him watch others play. You make him do that all day so that he can get a real sense of what he has in life when he isn't playing. "He'll never forget that day," Silverio said. "It killed him. But I couldn't permit that. I couldn't permit that kind of talk and lack of respect. There is no way he could get away with that in the United States." [12] So Miguel, who had grown up like wild grass, learned another lesson about American baseball. One he wouldn't forget. It changed him.

IN A WAY, Miguel's apprenticeship, his training to fit into an American system, was very Dominican. Baseball is the most visible example of the influence the United States has over a country about half the size of South Carolina. The game itself took root in the Dominican, was organized, institutionalized, and popularized in the early part of this century after the United States essentially took over the Dominican economy. American sugar barons had begun investing in the Dominican in the late nineteenth century, a time when a growing American nation—recovered from the Civil War—was starting to flex its muscles. In 1898, the United States drove Spain out of Cuba and Puerto Rico and found Dominican ports—poised between Spain's last colonial holdings—invaluable for strategic purposes. "The attitude that the Caribbean is an 'American backyard' and its southern first line of defense has been held by all U.S. presidents since James Monroe."[13]

By the first years of the twentieth century, an enduring relationship had been formed. "As its debts grew, the Dominican government gave over increasing amounts of its revenues and administrative control to American companies, and this helped foster the growth of the sugar industry. The government's burgeoning debt led it to exempt American companies from taxes, and to make up for the loss of revenues the Dominican government taxed its own farmers to the hilt. As a result, many smaller farmers were displaced, and their land was quickly bought up by American companies."[14]

As a result, dissension grew among the poor Dominican farmers who were angered by the loss of their way of life and the "ineptitude" of the Dominican government. There was rioting, looting, and violence. And so the United States sent in the Marines in 1916 to put down the revolt and protect their business interests. They stayed eight years, though it was hardly the first time the Dominican had been occupied.

Throughout history, the beautiful, nineteen-thousand-square-mile island of breathtaking beaches, mountains, and spectacular valleys, has been lusted after by larger, stronger nations.

Major league baseball is simply the latest powerful foreign institution to have designs on the place proclaimed by Columbus as "the fairest under the sun." Indeed, though you would scarcely know it in the United States, the Dominican has been a key outpost of history in the Western Hemisphere. "Not only was [the Dominican Republic] the first permanent colony in the

New World, it was also the site of the first cathedral, the first university. . . . It was additionally where Spain's first colonial, social, economic and political experiments took place: the . . . systems of exploiting native labor." [15]

After wiping out the indigenous Taino Indians, the Spaniards began importing African slaves in 1503. But years of prosperity for some began to end in the late 1500s when an earthquake destroyed many island settlements and many of the rest were raided by English pirates. Then, in 1586, Sir Francis Drake led an attack on the island, burning Santo Domingo to the ground. [16] For the next two hundred years, a time that saw massive burning, looting, and destruction, an indentured, two-tiered hierarchy was alternately fought over, controlled, and abandoned by Spain and France. From 1822 to 1844, neighboring Haiti occupied the Dominican in a bloody takeover that strains interisland relations to this day. And it wasn't until 1844 that an independence of sorts was secured. "The father of Dominican independence, however, was reluctant to wield the levers of power. While [Juan Pablo] Duarte procrastinated and was soon exiled, political power was consolidated in the hands of two self-appointed generals, Buenventura Baez and Pedro Santana. . . . Although it's difficult to decipher the national objectives of these two dictators, both had a vague design to restore the country to its earlier order and greatness and to develop close ties with a foreign protector. . . . Both feared the continous invasions of a more populous Haiti and they approached, in turn, England, France, Spain and the United States to offer an alliance and concessions as a way of safeguarding the country from invasion." [17]

"The protectorate idea and the concessions, however, also made the Dominican Republic a dependency—a virtual colony—of these larger powers." [18]

The turmoil that was the Caribbean led Thomas Jefferson to write, "History furnishes no example of a priest-ridden people maintaining a civil government. . . . America has a hemisphere to itself." [19]

So the Marines went in, and what they found were destitute people who already knew how to play baseball, having been taught by Cubans who learned it from Americans. "While the marines defended the sugar mills in the east and went into 'Indian country' to search and destroy, resistance in Santo Domingo took on a more refined cast." Guerrillas waged their hit-and-run campaigns [against the Marines] while Santo Domingo's youth played ball with them. Actually, they played more against them than with them. U.S. Navy teams had played against Dominican teams while on layover for years before the occupation began. And as U.S. interests on the island grew, especially during the tense years before the takeover, these vessels appeared more frequently. With the occupation, the number of North American military men skyrocketed. So, too, did the number of confrontations on the diamond. These games became a point of positive contact for Yankees and Dominicans, as well as a chance for the latter to measure themselves against their occupiers.[20]

In America, baseball was born a game of community and family, and at the time of the Dominican invasion, baseball stars were becoming national names while, at the grass-roots level, spirited players barnstormed from town to town in the tradition of the early American pioneers.

In the Dominican, baseball symbolized the American occupation.

Young Dominican men with no national identity to speak of after 1916 could do nothing as warships docked in their harbors and Marines stormed village after village. The only way they could measure up was by playing baseball. So they did. In this way, the Dominican is representative of the roots of Latin baseball, a game in which the stakes have always been higher, success more meaningful, and failure more painful—a brand of baseball that makes the word "pastime" seem trivial.

Beginning in Cuba, the game took hold after American sugar ship workers first played against locals in the mid-1860s. Once Cubans had been bitten by the bug, baseball took off largely through the efforts of a man named Emilio Sabourin. He helped found *La Liga de Baseball Profesional Cubana* in 1878.

And it cost him his life.

Cuba was still controlled by colonial Spanish forces, who got wind that Sabourin was using gate receipts from early baseball games to help fund the burgeoning Cuban independence movement led by José Marti. In December 1895, Sabourin and other baseball league officials were arrested, shackled, tried, and convicted by ruling Spanish authorities. Sabourin was shipped off to a penal colony in Morocco where he died miserably of pneumonia in 1897.

But baseball went on, moving across much of Latin America with the expanding influence of the United States throughout the hemisphere. Cuban enthusiasts helped the process of popularizing the game in the Dominican, Mexico, and Venezuela, but formal, organized indoctrination was carried out by Americans.

Almost all the nations and territories producing Latin players today have been invaded by U.S. troops in the last century: the Dominican Republic, Cuba, Puerto Rico, Mexico, Panama, and Nicaragua. And if it wasn't an invasion by American troops, it was American businesses that organized the sport. In Venezuela, U.S. oil interests helped popularize the game, and even today, Venezuela deals the United States middle infielders and petroleum. That Venezuela is the largest foreign exporter of oil to the United States is exemplified by the flashing neon CITGO sign visible over the Green Monster at Fenway. Citgo is a Venezuelan oil company.

Along with U.S. soldiers and sailors, U.S. railroads helped spread the game in Mexico. In Panama, it was workers in the Panama Canal Zone. All these nations view the United States with an ambivalent mixture of respect and resentment, a capacity for shifting degrees of love and loathing. The Dominican Republic is the nation that sends the most Latin players to the major leagues, and the story of the relationship of the Dominican and the U.S. contains every shade of gray in the complex tapestry that produced Miguel Tejada.

Those conflicting emotions are exemplified by Juan Bosch, who was elected president of the Dominican Republic in 1963—two years after the assassination of Rafael Trujillo, an iron-fisted dictator who carried out a reign of terror during a thirty-year rule. "The [1916] occupation did nothing for our game because our teams were already formed and playing by then. These games were not a form of collaboration with the North Americans, nor would I consider them acts of friendship. These games manifested a form of the people's distaste for occupation. They were a repudiation of it. And when a Dominican player would do something great, the people would shout their hoorays. The game was seen as a way to beat the North Americans," Bosch said.[21]

Over time, baseball also became the game for the poor in the Dominican Republic, one of the few avenues for recreation in lives marked by hard, back-breaking work in the sugar cane fields, the banana orchards, and the nickel mines. In the early years, shortly after the 1916 invasion, young Dominican men found solace in baseball, particularly after Marines disarmed the country and put down all resistance. "This mass disarming constituted a collective castration. . . . most Dominican males were to find some sort of substitute in bat and balls."[22]

Baseball also became associated with employment, wages, and jobs. Indeed, it was American sugar and fruit companies that built fields all over the Dominican and offered perks such as half days off so workers could play. The intent was to keep workers close to the land, and it worked.

Even Juan Marichal—the greatest Dominican player ever—got his start playing for a team sponsored by a subsidiary of the Boston-based United Fruit Company. In his 1991 book *Tropic of Baseball,* writer Rob Ruck quoted many prominent Dominicans who gave voice to the complex emotions behind the passion Dominicans have for baseball. One said: "Eight years under the invader's boots! This is a shameful thing for a country and there are scars on the body of our country. That is something for which the United States cannot be forgiven. . . . One can like a North American. One can love a North American. But with the government, one's warmth cools down, because it represents the state, and the state sometimes has a way of thinking that does not benefit the people. . . . Baseball is the national sport of the United States and it is the greatest thing that the United States has given us and the other countries of the Caribbean."

But the United States also gave the Dominican Rafael Trujillo, who seized power in his country in 1930 after being commander of a National Guard organized by the Marines to help keep resisters in their place.

At first a symbol of power and virility to a nation stripped of national honor, Trujillo became a despot, a cold-blooded killer of thousands, while receiving the backing of U.S. leaders through his support of American business interests and "anti-communist" credentials. One of the things Trujillo is most remembered for is ordering the massive slaughter of thousands of Haitians in the Dominican Republic in an effort to "whiten" the country. It is estimated that twenty-five thousand Haitians were executed, decapitated, or thrown into the sea in 1937.

Trujillo is also remembered for supporting baseball as a way of appealing to the masses—even though it is said he didn't much care for the game itself. By the mid-1930s, the greatest Negro League players of America were traveling to the Dominican, playing on the island in the winter. In 1935, the Cincinnati Reds became the first major league team to visit. And in 1937, a team bearing Trujillo's name won the fledgling Dominican League championship while boasting some of the greatest names in Negro League history: Josh Gibson, Satchel Paige, and James "Cool Papa" Bell were all on that team. All are now in baseball's Hall of Fame. Also on the team was Puerto Rican great Perucho Cepeda, the father of major league star Orlando Cepeda. Trujillo would watch games while perched regally in a special box, often decked out in full military regalia.[23]

Through the 1940s and 1950s, Trujillo consolidated his power, the poor of the Dominican remained poor, and baseball became part of the Dominican psyche. By 1961, the year Trujillo was assassinated, Dominicans had started reaching the major leagues, stoking the imaginations of poor Dominican youth. The country was also headed for its first truly democratic election in decades. When Bosch took office in 1963, the events of his short-lived but tumultuous presidency clearly illustrated the relationship between the United States and the Dominican Republic. "Bosch made a point of seeking aid and investment from European countries as a means of establishing economic independence and counterbalancing U.S. influence. Not surprisingly, some U.S. officials saw this as an affront."[24] Having also alienated elite Dominicans who feared his populist ways, Bosch was overthrown on September 25, 1963, seven months after he took office.

"The United States played a much more open role in this conflict than it did elsewhere. It not only agitated to oust Bosch but sent the marines into the country to make sure Bosch's supporters would not succeed in their efforts to regain power."[25] It was reported widely that the American ambassador to the Dominican Republic tried to contact U.S. military advisors to head off the coup but couldn't reach them by phone. Bosch later charged the United States with conspiracy to overthrow his government.

Pro-Bosch forces were put down by U.S. Marines in 1965.

The rest, as they say, is history. Since the mid-1960s the Dominican has continued on the same path as before—as one of the poorest nations in Latin America, despite a wealth of natural resources. By the time Miguel was born in 1976 it had become clear that baseball was the only hope for the economically disadvantaged Dominicans.

Because of this, most Dominican players are either black, like Miguel, or very dark. In the Dominican, "Race and class [are] closely tied together. The white element tends to be wealthier and to form the Dominican elite. The middle class tends to be mulatto. The working classes, rural and urban, tend to be black or dark mulatto." [26]

Today, an overwhelming 80 percent of the 8 million Dominicans live in abject poverty. [27] The country has the lowest per capita income in the hemisphere ($1,222 in 1991), one of the lowest literacy rates (68 percent), and one of the lowest rates of life expectancy (about sixty-three years). [28]

The legacy of the Dominican people can be found in a study released by the Dominican Planning Agency. It indicated that "the diets of 75 percent of the population were inadequate and that 50 percent had seriously deficient diets. Only 55 percent of the population has access to safe water." [29]

That study was released in 1978, two years after Miguel was born. By then the Dominican was known as a "company state" to the United States. All the major private sectors of the economy—agroindustry, mining, tourism, and light manufacturing—are controlled by foreign, mainly U.S. companies. So when major league baseball came calling, it was only following a well-traveled path to Miguel's country.

MIGUEL'S COACHES were hard on him because there were subtle changes the team wanted from him, changes that spoke to the two worlds Miguel had to bridge in order to achieve his dream.

For example, in the Dominican and in much of Latin America, that there will be a tomorrow is never assumed but always attributed to God's will. Considering the tumultuous history of the Dominican it's not hard to see why this is so. So when speaking of the uncertainty of tomorrow a Dominican boy like Miguel might say: "I will see you tomorrow, '*Si Dios Quiere.*' " If God Wishes. "Why," Dominicans will ask, "Do Americans never say *Si Dios Quiere?* Why do they always think there will be a tomorrow?"

The Athletics put psychologist Arturo Rodriguez to work on Miguel and the other boys: "Part of the psychology of poverty is that these boys never think about tomorrow, so we have to insist that they develop a goal. The poor man will think that he can do little about tomorrow. They leave tomorrow to God or they leave it to the lottery. . . . So we try to establish the mindset of a professional, to strive for excellence. All kids want to help their families, so we help them try to sort out those feelings. We tell them they shouldn't go over there to help their families but to help themselves. The money they pay for these kids is relatively small and if they are over there and are sending all their money home, they will have to live badly. So we teach them about organizing their lives, their money, and tell them that they aren't working for their families but for their careers."[30]

Miguel nodded as Rodriguez spoke to him but there was no way he could deny what was driving his desire—his hope of helping the family he barely had while growing up. So on the first day of the summer league season, all Miguel had were his thoughts as he watched from the bench. Lara, Polanco, and the other boys played well that day, their coaches scratching detailed notes into scouting reports on every pitch and play.

Miguel had gotten into the game late as a substitute. And when that first game was over, he was told he would play the next day. With a kid like Miguel there grows an expectation that he might have to play a second summer in the Dominican before being ready for the United States. But suddenly, there he was drilling a home run in his first at-bat of his first full summer league game. It was a line drive, a "tomahawk," as the cliché goes, and the coaches looked at each other in surprise, but not amazement. Amazement came later.

The next day, he hit another home run. Then another. And then still another. Miguel had five at the end of that first week, a startling turn of events for a league in which five home runs in an entire 74-game season is considered a good year. Because all the games are played at sea level and almost always in heavy, humid air, not that many balls fly out of the ballpark. It's mostly a doubles league, a league for stolen bases, live arms and flashy plays. "It was incredible," Silverio said. "Nobody hits that many home runs in the heavy air we have here. Nobody."[31] As is the case in most sports, the sight of a young phenom—particularly one who comes from nowhere—sets hearts racing. And Miguel had come from nowhere. While coaches can know the game, know situations within the game, and—at times—shape the game by their knowledge and instincts, there is an unknown quality about baseball that makes it intriguing. Often, the most highly touted prospects, the "bonus babies," are the ones who fall flat. And the kids who shine are the ones who come from nowhere.

Just within the Athletics, the fickle fortunes of young talent were on full display. Million-dollar "bonus baby" Todd Van Poppel, a Texas high-school phenom whose pitching arm reminded folks of Nolan Ryan's, was struggling and on his way to being one of the biggest busts in recent memory. Meanwhile, Mike Bordick had become a rock at shortstop after signing with the Athletics as a nondrafted free agent in 1986.

But Miguel broke the mold for surprises. One of the smallest, least impressive young players from a rag-tag bunch of Dominicans in an organization in which Dominicans were dropping like flies had the potential to become a monster on the field. "We didn't think he was going to do the things that he did," Silverio said. "If anyone had seen him, they wouldn't have thought so either."[32] Miguel had put on about ten pounds since reaching the complex and his desire had remained high, causing jealousy among other players who didn't put out as much as he did in practice.

And his confidence, always present, grew with each day. He developed a strut, a cocky air that turned off his fellow players at first. And it raised the eyebrows of his American coaches. "He would come on a little strong sometimes," Plaza said.[33] "I think he had an awful lot of confidence. He thought he was the star and he'd walk around like his shit didn't stink. We didn't want the other players to see this, and I'd tell him: 'Miggy, you have to have these things inside of you,' because we didn't want him showing off so much."

Plaza and the Athletics were concerned about discipline in general at the complex. While liked and considered good teachers for Dominican players, Silverio, Martinez, and the other coaches were sometimes considered too soft on players by Athletics management. "I know discipline went down after I left. Some of our [Dominican] coaches didn't know how to say no. I'd come back and say, 'Hey, where is so and so,' and they would respond, 'Oh, we let him go home.' And I'd say, 'You let him go home!' "[34] Plaza said.

It wouldn't be unusual to see scruffy kids with no obvious talent standing next to Miguel during drills. They would hang around, go through the motions, and hope they could spend the night in the complex dorms or eat in the cafeteria. Often, the Dominican coaches would look the other way and not say anything unless confronted by someone from the Athletics, such as Plaza. By the end of 1994, the team had brought in Raymond Abreu—an American of Dominican ancestry—to run the complex. Muscular, serious, with an air of authority and an eye for details, Abreu would become an effective enforcer. As an American, he carried an authority that made Dominicans stand up and take notice. But as an American of Dominican ancestry, he could always tell when someone was bullshitting him. "I'd go out on the field and see some kids running around like they had refrigerators on their backs," Abreu said.

"Then I would find out we hadn't signed them. The coaches here are nice, they feel sorry for these kids, but we have a job to do here."[35] Miguel was catching on to the job in a remarkable fashion. "In six months he went from being a kind of general person to being a star," Plaza said.[36] As he had done while growing up in Bani, Miguel was a master of adapting to situations. He could mold his personality and correct mistakes when they were pointed out to him while still retaining a keen natural intelligence. And eating solid meals, sleeping in clean quarters, drinking purified water, and lifting weights helped him develop a body he never knew he had.

There was also an added dimension to Miguel's game, a dimension coaches could only explain this way: "It's like his game would elevate from practice. He would get in game situations and all of a sudden he would show you things you wouldn't see in practice," Silverio said.

"Some of the other kids would practice really well, play really well, and then they would get in the games and it's like they would forget everything. It would be as if they hadn't practiced at all. Miguel would get in games and it's like things got easier for him. He would make adjustments. And once he started playing that summer league season, he went off like a bomb." [37]

By the second month, he was at 17 homers. "We started thinking, maybe he'll hit 25 or 30 home runs," said Martinez. [38] "It's like you would put him in a game and he would be transformed." Miguel seemed to practice even harder while he wasn't playing, lifting weights, taking grounders, taking batting practice. He had never played baseball for such a prolonged period of time and soon it was taking a toll. "Before the games, he would work a lot and he would get tired. In that last month of the season, he only hit one home run," Silverio said. [39]

While that Athletics team did not make the summer league playoffs, Miguel hit a league-leading 18 home runs. He also batted .294 and drove in 62 runs. That he also played a thrilling brand of shortstop only made his team even more excited. Shortstops are generally not expected to provide power, and when they do, stardom generally follows. Cal Ripken, Jr., and Barry Larkin had proved that by 1994, and a whole new crop of powerful major league shortstops soon followed. After that first game on the bench, Miguel never sat again. By the middle of the season, the other kids began treating him like a leader and with an affection that hadn't been there before.

And most exciting of all to him was the news that followed: He would be going to the United States in 1995—to spring training and the minor leagues.

Miguel couldn't have been more excited at the news, and Soto couldn't have been more proud. He would have plenty of competition waiting for him in the United States. At the major league level, Bordick was well established as the shortstop of the Athletics, a young talent with maturity who would only blossom in future years. In the minors, the Athletics had used two of their top draft choices in 1993 on a pair of infielders named Jefferey D'Amico and Michael Moschetti. And there were other young stars on the horizon as well. In the summer of 1994—just as Miguel began his career in the summer league—the Athletics had drafted and signed their number-one pick, a tall, skinny outfielder from Arlington, Texas, named Ben Grieve. One of the most heralded high-school players in the nation, Grieve was the second player chosen in the 1994 amateur draft. His dad—Tom Grieve—had been a first-round pick himself and at the time of the signing was general manager of the Texas Rangers.

The Athletics signed the younger Grieve for $1.2 million—more than it cost to buy and build "Campo Juan Marichal." They then sent Grieve to Medford, Oregon, that summer, where he batted an impressive .329 with 7 homers and 50 RBI. He was off to a great start and much was expected of him.

Because of where he was from and who he was, Miguel was still an X-factor to the Athletics. They were happy that he had done so well but he still had to make it in the United States. As Miguel prepared to leave on that first trip, he was only eighteen, and, except for Santo Domingo, had scarcely been outside Bani.

He was equipped with only as much English as he had learned while playing "Simon Says." He knew nothing of the press, of playing in ballparks in far-flung cities where no Dominicans lived. He knew little of his country's history with the United States and even less of the Latin players who had preceded him in their shared dream.

On the morning he boarded an American Airlines jet bound for Miami, then Dallas, then Phoenix, all he had with him were the few clothes he owned, curled up in a ball and stuffed into his duffel bag. As the plane lifted off Dominican soil and became airborne, Miguel's thoughts filled with the future. He was too young to know about the past.

Hundreds of young men like him had made this journey for almost one hundred years before Miguel left his island nation. They had left their countries, with histories much like Miguel's, to try to find their place in America. In large part, Miguel didn't know about this history—his history—because he was so young. But he also didn't know because much of it had been shrouded through the years by chance, by ignorance, and by fate. Maybe things would change in his generation. Maybe he would be able to accomplish things all those men couldn't. Nobody knew on that spring morning in 1995. About the only comfort Miguel had was his father's blessing, Soto's words of encouragement, and the saying *Si Dios Quiere*. If God Wishes.

Miguel put his faith in that feeling. It was all he had ever known in a life whose earliest childhood memory was the destruction of his home by a furious act of nature.

He hadn't been able to count on much after that. So he never counted on the future.

You'll be a star, people from *Los Barrancones* told him on the day before he left. Miguel thought for a minute, then answered honestly:

Si Dios Quiere.

5

"IT'S NOT OUR GAME"

THE SIGHT of Jackie Robinson in his white Dodgers uniform, leading off first base, bouncing up and down on the balls of his feet, darting toward second, and rounding the bag as his cap flies off in a trail of dust is perhaps the most enduring image of baseball in the twentieth century. Some historians might disagree, citing the greatness of Ruth, Williams, Cobb, or Mantle, but only one player had his number retired by every franchise in the game: Jack Roosevelt Robinson.

Perhaps what is most significant about Robinson's integration of baseball and breaking of the game's hallowed "color barrier" is that he transcended sport. Even people who don't like baseball know who Robinson was. They know what he did and what it meant, how important it was and how it was a precursor to the civil rights movement of the 1950s and 1960s. They know how every time Robinson flew around the bases, stole home, turned a double play, or hit a home run, the power of his spirit lifted all Americans to a higher moral place—even though many hated him for it at the time. So when the nation honored Robinson's memory in 1997, fifty years after he first suited up for the Brooklyn Dodgers, it seemed fitting that old number 42, that wonder from Pasadena, California, should take his place among the great Americans of this century.

Within the context of the game, Robinson's breakthrough and his success against overwhelming odds was the first chapter in the story of African-Americans in major league baseball, a clearly defined legacy that has marched alongside the times and the emergence of African-Americans in society.

The progress of African-Americans in the national pastime is exemplified today in the millions earned by the game's most marketable star, Ken Griffey, Jr. Dusty Baker and Don Baylor have excelled as managers after decades of racist perceptions that they weren't smart enough to do the job. Bill White was president of the National League. And Bob Watson, former general manager of the New York Yankees, burst through the glass ceiling of baseball's front offices when he assembled a World Champion in 1996. In the wild celebration of the Yankees clubhouse after they defeated the Atlanta Braves in six games, one of the first things Watson did was to eloquently pay tribute to Robinson. While there is undoubtedly much more room for progress, it truly has been a long road since 1947.

The Latin story in major league baseball is not so clear-cut. It is a story with muddled chapters and missing pages, significant events lost through the years because, until now, they were primarily known only in Spanish. And one fundamental reality has been untouched by progress or the passage of time—the Spanish-speaking pioneers of the game were recruited as cheap labor just as Miguel Tejada was in 1993. Of course, there has been progress for some, like Pedro Martinez—once as poor as Tejada but now earning $12 million a year for the Boston Red Sox.

Sammy Sosa thrilled America in 1998 by hitting 66 home runs. And Orlando "El Duque" Hernandez floated off the Cuban isle, found an agent, and signed for $6 million with the Yankees, and the media ate it up.

But all are products of a legacy devoid of heroic beginnings to light the way for history, context, or understanding. Who can remember the first Latin to play in major league baseball? What was his name? Where did he come from? Whatever happened to him? The casual fan might answer Roberto Clemente, the great Puerto Rican who starred in the 1960s before dying in a tragic plane crash while rushing relief supplies to Nicaragua. People in their fifties and sixties might think it was Minnie Minoso, the colorful Cuban Gold Glove outfielder and stolen base champ of the "go-go" Chicago White Sox of the early 1950s.

Others might say Orlando Cepeda of Puerto Rico or Juan Marichal of the Dominican Republic or Luis Aparicio of Venezuela, standouts in the era right after Robinson's break-through. But a full forty-five years before baseball's color barrier was officially broken, Louis R. Castro, the Jackie Robinson of Latin America, made his debut in major league baseball, play-ing 42 games for the Philadelphia Athletics in 1902. There is al-most nothing in the official records to distinguish this pioneer, a significant omission considering that this man broke racial and ethnic barriers that would lead to the powerful presence of Latins in baseball today. History tells us this was not insignifi-cant.

After all, while through the years a small number of Asians, Canadians, Europeans, Australians, Native Americans, and a handful of others have played major league baseball, by and large the game has been made up of three kinds of people: whites, blacks, and Latinos.

It goes without saying that the history of white Americans in baseball is well known. And Robinson's brilliance was so great, the integration of African-Americans he symbolized has become an integral part of baseball lore and American history. In recent years, there has also been extensive documentation of the lives and experiences of men who played in the old Negro Leagues, men who never got the chance to compete in major league baseball because of their color.

But what of Latinos?

In a sense, the metaphor for their story is a missing history, the one belonging to Louis Castro.

Castro was born in 1877 in Cartagena, Colombia. When and where he died is not documented in this country. Castro was said to have stood five feet seven inches that summer of 1902, when he would have been twenty-five.[1] He threw right-handed, hit right-handed, and was given the nickname "Jud," just as years later Clemente was identified on baseball cards of the 1960s by the first name "Bob."

Of course to call Castro a Latin Jackie Robinson is to be facetious. Aside from being credited as the first Latin and African-American players to play major league baseball in this century, the only thing Castro and Robinson have in common is that they technically weren't the "first" nonwhite players to compete against whites on the playing fields of America. In the late nineteenth century, in leagues that were the forerunners to the major leagues we know today, men like Bud Fowler, Frank Grant, and Moses Fleetwood Walker were among roughly seventy African-Americans who played organized baseball. About half of those men performed on integrated teams until all were systematically forced out of organized baseball by 1898—a ban that would hold firm until Robinson came along forty-nine years later.[2]

Meanwhile, in the early 1870s, a Cuban named Esteban Bellan played in the old National Association for a team called the Troy Haymakers. He also played for the New York Mutuals. But Bellan went back to Cuba around 1874 and no Latino would play in the United States until Castro suited up in 1902.[3]

Since organized baseball was the domain of white America, early African-Americans and Latinos were viewed as interlopers, unwelcome outsiders. But from those turbulent beginnings, the differences between the histories of African-Americans and Latinos are symbolized by the differences between Robinson and Castro.

While the memory of Robinson grows with each year, what is known about Castro couldn't fill a decent newspaper obituary.

According to the *Baseball Encyclopedia,* Castro had 35 hits in 143 at-bats, of which 8 were doubles and 1 was a triple. He is also credited with hitting a single home run. He had 15 RBI, scored 18 runs, drew 4 walks, and had two stolen bases. Playing 36 games as a second baseman, 3 games in the outfield and 1 as a shortstop, Castro had 75 putouts in 86 attempts, committing 17 errors while helping turn 10 double plays. In 2 other games, he appeared only as a pinch hitter. He went 0–2.[4]

While the Philadelphia Athletics finished atop the American League standings in 1902, the first World Series would not be played until the following year.

Not much more is known.

To this day, Castro may have the smallest, thinnest file of any big leaguer catalogued in the thousands of volumes at the Baseball Hall of Fame and Library in Cooperstown, New York.

There, under an entry compiled by the Society for American Baseball Research, there is a single paragraph of information gleaned from a 1976 item about Orlando Ramirez, a Colombian who played for the California Angels in the mid-1970s. It reads simply, "It turns out shortstop Orlando Ramirez isn't the only native of Colombia to reach the major leagues. Louis (Jud) Castro played for the Philadelphia A's in 1902 and disappeared."

The only other significant reference to Castro was printed in 1998, in Samuel O. Regalado's book *Viva Baseball*. According to Regalado, Castro was the product of a wealthy family, a rich kid who took up baseball while attending Manhattan College in New York City.

His on-field legacy? The legendary Connie Mack, who ran the Philadelphia Athletics for half a century, pegged Castro a bench warmer, "for which position he was immensely fitted." Almost everything else about Castro remains lost.

And sadly, so is his historical significance.

Indeed, based on the facts, the legacy Castro represents is the last, great untold story of baseball. It is a story of a people living on the fringes of America, heroes at home, marginalized in the United States. A people who have never fit America's increasingly obsolete way of defining race and culture—as an issue of black and white. The result? Off the field, the diverse experience of a people defined as Hispanics by the U.S. Census—a population now 28 million strong—seemingly waits to fully register on America's cultural radar screen while the nation wrestles with its "black/white" issue.

And on the field, in the game linking Americans and Latins more than anything else?

Just remember Louis Castro.

No one does. Just as no one remembers the meaning of his experience. People forget that Latins were around forty-five years before Robinson. They forget that some of those early Latin major leaguers were identified as "light-skinned black men" in the African-American press, that some were considered black by their white teammates, and that two, named Jacinto "Jack" Calvo and Jose Acosta, pulled a most unusual feat—playing in both the segregated major leagues and the Negro Leagues. These were all men who learned the game not in communities where baseball was a focal point of civic pride, as it is in the American ideal, but rather under American expansionism and "manifest destiny."

Blood has been spilled in Latin America over the game, just as thousands of young boys have come to depend on it to eat, to live, and to dream. Add to that the struggle of being a Latin immigrant in the United States, the faith that such people put in an America that has been both conqueror and reluctant host, and you barely begin to understand a people whose courage, strength, complexity, and talent are too often lost in the translation from Spanish to English.

It all begins with Castro in 1902, when baseball was a game for white America only. But even though Castro's skin must have been fair enough for him to slip past baseball's racist policies of that day, he was still different, both culturally and racially. And he would not be alone. After Castro, forty-four Latins would play in the major leagues before 1947 and Robinson's historic debut, all of them a world apart from their white teammates.[5]

In 1911, two Cuban men, Rafael Almeida and Armando Marsans, were signed by the Cincinnati Reds' Clark Griffith, a miser who in later years, as owner of the old Washington Senators, would become the leading importer of Latin players to the United States.[6]

From the outset, the Griffith-led Reds made their feelings known about what the two Cubans were worth. "We will not pay any Honus Wagner price for a pair of dark-skinned islanders."[7] Almeida and Marsans did, however, raise eyebrows for the "olive skin," and were not allowed to play until the Reds sent for and received written proof from Cuba that they were of Castilian and not black descent.[8] Still, the first time the two Cubans played before the home fans in Cincinnati, someone was heard to shout, "Get that nigger off the field!"[9]

Two years later, in 1913 (and again in 1920), another Cuban, Jacinto "Jack" Calvo, played briefly for the Washington Senators. Like fellow Cuban Jose Acosta—who pitched for the Senators and Chicago White Sox between 1920 and 1922—Calvo's skin color was a source of much controversy. And with good reason. In 1915, both men played in the Negro Leagues.[10] And yet, in 1920, the two Cubans suited up for the big league—and supposedly segregated—Washington Senators. To this day, they are recognized by historians as the only men to have ever done this.[11]

Yet the two were never recognized as racial pioneers. What little is remembered of either is a particular exhibition game Acosta pitched in 1920—a game in which he struck out Babe Ruth three times.[12]

Racially, Latins have been the odd men out in America, their varied skin colors the products of a mixture of African, European, and Indian bloodlines. While they didn't fit to the rigid American definition of "black," they weren't exactly white either.

But as is the nature of any kind of history, there is what is written and what is known. And in the case of Latins playing in the American pastime of baseball, there has been a significant amount written on Latin players bending, hiding, and sneaking past the color barrier before Robinson. It's just that none of it has taken hold in American consciousness. It is relegated instead to the fine print of history.

The trail of those now-missing stories began when Latin men began arriving in the majors and were touted in the African-American press as a hopeful sign that the Latins would open the door for American blacks.

In 1970, in his heralded book *Only the Ball was White*, Robert Peterson published the following quotation that he found pasted in the scrapbook of an old Negro League player. It read: "Now that the shock is over it would not be surprising to see a Cuban a few shades darker than Almeida and Marsans breaking into the professional ranks, with a coal-black Cuban on the order of the crack pitcher, [Jose] Mendez making his debut later on. . . . With the admission of Cubans of a darker hue in the two big leagues it would then be easy for colored players who are citizens of this country to get into fast company.

"The Negro in this country has more varied hues than even the Cubans, and the only way to distinguish him would be to hear him talk. Until the public got accustomed to seeing native Negroes on big league [teams], the colored players could keep their mouths shut and pass for Cubans."

Noted African-American writer and editor Art Rust, Jr., argued, "I have always been convinced that Jackie Robinson was not the first black man in the modern major leagues. The Washington Senators in the mid-thirties and forties were loaded with Latin players of darker hue, who because they spoke Spanish got by with it."[13]

Rust wasn't the only one who held this opinion.

In 1980, Hall of Fame sports writer Bob Addie of *The Washington Post* wrote in his autobiography, "Long before the color line was supposedly broken in modern times by Jackie Robinson, the Senators had a player who today would be called 'black.' He was an outfielder named Roberto Estalella." (Estalella reached the majors in 1935.) "Bobby was a cafe au lait type and nobody asked questions when he was inserted in the lineup. But there are those who say Estalella crossed over the line when it was considered hopeless for a black man ever to play major league baseball."[14]

After he had retired, Washington Senators outfielder John Welau said openly that most of the team considered Estalella and other Latin Senators from the early 1940s to be black—and they were treated as such.[15]

Howie Haak, one of the earliest and most effective major league scouts in Latin America, scoffed at the notion that baseball's "color barrier" wasn't challenged until 1947. Haak spent more than a quarter century "mining" the Dominican Republic, Puerto Rico, and Cuba for the Pittsburgh Pirates, signing and scouting a raft of players including the great Roberto Clemente. A Cuban pitcher named Tomas "Tommy" De La Cruz stood out in Haak's mind. De La Cruz posted a 9-9 record for the Cincinnati Reds in 1944, three years before Robinson's debut. But De La Cruz's dark skin color made baseball men feel uneasy and the Reds didn't ask him back the following year, even though in 1945, America and its best ballplayers were still at war and the Reds had a very thin pitching staff.[16]

Major League baseball "had this phony form sayin' [Latin] players were of white ancestry. But, hell, Tommy De La Cruz was as black as they came," Haak said in 1989.[17]

And then there are Calvo and Acosta, symbols of America's muddled categorizations of Latins, two men black enough for the Negro Leagues in 1915 yet white enough for the majors in 1920. Like so many other aspects of the Latin history in baseball, these stories have never taken hold.

Perhaps there is concern that, once told, they appear disrespectful to the memory of Robinson's achievement, that they somehow diminish what Robinson did. But there is no way that could happen.

Robinson is rightfully a hero. He not only performed on the field with Hall of Fame talent, he did so under enormous adversity and triumphed even while being subjected to ceaseless hatred by people intent on bringing him down.

Whether he technically was or was not the "first" black man in major league baseball is a complex, muddled question that will always be debated by historians. After all, there were African-Americans who played against whites in the nineteenth century. And some of the Latins who reached the major leagues before him might be considered light-skinned black men today. There is no doubt that Robinson had very dark skin and that dark-skinned African-Americans who preceded him were kept out of baseball. And what should be remembered is that scores of immensely talented dark-skinned blacks from Latin America suffered the same fate until after Robinson's debut.

But over and above unanswerable questions of who was black and who wasn't stands the reason Robinson is a towering figure today: He never backed down on the playing fields even as ignorant, hateful men spiked him, spit at him, and assaulted his humanity. What's more, as a player, his combination of speed and power changed the game, made the stolen base an art form that rattled pitchers and forced everyone to play differently.

And after his career was over, Robinson dedicated his life to the ideals of social justice.

It is hard to imagine that such a man could be diminished by pulling Calvo, Acosta, De La Cruz, Gonzalez, Estalella, and a few other long-forgotten Latins out of obscurity. Theirs is simply another story.

In retrospect, the question of who was the "first black" seems like a red herring, far less significant than Robinson's courage and the fact that all Latin players before Robinson— light-skinned and dark-skinned—have never found their rightful place in baseball history.

Why is this important?

Robinson used to say that his breakthrough in baseball was not an important story of one man, but an important story for an entire race. History has proved him right.

But applying that same principle to Latins in major league

baseball, what can be said upon reviewing the history of Castro and the rest?

From the Latin perspective, the answer can be found today in the words of Miguel Tejada when discussing the game that has been the focus of his entire life. Shared by up-and-comers like Tejada and superstars like Juan Gonzalez, there is a saying among Latin players that crystallizes that feeling:

"Este juego no es de nosotros. Es de ellos, del Americano." [18]

It's not our game. It is theirs, it belongs to the American.

Even though Tejada has never heard of the Latin men who blazed a trail for him, that feeling has been passed down to him and become second nature, carried through the years since before Castro's time. It is born of the omnipresent relationship the United States has with most Latin countries. Scholars and experts on the Hispanic experience in America have long viewed a lack of entitlement, of political participation, and the high dropout rate among Hispanic students as symptoms of a larger problem—of not having a stake in the United States.

On the field, a lack of ownership of the game is the essence of the Latin experience, and it has its roots in how baseball was brought to Latin America and how Latin players were treated once they got here.

With Latins now comprising 25 percent of major league rosters and men like Pedro Martinez, Raul Mondesi, Sammy Sosa, and Ivan Rodriguez commanding huge contracts, there is evidence that the tide for Latins has turned and a new era is at hand.

But to retrieve the past is to remember the saddest kind of brave men—the ones who have been forgotten. And it seems that they were forgotten at the very moment when they arrived, when they became a kind of counterfeit player. Indeed, the most significant commentary made about the early Latin players—aside from mocking their English—was when it was written that lucky African-American players might be able to "pass" as Cubans by "keeping their mouths shut."

To be Latin was to be a curiosity, a person somehow less repugnant to the racist mind yet still stripped of all legitimacy as man and player. Consequently, the identities of Latin players were a blur from the very beginning, shrouded in whispers and innuendo.

When Jackie Robinson broke into baseball he was called a "first," and in a crucial sense he was—no one tried to deny who he was and what he was and no one tried to sneak him through a back door.

Brooklyn Dodgers President Branch Rickey effectively said: Robinson is a black man, he is going to play for the Dodgers, and that's that. But from the very beginning, Latin players were like low-income Latin immigrants entering the U.S. workforce today—they were sneaked into baseball via "phony" papers and were the constant focus of suspicion.

Consequently, they never achieved any racial firsts because, they had to not only deny who they were but outright lie about it so they could play.

"The idea of passing was very common in those days. African-American players tried various tricks to make themselves acceptable. In 1885, players on the first all-African-American baseball teams called themselves the 'Cuban Giants.' Because so many Cubans and Caribbean and Central American people were of mixed descent and consequently less African looking, the black players spoke gibberish on the field to pretend they were passing for Spanish." [19]

In 1945, sportswriter Joe Williams wrote: "It is no secret that players of suspected Negro parentage have appeared in the major leagues. They were presented as Indians, Cubans, Mexicans and you name it." [20]

The result: Early Latin major league players were like novelties, their presence more a source of nonthreatening amusement. They were treated like comic relief.

A typical depiction can be found in a 1940 article written by sportswriter Vincent X. Flaherty. It's about Washington Senators pitcher Alejandro Carrasquel, the first Venezuelan to play in major league baseball.

"Those of you who would search a little deeper into the catacombs of Alejandro Carrasquel's past, haul up a chair, ignite a panatela, cup the ear and hearken to the findings of our bureau of research. This sad-eyed Latin, whose heavy brow, parenthetical lines at his mouth corners and worrisome wrinkles give him a look of perpetual sorrow, paraded into Washington last April with all of the pomp and circumstance of a church mouse. He was the least attraction in [Senators owner Clark Griffith's] sideshow of geographical freaks. He seemed to take umbrage at his all-consuming obscurity, and he penned himself away from the rest of his fellows like one whose chosen penance was solitary confinement. During those springtime travels of the [Senators], Carrasquel carried his internal gnawings to the secluded corners of hotel lobbies, where he seemed to sit and brood for endless hours. He stirred at the slightest sound and tossed picture magazines around in confetti flurries. At night he would shy away to Spanish restaurants, where he cremated his woes in hot condiments and fiery sauces. And when he returned for the night, he would thread through the lobby, feed himself to an elevator and disappear as the steel doors devoured him."

By the end of the 1940 season, twenty-five Latins had played in the major leagues, all of them Cuban except Carrasquel and Louis Castro and two Mexican players, Mel Almada and José Luis "Chile" Gomez. Eight of the twenty-five had played for the Senators, who would import seven more Cubans during the "manpower shortage" war years between 1941 and 1945. This while other squads could count on one hand the number of players they had promoted from the Caribbean.[21]

His long-standing views solidified by the Great Depression and World War II, Griffith was able to use Cuban players to maintain his Senators on a shoestring budget. In a 1952 *Saturday Evening Post* profile called "Baseball's Improbable Imports," an unidentified "baseball man" was asked about the increasing presence of Cubans in major league baseball. He replied, "Those Cubans may have been crazy, but at least they were fast."

Beginning in the early 1930s and for a quarter century, the Senators cornered the market on Cuba with the help of a legendary character named Joe Cambria, who outshone his competition by being about the only American scout who dared venture out of downtown Havana in search of talent. "Papa Joe" was said to arrive regally at dusty Cuban playing fields in a stretch limousine, often wearing a white linen suit and chewing on a fat cigar. A typical recruiting trip was reported this way in 1952: "Cubans ran smack into the loving arms of Joe Cambria, a long-time Cuban ivory hunter for the Senators. . . . Cambria, it seems, strung up some lights last winter in an abandoned ballpark in Santiago, Cuba's second largest city, and announced the formation of a four-team baseball league and called loudly for players. The result . . . to the summons was a four-star miracle."

"Why, they just jumped right out of the jungle," Cambria said, shaking his head at "the wonder of it." In the mid-forties, Cambria spotted a tall, skinny Cuban pitcher with fiery eyes and a weak arm, an arm Cambria thought would serve up too many bleacher bombs. So he turned him down—twice.

That pitcher's name: Fidel Castro.[22]

Cambria's players who did make it to the big leagues in those years didn't make much of a dent either. Most of them bounced to a number of teams after the Senators dumped them.

In 1935, "cafe au lait" colored Cuban Roberto Estalella was Cambria's first discovery to reach the big leagues and was promptly nicknamed "Bobby" by his teammates, who thought of him as a kind of sideshow attraction. "Bobby," who was also known as "Tarzan," was often ridiculed in the press for his peculiar habits. Often, the reports framed Estalella as a backward, funny-talking foreigner—too silly to be much of a threat, despite his nonwhite skin color. One such report documented his minor skirmishes with modern-day America. One day, Estalella "was found standing next to a mailbox in Detroit, frantically flapping his arms while passers-by stared at him in amazement. In the absence of the club interpreter, it took the combined efforts of most of the Washington team to figure out Bobby wanted to send an air-mail letter to Cuba, but didn't know how to go about it." Estalella was also mocked in the Washington press for stopping ground balls from his third-base position with his chin or his chest.

At one point, Harris banished Estalella to the outfield. But the five-eight 180-pounder resisted. "I will fine," Estalella was reported to have said in protest. "Get to the outfield!" came Harris's response. "I hope you will fine, too," Estalella replied with a "smile." According to the papers, the incident ended when "Harris picked up a bat and brandished it menacingly at Estalella. Reluctantly, the Cuban agreed to become an outfielder."[23]

By 1940, Estalella had bounced up and down between the Senators and the minor leagues, this despite finishing a nine-season career with a respectable .282 batting average. During those years, he had been joined on the Senators by fellow

Cubans Fermin "Mike" Guerra, Rene Monteagudo, and Carrasquel. The Latins on the Senators were ostracized from American white players and often heard the shouts of "nigger" when they were on the field. In the spring of 1943, Hall of Fame sportswriter Shirley Povich described the atmosphere surrounding these very lonely men. "Ballplayers are notoriously narrow minded anyway. They resented the presence of [Carrasquel]. They were fed up, in fact, with all the Latins the Washington club was importing. The 1000 percent Americans on the club viewed the influx as bread being taken from their mouths. Even the locker room attendants grumbled when Carrasquel and the other Latins sought the routine services in the clubhouse, towels, under socks, and perhaps a dry sweatshirt. The clubhouse boys who leaped at the bidding of other players, gave the Spanish-speaking lads a brutal run around. The Washington Senators couldn't pin anything special on [Carrasquel]. They didn't like the cut of his clothes, with his fancy padded shoulders to be sure. But the fact that he looked like a Spaniard and couldn't speak English was enough. [Carrasquel] isn't exactly a handsome guy. As somebody once said, he looked like a guy off a Spanish galleon who wouldn't be out of character climbing up the side of a pirate ship with a knife in his teeth. They didn't let [Carrasquel] into their card games, and he was forced into the role of loner even when he was winning five games in a row for the [Senators] during the 1941 season. Eventually, officials of the Washington club stepped in and demanded that Carrasquel get some of the common courtesies."

Despite the way they were viewed by fans and the media, these were men who didn't simply roll over on the field. On one occasion in 1941, "Mike" Guerra got into a heated argument with a St. Louis Browns catcher named Tom Turner, an argument that resulted in a challenge by Turner to fight. But before a single punch could be thrown, fellow Cuban Roberto Ortiz stepped in and told Turner, "You no fight Mike, you fight me." The papers then described the incident this way: "Turner accepted with ill-considered alacrity and promptly received an old-fashioned Cuban lacing from Ortiz. . . . After Ortiz finished the ceremonies, the attitude of certain American players toward the Cuban element underwent a marked change."[24]

These were not cowards, they were work-hardened men

desperate to sign contracts just as Miguel Tejada was in 1993. But there were some things they couldn't control, like the league-wide reputation that was being forced upon them. Before America had taken up arms to fight World War II, that reputation had been set in cement.

It was put into words by Harris, who was asked in 1940 what he thought of Latin players. As the manager of the organization with the most Latins, he gave voice to widely held views of what Spanish-speaking players were worth. "They're trash," he said. "They're doing no good and they aren't in place here. They don't fit. . . . If I have to put up with incompetents, they better at least speak English." By the time Harris had made his comments in the newspapers, Carrasquel had anglicized his name to Alex Alexandra amid a torrent of racial slurs that accompanied him every time he took the mound as a pitcher for the Senators. But name change or no, reporters made sure everyone knew that Carrasquel was different by always referring to him as "Carrasquel the Venezuelan." [25]

MOST LATIN PLAYERS of the pre-Robinson era were shuttled around from team to team, hardly making an impact on the field. In numbers of players, Latins were still far in the minority. It is a fact of that era that the very best Latin players had very dark skin and, therefore, were not allowed to reach the major leagues.

In fact, the only true Latin impact player of that time was a Cuban pitcher named Adolfo Luque, who in 1923 led the National League with a whopping 27 wins. He also posted a league-leading 1.93 ERA, led the league in shutouts with 6 and struck out 151 batters. In a twenty-year career, in which he enjoyed most of his success with the Cincinnati Reds in the 1920s, Luque led the National League in shutouts three times. Twice, he was league ERA leader. And between 1920 and 1930, he posted four 13-win seasons, plus seasons with 27, 17, 16, and 14 wins. That kind of a run would earn today's pitchers $7-million-a-year contracts. But Luque once haggled with the Reds over the ninety-five hundred dollars a year he wanted in 1925. [26]

By the late 1920s, he and "Mike" Gonzalez were about the only Latins playing in major league baseball—most of the others had been released. At five-seven and 160 pounds, Luque stood up to any and all comers, never flinching at the racist cat-calls of opponents or even the home fans in Cincinnati. And with his success, he became a kind of mythic figure. "When Luque got on the mound," wrote Pulitzer Prize-winning sports-writer Arthur Daley of *The New York Times*, "his blue eyes blazed malevolently at each hitter and he defied them. He was a mean cuss at times and they said he never threw a beanball by accident. Whenever he hit a batter with a pitched ball, it was because he intended to do it."

Luque was the consummate competitor and took an in-tense pride in who he was and in his talent, qualities that were often challenged by his opponents. On a hot summer day in 1922, those qualities were pushed farther than Luque could allow. Pitching in Cincinnati against the old New York Giants, Luque was being mercilessly hounded by the entire Giants bench, who sat closer than usual on the field to accommodate an overflowing crowd. "Words were uttered that no descendant of the Spanish grandees could endure," Daley wrote later.

One of the Giants cursing Luque was Casey Stengel, who years later became a Hall of Fame manager while leading the New York Yankees to seven World Championships and ten World Series between 1949 and 1960. Frank Graham of the old *New York Journal-American* wrote, "The Giant bench warmers were riding [Luque] savagely and most savage of them all was Bill Cunningham, an outfielder. [The Giants'] Ross Youngs [a future Hall of Famer] was at bat when Luque took off his glove, placed the ball in it, put it on the ground and, walking straight to the Giants bench, punched Casey Stengel in the eye, Casey having the misfortune to be sitting next to Cunningham. When the free-for-all that followed had been settled, or so the umpires thought, Luque was put out of the game. A moment later he was back, bat in hand, intent upon clearing the Giant bench. This time he was led, struggling, from the field by four policemen."

There are those who say the bat incident haunted Luque, diminished his talent, stripping him of the notoriety he de-served. Years later, baseball historian Peter Bjarkman wrote, "What passed for comic interlude had dire circumstances as well. Luque suddenly and predictably played an unfortunate role in fueling the very stereotype that has dogged his own ca-reer and that of so many of his countrymen." Ironically, forty-three years later, Dominican and star pitcher Juan Marichal would be involved in a fight in which he brandished a bat against Los Angeles Dodgers catcher John Roseboro, an incident that would also haunt Marichal and detract from an otherwise Hall of Fame career.

Instead of shrinking away, Luque grew tougher—posting his phenomenal 27-win season the very next year in 1923. But he did it while being the focus of intense derision in some quarters of baseball, even by some of his fellow Cubans. In Luque's file at the Baseball Hall of Fame, there is a letter written in January 1923 by the sports editor of a Havana daily, who, through this missive, was reporting Luque's movements and thoughts to the president of the Reds. The letter reads, "Between you and me (please keep this letter a secret) Adolfo has grown a head large-enough to wear a number 47 hat. I read your letter to him and as he is the most illiterated [sic] man on captivity, he raised cane [sic] and started to say at the top of his voice that you and [then Baseball Commissioner Kenesaw Mountain] Landis could go pllump [sic] to . . . Outside of his ability to pitch [he] is a most perfect jack-ass. He packs a 'gat' and tries to make everyone believe that he is a sort of a Demi-God. . . . He is a good man at heart but a most perfect savage."

So Luque—solitary, proud, unrelenting—became known as a hot-headed "savage." Years later, Branch Rickey would admonish Jackie Robinson not to fight back against the racism he faced every day, and Robinson acquiesced. Perhaps Rickey was drawing on Luque's experience.

It is impossible to imagine what it must have been like to be proud, to be alone, to be cursed and insulted daily, and to be from another world. Looking back on that time now, it is not difficult to see the similarities between what Luque endured in the 1920s and what Robinson endured in the 1940s and 1950s. As his fight with the Giants indicated, it didn't seem to matter to American players that Luque's skin was light enough for him to play alongside them. They hated him just the same.

But the difference between Luque and Robinson is that Luque was a "foreigner" in America. Without Robinson's passionate, articulate ability to speak out against injustice in a way Americans could understand, all Americans saw of Luque was rage. And then he was gone.

"Luque was a usually quiet and iron-willed man whose huge contributions to the game are unfortunately remembered today only by a handful of his aging Cuban countrymen. So buried by circumstance are Luque's considerable and pioneering pitching achievements that reputable baseball historian Lonnie Wheeler fully reports the infamous Luque-Stengel brawl in his marvelous pictorial history of Cincinnati baseball . . . then devotes an entire chapter of the same landmark book to The Latin Connection in Reds history without so much as a single mention of Dolf Luque or his unmatchable 1923 National League campaign in Cincinnati." [27]

Luque finished his career with a record of 194-179, pitching for mostly mediocre teams. He did, however, pitch on the winning side in two World Series, including the infamous 1919 "Black Sox" Series, in which his Reds beat a Chicago White Sox team loaded with players later banned from baseball for accepting bribes from gamblers. In that series, Luque pitched five scoreless innings in two games. When he died of a heart attack at the age of sixty-six in 1957, his passing drew praise that often eluded him during his life. "Adolfo Luque is dead?" wrote the *New York Journal-American*. "That's what it said in the paper. Still, it's hard to believe. Adolfo Luque was much too strong, too tough, too determined to die at the age of 66. The paper said he died of a heart attack. It sounds absurd. Luque's heart fail him in the clutch? It never did before. How many close ball games did he pitch? How many did he win . . . or lose? When he won, it was sometimes because of his heart. When he lost, it was never because his heart had missed a beat. Some enemy hitter got lucky . . . or some idiot playing behind Luque fumbled a ground ball or dropped a sinking liner or was out of position, so that he did not make the catch that should have been so easy for him . . . [Luque] was the elder statesman of Cuban baseball, the first of the Cuban pitchers to make the major leagues. His life was dedicated to baseball, summers in this country, winters in Havana."

That Luque was able to play in the major leagues at all was because, as some newspapers said, he could be described as, "looking more Italian than full-blooded Cuban." That capricious reality was illustrated by an event soon after Luque's brilliant 27-win season in 1923. Welcomed home to Havana as a conquering hero, Luque was paraded through the streets of the Cuban capital by adoring fans. He was then taken to Havana's Gran Stadium where more adulation rained down on him. And then, in a ceremony at home plate, he was presented with a new car. As he was being honored, Luque picked out a face in the crowd, a dark-skinned face, a fellow Cuban, a fellow pitcher. His name was Jose Mendez.

The racial realities of that day struck Luque upon spotting Mendez and, as was his custom, he spoke directly. "You should have gotten this car. You're a better pitcher than I am. This parade should have been for you."[28] Mendez never got any parades in his lifetime, just as he never played in major league baseball. Unlike pre-Robinson Latins in the big leagues, there was no ambiguity in his face. The newspapers used to call him "coal black."

Similar descriptions were used for fellow Cubans Cristobal Torriente, Martin Dihigo, and Luis Tiant, Sr. And they were also used for Perucho Cepeda and Francisco Coimbre of Puerto Rico, and for Dominicans Tetelo Vargas and Horacio Martinez. There were many more black Latin players who barnstormed America in the Negro Leagues during the era when baseball was segregated. But these were the greatest. Hall of Fame manager John McGraw was once said to have placed a value of fifty thousand dollars on the right arm of Mendez, who beat the greatest white pitchers of the early twentieth century in exhibition games—including Hall of Famer Christy Mathewson.[29] In 1909, while pitching for the Cuban Stars, Mendez posted a mythical won-lost record of 44-2.[30] In those years, white major league players took on all-star teams made up of Latin and African-American players 65 times. The final tally was 32-32-1, with Mendez picking up 8 of those wins.[31]

Dihigo, whose prime was in the 1930s and early 1940s, was cited by Negro League Hall of Famer Buck Leonard as "the greatest player of all time." At six-one and 190 pounds, Dihigo played all positions but was best known as a gazelle in the outfield who had a deadly accurate arm. In 1929, Dihigo batted .386 against the best Negro League pitchers around.[32] And in 1977, six years after his death, Dihigo was enshrined at the Baseball Hall of Fame in Cooperstown, New York. Of all the Cubans to play baseball in America he is the only one in Cooperstown. He was also the second Latin to receive baseball's highest honor, after Puerto Rican Roberto Clemente—who was also enshrined posthumously. While Dihigo may be the least known man in Cooperstown, his exploits on the field were such that his bust also hangs in the Cuban Baseball Hall of Fame, the Mexican Baseball Hall of Fame and the Venezuelan Baseball Hall of Fame, the only man to have accomplished that feat.

But there was no hiding his blackness. As with their African-American teammates, blackness nullified the greatness of all black Latin players unlucky enough to have reached their primes before Robinson entered baseball. In the 1920s, Torrienti was lighting up the Negro Leagues, launching towering home runs at the same time Babe Ruth was becoming a household name in America. A veritable bull of a man, Torrienti was five-ten, weighed 190 pounds, and was a Negro Leaguer from 1914 to 1932, playing mostly for the Chicago American Giants. And when he played, he stood out from the rest by defiantly wearing a red kerchief around his neck and a bracelet around each wrist.[33] So imposing was Torrienti that a rival manager once said, "If I should see Torrienti walking up the other side of the street, I would say 'there walks a ball club.' " At this point, some reporters took to calling Torrienti the "Cuban Babe Ruth."[34] And in exhibition games played against major leaguers in Cuba, Torrienti added to that legend by blasting 3 home runs before squaring off against Ruth himself, who inserted himself into one game as a pitcher just so he could face Torrienti. Before he became an immortal power hitter, Ruth was one of the more promising pitchers in the game. But he was overmatched on this day.

Torrienti lashed a double off the Babe.

But it didn't matter. After the game, Ruth correctly assessed Torrienti's place in the world by dismissing him as being "as black as a ton and a half of coal in a dark cellar."[35]

During Torrienti's heyday, a New York Giants scout was following him with interest and, contrary to Ruth's assessment, there even appeared a chance he could sneak into major league baseball. But that never happened and the reason was that his hair made him look "too black."

"He was a light brown, and he would have gone up to the major leagues, but he had real rough hair," a teammate recalled.

Years later, Hall of Fame New York Giant and St. Louis Cardinal Frankie Frisch would say, "Torrienti was a hell of a ballplayer. Christ! I'd like to whitewash him and bring him up."[36]

Unlike some of their African-American contemporaries brought to life through the work of writers like Peterson, John B. Holway, Jules Tygiel, and Donn Rogosin, the Latin blacks of the pre-Robinson era have not been so lucky.

Torrienti died in obscurity of alcoholism and despair, spending his final years roaming the streets of Chicago rescued briefly by Dihigo, but dead by his early forties in 1938—nine years before Jackie Robinson's major league debut. Mendez died a decade before Torrienti, likely of tuberculosis, at the age of forty. Pitching as late as 1924, Mendez's magic arm was dead near the end as he gutted his way through Negro League games on guile and bravado.

Francisco Coimbre—a Puerto Rican two-time Negro League All-Star—perished horribly in his own home in Ponce, Puerto Rico. Living in a dangerous neighborhood, Coimbre had iron bars attached to his windows to keep burglars out. Instead, they trapped him inside, set his house afire and he was engulfed by flames.[37]

Fellow Puerto Rican Perucho Cepeda—father of major league great Orlando Cepeda—refused to play in America. "They wouldn't let him play in the major leagues so he wouldn't go to America," said his son, a former National League Rookie of the Year, MVP, and eight-time All-Star. As great as Orlando Cepeda was, his father was considered even greater by the people of Puerto Rico. But Perucho Cepeda was only forty-nine when he died in 1955. "It tore him up that he couldn't play here. That's why he died so young," Cepeda said.[38]

When Orlando Cepeda signed with the Giants that same year, the ban that had kept blacks out of baseball had already been dropped. The Giants offered Cepeda five hundred dollars to become a professional and he took it. But he didn't spend that money on himself. He used it to pay for his father's funeral.[39] That's as close as Perucho Cepeda or any of the others got to the major leagues. For them and other Latin men, the major leagues have always been a mirage—like the promise of America, a promise unfulfilled.

Ever so briefly, before he chose Robinson, Branch Rickey

had sent scouts to Cuba in search of a black player to integrate the major leagues. And, according to published accounts of that era, a Cuban shortstop named Silvio Garcia had gotten some consideration by the Brooklyn Dodgers. A three-time Negro League All-Star, Garcia stood six feet tall and weighed nearly two hundred pounds in his teens, and was known as a "deadly" opposite field hitter.[40] Garcia is remembered in Cuba as one of the great black players of the pre-Robinson era. He played in the United States for the New York Cubans of the old Negro Leagues between 1940 and 1947 and was also a star in his own country. Rickey was said to have become fascinated by Garcia, and there have been various published stories that he sent people from the Dodgers to Cuba in 1943 with twenty-five thousand dollars at the ready and instructions to sign Garcia "at any cost."[41] There have also been stories that Garcia's chance to set baseball history was derailed by his induction into the Cuban military. And still other stories say that the Dodgers were scared off by Garcia's age—he would have been thirty in 1944—and by his alleged drinking and womanizing.

But Jules Tygiel, author of the noted book *Baseball's Great Experiment: Jackie Robinson and His Legacy,* wrote that, in the end, Rickey simply didn't think baseball should be integrated by a player from Latin America.

"It's tough enough for a colored boy if he can speak the language," one of Rickey's aides said back in the mid-1940s. "So it's going to be doubly tough if he can't."[42]

Rickey knew that for a black player to make it in the major leagues, he would have to generate sympathy amid the racists. An intelligent, well-spoken former Pasadena Junior College and UCLA student, Robinson was more than able to do that.

But like Adolfo Luque and all the Latin men before him, there was no way Silvio Garcia could. If he had come to America and played with white men in the major leagues, Garcia undoubtedly would have been spit at, spiked, segregated, and persecuted just as Robinson was. But then after games, when it came time to put his experience into words, he would have come up short. His words would have been translated to Americans in fumbling fits and starts through sports page stories filled with mocking condescension or in a way that would have put Garcia squarely in his place—as a foreigner in America. In the eyes of 1940s America, he was more than black enough to be hated, but his pain, his suffering, and his courage would somehow have been less valid or less important. The American justification for the treatment of its newly arrived immigrants is familiar: Garcia would have been "lucky" to be here. What was his alternative, cutting sugar cane?

And Garcia probably would have been like most Latin immigrants—eager and anxious to grab his piece of the American dream just like immigrants from other parts of the world. We'll never know, because he never got the chance. After playing in the Negro Leagues in 1947—the same year as Robinson's spectacular debut—Garcia never played in America again. But many other black Latin men did live the experience that would have been Garcia's. While in the eyes of much of America there was little difference between them, these men came from a variety of places: Cuba, Puerto Rico, the Dominican Republic, Venezuela, Mexico, Panama, Colombia, and Nicaragua. Despite their diversity, they had three things in common: their language, a shared dream of America, and a door opened by Jackie Roosevelt Robinson.

6

FOLLOWING
JACKIE'S LEAD

JACKIE ROBINSON opened the door for Latin players when he integrated baseball in 1947. Two years later, Saturnino Orestes Arrieta Armas Minoso walked through that door, and once inside, he ran down outfield flies with a flair no one had ever seen. He stole bases so brazenly, the home fans changed his name. They called him Minnie—as in "Minnie the Moocher"—and they screamed it out over and over until nobody remembered the name Saturnino.[1]

The new chant came from the south side of Chicago, from Comiskey Park, from blue-collar White Sox fans—children of Polish, Jewish, Italian, and German immigrants. All of them yelled together for a black man from Cuba who grew up cutting cane for sugar they sprinkled on their morning cereal.

"Go Minnie Go! Go Minnie Go! Go Minnie Go!"

Minoso started his career in Cleveland but became a hero in Chicago as the first black to play in America's second city. But first he lived the experiences of Jackie Robinson—segregated, cursed, targeted, denigrated.

But Minoso's ordeal went deeper than that.

He shouldered that same extra burden Branch Rickey had predicted for Silvio Garcia—he didn't have the English words to express his struggle. And what words he had were often mangled, making him appear unintelligent. So he did as he had always done, he "danced the Cha Cha Cha." When pitchers bruised his ribs or bounced fastballs off his magical legs, he would pick up the ball, smile, and toss it back. When hotels or restaurants closed their doors in his face, he turned and went where he was welcome. At game time, in uniform, he outran ignorance, slid out of the way of racism. Afterward, he would slip into stylish suits befitting a movie star.

A sunburst of charm in a beer-and-a-shot city, the *Chicago Sun-Times* gushed, "Minnie is a never-ending source of fun and amusement."

He was a new fascination of the early 1950s, the new attraction. He was different, he was colorful, he was exotic, he was exciting. And he reveled in that newness, shaped it to his liking, all the while making fans happy while posing no threat. During those magical years right after Robinson's debut, Minoso became something unheard of in baseball—the Latin star player. But unlike Robinson, Minoso didn't have cultural giants like Richard Wright, Ralph Ellison, or James Baldwin acquainting white Americans with his experience. On the field, he had no crusading African-American writers like Art Rust, Jr., or Wendell Smith lobbying his cause. When Minoso played his first major league game with the Cleveland Indians in 1949, he hit a home run and ran around the bases in a historical vacuum. All he had were the ghosts of Louis Castro and Bobby Estalella, which is to say, he had no history at all in the eyes of America. It was as if he suddenly appeared one day, dropped from the sky in a baseball uniform, his skin as black as that of any man called a "nigger" and even more distant.

All he could do was play, and play he did.

Minoso batted over .300 eight times. He drove in more than 100 RBI four times. He scored over 100 runs four times. In five other seasons, he scored 90 runs or more. An everyday starter from 1951 to 1964, Minoso led the American League in stolen bases three times and won three Gold Gloves for his outfield play. Had baseball begun awarding Gold Gloves before 1957, he likely would have won more. As it was, in that inaugural year, a single Gold Glove outfield was recognized: Hall of Famer Al Kaline of the Detroit Tigers, the immortal

Willie Mays of the New York Giants, and Saturnino Orestes Minoso.

Minoso achieved unparalleled acceptance for a Latin player. "Minoso's immediate popularity in Chicago translated into record breaking attendance—1,328,000 fans—for the White Sox in 1951. An expression of thanks, the team honored him late in the season with Minnie Minoso Day, a gesture unprecedented for a rookie. He was given a brand new Packard automobile and the deed to a lot in Chicago."[2] There was also a Minnie Minoso-Cuban Comet Fan club.

Newspaper articles on Minoso took forms never seen in the rich history of baseball writing—stories describing the way he moved, the way he ran, the daring of his baserunning, the way his hat flew off while chasing fly balls. Even sex made its way into the stories. "Merrylegs Minnie is what the gals call Saturnino Orestes Arrieta Armas Minoso," wrote Virginia Marmaduke of the *Chicago Sun-Times* in 1953. "They like the way his uniform fits, the way he smiles, and the cute way he seems to have one pants leg lower than the other."

But Minnie was more than just an attraction.

"Minnie is to Latin players what Jackie Robinson is to black players," said Orlando Cepeda. "He was the first Latin player to become what in today's language is a 'superstar.' "[3]

But Minoso's name grows fainter each year, connected mainly to the colorful things he did and not to what he meant to the game and to Latin ballplayers everywhere. This can be traced to his heyday, when his escape from Cuba's sugar cane fields and dignity in the face of constant beanings took a backseat to comical characterizations reeking of stereotypes.

In 1949, a *Cleveland News* article described the time Minoso chose a three-hundred-dollar-a-month salary in the American minor leagues over twice that offered by Jorge Pasquel, former president of the Mexican Baseball League as follows: "Pasquel say, I give you six, seven hunder dolla. I say no, I no want play Mexico. Pasquel take my arm, go in car. . . . He open big bag, full money. He say, here take, yours."

In Spanish, Minoso describes the event this way: "If my mind had been filled with dollars, I would have gone to Mexico. But I wanted to see the United States. I fell in love with the name: United States. And for me, playing baseball has been like a war and I was defending the uniform I wore. Every time I put on the uniform I respected it like it was the American flag. I wore it like I was representing every Latin country."[4]

He wore it so well, baseball's link to Latin America was solidified, forever opening the door of opportunities to other Latins.

That distinction and his exploits on the field have gotten Minoso scarce attention from Hall of Fame voters.

But despite this slight, Minoso still embodied baseball's Latin experience in the modern era: In all those years, an unbroken chain of Spanish-speaking men have appeared on major league diamonds and taken positions somewhere between two worlds. Their very presence went against the grain. The way they played went against the grain. Their motivations went against the grain. Men like Minoso could laugh on the field and still be competitive in their hearts. They could play tricks Americans considered underhanded and still respect the rules. They could display their friendship with an opponent during a hard-fought game. They could laugh in the dugout when a teammate struck out. They could talk back to their manager while still respecting authority. And they could accept a game-costing error and whistle while walking off the field. Most of all, they could play on a team while still defining themselves as individuals. Given the era in which Latin men became significant players in the game, these characteristics could not have been more diametrically opposed to the kind of country America was and the way baseball was played.

When Minoso reached the big leagues, America had just come home from World War II and was in the process of "policing" Korea—and it showed on the field. Baseball was filled with ex-GIs who played a blood-and-guts, full-steam-ahead brand of baseball. Indeed, the essence of American baseball—the ultimate team game—was an extension of the collective, "We the people."

With Minoso and other early Latin stars came a new style, a flamboyant, individualistic mixture of speed and grace, joy and aggression that punctuated the game about as subtly as an interlude of salsa on a radio station that plays only military marches.

"The majority of players [of that era] came from military

bases," said Alfonso "Chico" Carrasquel, a teammate of Minoso's on the White Sox. "I remember [Hall of Fame pitcher] Early Wynn. Why, he would bear down from the mound like he wanted to fight me and I would call time out and say, 'What's wrong with him?' In their minds, they were always trying to prove who was more of a man, who was stronger. And we Latins had to adapt to that kind of living."[5]

It was in that adapting, that wrenching push from one world to another, that clash between one style of play and another, that stereotypes were formed, opinions hardened, careers completed, and history written. And the history of Latin major leaguers since Robinson's integration has been, like the story of Minoso, one in which only half the man was ever really captured in print. With each man following Minoso's lead, this new player came to be known by words like "showboat," "temperamental," and "not a team player"— about the worst label that can be attached to a ballplayer.

Against this backdrop roughly two thousand men have played: five Hall of Famers, scores of All-Stars, Gold Glove winners, cult players, fan favorites, also-rans, and men only historians would remember.

One undisputed Latin legend stands out in the minds of most Americans—Roberto Clemente. But as great as Clemente was, even he had to die to achieve that status.

After Minoso began dancing his "Cha, Cha, Cha," "Chico" Carrasquel became the first Latino to be selected to an All-Star team. Then came Luis Aparicio, who would go on to a Hall of Fame career at shortstop. In 1954, Mexican Alberto Avila, whom the press dubbed "Bobby," won the American League batting title with the Cleveland Indians. In 1955, Clemente broke in with the Pittsburgh Pirates. And in the late 1950s, the Dominican Republic was being discovered for its talent pool of Latin ballplayers.

By 1965, the influence of this new wave was evident: Eight Latin players were selected to the major league All-Star team that year.

These men would start traditions that remain strong to this day. On Minoso's White Sox team, for example, was the granddaddy of an enduring lineage of flashy, balletic Latin shortstops, Alfonso "Chico" Carrasquel. Chico's uncle—Washington Senator Alejandro Carrasquel—had been the first major league player from Venezuela. And when he took the field for the White Sox in 1950, he helped change the way the shortstop position was played.

Graceful and fluid at six feet tall, Carrasquel turned double plays by gliding effortlessly toward second base, becoming airborne, and throwing the pivot sidearm toward first base. While all shortstops do it that way now, this was a radical change in the early 1950s. On double plays back then, most shortstops stood planted at second, throwing overhand toward first with runners barreling toward them, spikes up.

"When I [came along], baseball was automatic. It was mechanical," said Carrasquel in 1993. "The infielders went this way and that, all the same. [Latins] added flavor to the game. I was one of the first shortstops [to] throw the ball from second to first underhanded during double plays. [Before that] somebody would always spike me. Every time! And so I said, 'I have to defend myself.' Throwing underhanded, the runner would have to slide or get hit with the ball. The first time I did that was to [former New York Yankees great] Hank Bauer. He got mad. But he also got scared. He said, 'Chico, god damn it!' "[6]

Carrasquel was so good, his talent so exciting, he displaced White Sox legend Luke Appling in 1950, after Appling had spent twenty years of a Hall of Fame career at the position. But the road Carrasquel took to the majors was hardly the stuff of All-American baseball lore. As a child, Carrasquel learned of America through the stories of his uncle. By his teens, he was working in a Caracas rubber factory when he was discovered by the Brooklyn Dodgers. "The Dodgers offered me $1,000. [Earlier] the [Detroit] Tigers wanted to sign me. You know what their offer was? A baseball glove. I almost signed it because I had so much desire to play baseball." In the spring of 1949, the Dodgers dispatched Carrasquel to Fort Worth, Texas for a stint in the minors. "I made $600 a month back then and when they gave me my first check it was for $200. And I said, 'no, that's not enough.' So the secretary said to me: 'Uncle Sam.' And I said, I don't have any uncle here, I'm Venezuelan. She kept saying, 'Tio Sam. Tio Sam.' I kept saying, 'Look, I don't have any uncle here and if I did his name sure wouldn't be Sam.' "[7]

On the field, Carrasquel batted .315 that year. Off the field, he led a different existence from his American teammates. Once "in San Antonio I wanted to order food without help. When the waitress came by I said, 'I want a glass of orange juice, a glass of milk, ham and eggs and I want my eggs scrambled and a cup of coffee. Co-FEE. OK?' She understood really well. I was happy. But I noticed I didn't have any utensils. So I started thinking to myself, how do you say fork in English? I figured it out and I asked (the waitress) for one."

In his linguistic triumph, Carrasquel hadn't factored in his thick accent. He meant to say fork, but it didn't sound that way. "What the waitress heard was, 'I want a fuck.' She screamed, 'What!?' I looked her in the eye and said, 'I need a fuck.' She started screaming and before I knew it I was being arrested. They were taking me away! Luckily at that moment our manager arrived. He spoke Spanish and he kept saying, 'Chico, *que pasa?*'"[8]

The incident cleared up, and Carrasquel went back to starring on the diamonds of Texas. As successful as he was, Carrasquel looked to join Jackie Robinson and the Dodgers, but the team was strapped for cash, so Branch Rickey sold Carrasquel and two other players to the White Sox for twenty-five thousand dollars.[9] Soon he was in the starting lineup. "Once in the majors, Chico's rise was meteoric," wrote *Colliers Magazine* in 1951. "Red Rolfe, manager of the Tigers, said: 'He's the most uncanny defensive player I've ever seen. Here he is in a strange land, playing his first year in the majors and he moves like a veteran of 10 years. You have to be born with that kind of talent. He's a picture to watch.'" In 1951, Carrasquel was selected to play for the American League in that year's All-Star game— the first Latin player to receive such an honor.

He would be selected for three more. Like Minoso, Carrasquel was noticed for playing his position differently, as if he had reinvented it. He would go deep into the hole between second and third, robbing batters of sure hits. He would make double plays and fly over the heads of runners trying to spear his legs. "Don't ask me how he gets in front of those ground balls or where he comes from," Casey Stengel was quoted as saying in 1951. "I only know he's always there."[10] At the end of the 1951 season, there were even printed reports that the Boston Red Sox were ready to trade the great Ted Williams for Carrasquel in an even swap. Red Sox manager Lou "Boudreau's willingness to yield Williams in an even trade for Chico Carrasquel created considerable surprise around here," wrote Hall of Fame sportswriter Dan Daniel in the *New York World Telegram and Sun.* "Carrasquel threatened [Yankees great] Phil Rizzuto's position at the head of the loop's shortstops in 1950. The former Brooklyn farm hand went deep behind third base, to make amazing throws and he batted effectively, especially against the Yankees." In the end, the White Sox refused to trade Carrasquel for Williams. Whether Williams's $90,000-a-year salary was what really nixed the deal was only hinted at, but for a time Carrasquel was a marquee player. He got that $20,000 salary, a big bump from the $12,500 he was earning.

During those years, Carrasquel was a free spirit, a jovial, good-natured field magician who played the game with unabashed joy. But that very attitude often drew intense derision from American opponents. He was just playing the way he had always played. But it wasn't long before he realized the brand of baseball he had learned on the streets of Caracas was far different from the one he encountered in the major leagues.

"I remember once we were tied in the ninth inning in Boston. [Former Red Sox catcher] Sammy White hit a double and was standing on second. And I pretended to throw the ball back to [the pitcher] but I kept the ball in my glove. [The pitcher] was standing on the mound, pretending he had the ball. So I went over to White and said, 'Hey, let me dust off the bag.' He took his foot off and I tagged him. Wow! The crowd went crazy. There were 30,000 people in Fenway Park and they had to send me to the dugout. They were going to lynch me. Since then you can't do that," Carrasquel said. "But we Latins used to do it all the time. All those things added flavor to the game. But especially in that time, Americans would never do that. They would want to fight you. Pitchers would curse you after you hit a home run. And we didn't have batting helmets then." Pulling his pants leg up to show off numerous scars, Carrasquel said, "This is Hank Bauer. This is [former New York Yankee] Gene Woodling. This is [Hall of Famer] Mickey Mantle." [11]

Though he continued being selected to All-Star teams, the joyride began to end for Carrasquel in 1955, shortly after the White Sox hired manager Marty Marion. With Marion at the helm, the White Sox began to sour on Carrasquel's style, which they saw as less than serious. He was accused of being "indifferent," "lazy," and of "not having his head in the game." In 1955, United Press wrote that Marion was angered by his failed attempts to turn "easygoing" Carrasquel into a "take-charge guy." Carrasquel was selected to another All-Star team that year but it didn't matter—Marion was still ripping him in the press. "He's not doing his job," Marion told the Associated Press on July 11, 1955. "Balls which he would have gobbled up last year are going through for hits."

Marion thought Carrasquel's good humor and affability were signs of weakness. Chico believed he was playing with everything he had. But somehow, that never translated from Spanish to English. So despite his credentials, and the fact that he was only twenty-seven, Carrasquel was traded to the Cleveland Indians at season's end. To this day, Carrasquel is convinced the cultural divide between him and 1950s America soured his once rosy relations with the White Sox. Looking back, Carrasquel thinks he was the odd man out, indecipherable to hard-nosed coaches who were dismissive of players not fitting a certain image. The essence of who Carrasquel was, the way he played, was what turned Marion off, despite his success. What Marion missed, Carrasquel said, was his desire to play.

"When I was a kid, the first baseball uniform I wore was made of flour sacks with the Gold Medal label on it. They used to give them away and so us kids formed a team we called 'Boston' and we wrote Boston on the front of those uniforms. The first time I got to Yankee Stadium I stood in the hallway, thinking to myself, I started out wearing a flour sack and now I'm wearing a White Sox uniform in Yankee Stadium. For Latins nothing in life is easy. You have to fight for everything." [12]

When Carrasquel was traded, the White Sox had another Venezuelan shortstop, named Luis Aparicio, waiting in the wings. He would go on to a Hall of Fame career, while injuries ended Carrasquel's playing days after the 1959 season. While Aparicio is remembered, Carrasquel really isn't. Yet there is no denying the tradition he started. There have been many distinguished Gold Glove Latin shortstops, many of them repeat winners, including Aparicio, Zoilo Versalles of Cuba, Ruben Amaro of Mexico, Leo Cardenas of Cuba, Dave Concepcion of Venezuela, Afredo Griffin and Tony Fernandez of the Dominican Republic, Ozzie Guillen and Omar Vizquel of Venezuela, and Rey Ordonez of Cuba. Scores of other Latins have also gravitated toward the position over the years, following Carrasquel's lead. At one time, Latins were routinely smaller than American players and used their quickness to the fullest advantage in a position where speed and fluidity are musts. And once Carrasquel set the standard and Aparicio became a star, others followed the path where Latins had the most consistent success.

Living in a tiny house on the south side of Chicago today, Carrasquel remains close to the game as a Spanish-language broadcaster working home games for the White Sox. "It doesn't bother me that I didn't get the recognition of being the first Latin to play in an All-Star game. Jackie Robinson was the first to break a racial barrier, I was the first Latin to play in the All-Star game and that [broke a barrier]. We Latins in the 1950s were pioneers also and when I see these Latin guys making millions now, it makes me proud." [13]

A soft-spoken man, Carrasquel is representative of early Latin players who broke in right after Jackie Robinson. But it wasn't long before there was a new type of player—outspoken, colorful men who paid a price for their style, as the image of Latin players became solidified in negative terms.

The first "showboat" was a Puerto Rican named Victor Pellot, who broke into the majors with the Kansas City Athletics—a black man known to Americans as Vic Power. "I played in Canada before I played in the U.S. but up there people got really concerned because somehow when you pronounced my last name in French, it sounded like an intimate female body part. So they decided to change it to Vic Power, which doesn't make sense because I am Puerto Rican." [14]

During his twelve-year career for five different teams, Power was one of the best defensive first baseman ever. From 1958 to 1964, he won seven consecutive Gold Glove awards. He was also chosen to five All-Star teams. And there will always be the question of how great he could have been had his dark skin not kept him toiling in the minors long after proving he was a big leaguer.

Coming of age on the heels of Robinson, only a trickle of

black players were reaching the majors when Power signed with the New York Yankees, baseball's premier franchise, in 1951. In fact, Power looked to become the first black player to wear the fabled Yankee pinstripes of Ruth, Lou Gehrig, and Joe DiMaggio. In his first year in the minors, he batted .334, hit 14 home runs, and drove in 105 runs. But there was no call from the Yankees. In 1952, Power hit nearly .300 and drew raves for his defense. Still no call. In 1953, he hit .331 with 16 home runs and 109 RBI. By that point, New York writers were pounding the Yankee brass, suggesting they were racist. But the lordly franchise wouldn't budge: "We have been looking for a Negro player for some years," said then-general manager George Weiss in 1952.[15] "But when he makes our club it will be on the merit, and not because of our giving in to certain pressure groups. Right now, there is a sharp division of opinion on Power as a potential big leaguer."

Back then, Power lived the life of the black man in 1950s America, though always with a wry twist of humor. "I became the first black player in the Yankees organization. The Yankees always wanted the best so they made sure I was in the best place in the black section, which often meant living in a funeral home. That's where I lived. I used to sleep in the front room with all the cadavers."[16]

By the latter stages of the 1953 season, when Power was blazing through his best year, the Yankees still resisted. And in August of that year, they called a press conference at which manager Casey Stengel said, "Throwing the Puerto Rican into the current tense situation could turn out to be a losing gamble for the Yankees and the player." And it got worse. In his 1975 best seller, *Dynasty: The New York Yankees, 1949-1964*, Peter Golenbock wrote, "A media blitz by the Yankees accused Power of being stupid, hot-tempered and a show boat. There was also talk that he liked white women."

Power grins today at the last point. "I do. I like all women." A beefy six-footer who was listed at 190 pounds during his playing days but probably weighed more, a gregarious, fearless man with a booming voice and the soul of a poet, Power was a terrifying combination to the smallest minds of 1950s America. He was a dark-skinned black man who possessed no prior experience with Jim Crow and, therefore, would not be cowed in its presence.

When pitchers threw at him, he would rush the mound. If opposing players cursed him, he cursed back. In the end, when Power wouldn't yield to intolerance, the Yankees traded him rather than promote him. He was shipped to the lowly Philadelphia (soon to become Kansas City) Athletics for first baseman Eddie Robinson and pitcher Harry Byrd, who had lost an American League–leading 20 games for the Athletics in 1953. While Power started his string of Gold Glove, All-Star years, Byrd went 9-7 with the Yankees before being shipped to the Baltimore Orioles, winding up a sub-.500 pitcher. Robinson, a journeyman infielder, did no better. Meanwhile, the soft-spoken Elston Howard became the first black man to play for the Yankees in 1955. And Power? In his first game at Yankee Stadium, on April 15, 1954, he got his revenge. He lashed two hits that day, prompting New York headlines like, "Maybe Yanks Let Good One Get Away." But it was a throw Power made from left center field after robbing Mickey Mantle of extra bases that stood out. Power fired a perfect strike from one the deepest parts of the outfield to cut down Bill "Moose" Skowron—the very man the Yankees had chosen over Power to play first base—at home plate. Dan Daniel wrote, "It was one of the finest throws seen in the Stadium in some time, and made some of the fans hark back to 1936 when Joe DiMaggio cut down a Detroit speedster who was trying to score on a fly ball to left field." After the game, Stengel conceded, "We figured Skowron, who is a fast runner, would score with ease, but Power certainly showed us an arm." [17]

Soon, Power moved to first base, where he'd play for good. And in time, he stood apart from other first basemen by snaring ground balls with his glove hand only. Daniel described this groundbreaking style by dubbing it "one-handed legerdemain." Up until then, most players were taught to always use both hands while fielding. But on soft or screaming grounders, Power would stylishly stab the ball with his glove hand and nonchalantly step on first base for the out. He would play much farther behind the bag than others at his position, fielding high bounces and reaching the bag faster than his contemporaries. It was all in the way he moved, the effortless manner in which he shifted his big body that stood Power apart. And then he would grin. Not a feckless grin or a subservient grin, but a big, worldly "I'm just as good as you are" grin. Without apology, Power represented a marked departure from the type of player common in 1950s and 1960s major league baseball. In 1962, when Power was a member of the Minnesota Twins, sportswriter Stan Isaacs quoted an unnamed Minnesota baseball official as saying, "I used to hate his guts when he was with other teams because of the way he used to catch everything with that one-handed showboating flair of his. But damn it, he never misses."

Power's style was influential.

Isaacs wrote: "Wherever Power goes he becomes something of a pied piper. He is adored in Minneapolis and inevitably, kids all over Minnesota are catching balls one-handed." Said Power, "I remember one writer asked me why I was such a clown, why did I catch the ball with one hand? I told him if the guy who invented baseball wanted us to catch with two hands he would have invented two gloves. I don't want to say they are racists. I understand that baseball is structured for one group of white players. . . . A group of us Latinos showed up and they gave us a little space to fill and a few African-Americans to fill other spaces. But baseball was maintained as a white game even though they know there is talent in the African-American community. They know there is talent in Latin America. But they have remained guarded even as the room filled with water."[18]

The essence of Power's inner strength, of his courage, was captured in 1963 by sports journalist Leonard Shecter, who later gained fame as the editor of the best-selling baseball book by Jim Bouton, *Ball Four*. In a magazine article, Shecter described a bitter cold, Minnesota day when the temperatures dipped to fifteen degrees below zero and Power—stylish, outspoken, black, Puerto Rican—stood before "200 hushed men, women and children, farm people most of them," in the basement of a church in rural Jordan, Minnesota. In those days, Twins players would fan out across Minnesota to promote the team during the off-season, assignments Power relished, particularly on this day. "In his heavy, charming Spanish accent, Power told [the crowd] of his arrival in this country and of being sent to play his first game in the U.S. in Little Rock, Arkansas. . . . [Power] went to a restaurant . . . only to be told by the waitress, 'I'm sorry, we don't serve colored people here.' "

As Schecter described it, "The embarrassment in the big,

low ceilinged room was almost palpable. The people weren't sure whether Power was about to indict them, lecture them, or make them cry. And he wasn't telling right away. He had them in the palm of his hand and he let them roll around like a set of dice. Finally, he said, 'I have not much English then and I have hell of a time telling her is OK, I don't eat colored people.' There was a relieved burst of laughter and applause. They were all having a good time again, but no one was enjoying the whole thing more than Vic Power. And that answered, in part at least, one of the questions I had come to Minnesota to ask Power. What had made him forsake the warm blue of Puerto Rico for the frozen white of Minneapolis-St.Paul?"

That question is important because it reflects the lack of understanding, the distance between early Latin players and the American public and press. Mixed in with the talent of Vic Power was always a sense of the unknown—because he and others came from another world.

Americans could understand that Power had black skin, but he and other Latins weren't from the same history as Jackie Robinson, Willie Mays, Hank Aaron, or other pioneering African-American players.

Throw in language and cultural barriers and you have the subtext of Schecter's question: Who are these guys?

Reflective of the era, few white Americans were interested in the answer. Instead, by 1965, the same year eight Latin players were selected to the All-Star team, the image of Latin players could not have been worse.

That year, Robert H. Boyle of *Sports Illustrated* wrote: "Baseball is a team sport, but to the dismay of American baseball men, Latins sometimes play with a reckless individuality. Indeed, it is the individuality in baseball that they like." In Boyle's piece, Buck Canel, a famed Spanish-language broadcaster, said, "Essentially, baseball is a duel between two men, the pitcher and the batter. Latins realize that baseball is a team game technically, but for every player there is a moment of individual glory, to hit a home run, to win the game or the chance to strike out a guy with the bases loaded."

By the time Canel said those words, the team with the most Latin players in the game—the San Francisco Giants—was being torn apart by a clash between the American game and the way Latins played it. That reality is a source of deep regret for the former standout Latin players of the Giants, a group that still ranks among the most talented ever produced in the Caribbean basin. It is also deeply felt by their old manager, long-time baseball man Alvin Dark. For it was the rift between Dark and his largely Latin squad that symbolized the failed championship dreams of the winningest team of the 1960s and exacerbated disturbing questions and stereotypes about Latin players that linger to this day. Along with bad management and bad luck, the Giants were undone by bad chemistry. And the Latins on the team were accused—both subtly and overtly—of not being "team players."

"The teams that win are the ones who maintain unity and that is something that we didn't have," said Jose Pagan, who played with the Giants from 1959 to 1965 before being traded.[19] At the heart of it all was the very identity of the Latin men wearing the black and orange of the Giants. "Alvin Dark told us we couldn't speak Spanish. . . . He was afraid that Americans would think badly when they heard us speaking our language. It was ridiculous," remembered Felipe Alou, who played with the Giants from 1958 to 1963 before being traded.[20]

Said Orlando Cepeda in one of his two autobiographies: "The first thing I saw was a sign that said, 'Speak English. You're in America.' " While Cepeda was clearly the most vocal, the other Latins on the Giants resisted as well. "We told him no," Alou said. "Marichal, Cepeda, me. We said we wouldn't accept that and we kept speaking Spanish."[21]

But the problems didn't stop there. There were other divisive issues born of ignorance and misunderstanding that chipped away at a very talented club, such as the way Latin players approached the game. "I can say that when there is a group of Latins playing together there is no pressure," Pagan said. "If we had a bad day, if one of us was down, the others would pick him up. I remember once Felipe Alou struck out, one of four times on this particular day. The last time, all the Latins were going crazy. We were rolling on the ground laughing. . . . The Americans, they take the game home with them. But you need to leave it at the park. What can I do about yesterday?"[22]

A former Marine officer and stellar major league shortstop,

Dark recoiled at the attitudes of his Latin players, which he and other baseball men saw as frivolous and counter to long-standing American views on teamwork. One of Dark's old big league roommates once said, "Baseball is [Dark's] life. He lives, breathes and talks baseball most of the time. Many times when he sets baseball aside, he reads his Bible."[23]

To say the two worlds of the Giants didn't mix is an understatement. But maybe the clash was an accident waiting to happen, because the Giants team Dark took over in 1961 was different from any other in baseball history at that time. While Hall of Famer Willie Mays was the greatest Giant there was, the Latin Giants were stars in their own right, everyday standouts, fan favorites. They were not like the heavily Cuban Washington Senators of the 1940s and 1950s because they were not bench warmers or "geographical freaks." At first base stood Orlando Cepeda, Puerto Rican, the 1958 Rookie of the Year, an All-Star in 1959 and 1960 and wildly popular in San Francisco. At shortstop was Pagan, also Puerto Rican. He was solid, steady, durable. In left field was Felipe Alou, a Dominican and beginning a successful seventeen-year career. He was joined by his younger brother Mateo or "Matty," later traded to Pittsburgh, where he won a batting title and hit over .300 six times. And greatest of them all was Marichal, a Dominican headed for the Hall of Fame.

The first hint of trouble surfaced at the end of the '61 season, the greatest in a Hall of Fame caliber career for Cepeda. Batting .311, Cepeda led the National League in home runs with 46 and RBI with 142. While the Giants finished eight games behind the pennant-winning Cincinnati Reds, Cepeda had a legitimate claim for the 1961 MVP award. But the winner was the Reds' Frank Robinson, who batted .323 with 37 home runs and 124 RBI. Had Cepeda won, he would have been the first Latin MVP. As it was, he was the first Latin home run and RBI champion. In his autobiography *High and Inside*, Cepeda wrote that 1961 was a great year for him, but "But Alvin Dark managed to spoil even that for me. . . . When some sports writers came to Dark and asked if I was really the MVP of the league, he said, 'No, Frank Robinson is. My own manager.' "

While this could be dismissed as a petty dispute between manager and player, it was a prelude of things to come. In 1962, the year the Giants were National League champions, it got worse. Before a road game in Milwaukee, Dark benched Cepeda for missing the team bus.[24] Cepeda was furious, and when called on to pinch hit, he caused a firestorm by not running out a ground ball. Alou said, "After the game, Dark called a meeting and said, 'I'm going to fine you $100. And Orlando said, 'Fine me $1,000 if you want. $1 million!' " This was a Latin man! A black man saying this to a white man in baseball, which is a game of authority! "People don't realize it today but authority in those days had unlimited power. Those were things that made men tremble and even Willie Mays couldn't believe what he was hearing."[25]

But even more divisive was the reported rivalry between Cepeda and Mays over who was "the man" on the Giants. While denying then and now that he was ever jealous of Mays, Cepeda was nonetheless accused of that in print. The seeds for rivalry were planted when the Giants moved west in 1958.

Cepeda "made San Francisco his personal playground in the Giants first year in town," wrote *Sports Illustrated*'s Ron Fimrite in 1991. "It was Orlando Cepeda, the new kid, and not the established star, Mays, who first won the hearts of San Franciscans. . . . Mays was still regarded as a New Yorker, and because he was such a private man, he didn't get around town as much as San Franciscans would have preferred. . . . Cepeda was all over the place, earning his nickname Cha-Cha as he danced and pounded the conga drums at the Copacabana or swayed to the sounds of Dave Brubeck at the Blackhawk. Cepeda was an exciting young presence, a Latin charmer, and the city embraced this 20-year-old Puerto Rican as if he were a native son."

By 1959, suggestive news stories baiting a rivalry began to appear in the papers, like this one from Associated Press: "Say hey! Look at Orlando Cepeda muscling in on Willie Mays' racket. The job of leading the Giants in homers and runs batted in has been Mays' responsibility since he played his first full season in 1954, except for [1958]. That's when Cepeda, 21, tied Willie for the San Francisco team RBI lead [96]. Now the big first baseman has left Mays behind in home runs and RBI." The headline for that article: "Cepeda Out-Mays Mays." By '62, talk of a rivalry between Cepeda and Mays was taking on disturbing tones. That was the year of the expansion New York Mets, the first time in five years National League baseball was played in New York City. And the first time the Giants traveled to Manhattan, Mays was welcomed like a hero. Of that day, Arthur Daley of *The New York Times* wrote, "In the language of the clubhouse, the best ballplayer on any team is always respectfully referred to as the 'big man.' It has applied over the years to superstars from Babe Ruth to Mickey Mantle. Lionized though Cepeda was . . . his first trip to New York in 1962 had to jolt him. He walked down the clubhouse steps . . . unnoticed. But the instant Mays stepped out the door, pandemonium broke loose. [A Giants official] nodded toward Cepeda. 'I guess that the big man just discovered who the big man really is.' "

That kind of talk would fester and then explode in a controversial *Look* magazine article in early 1963, in which sports editor Tim Cohane quoted an unnamed Giants executive suggesting that Cepeda's production trailed off in the 1962 season after he had his feelings hurt in New York. "Orlando didn't get over that for quite a while," the executive was quoted as saying.

Bob Stevens of the *San Francisco Chronicle*, wrote, "The [*Look*] article indicated Orlando didn't give it his best all the time, that he failed in the clutch. . . . In the meantime, his emotions stirred and his feelings battered, Orlando has tried to keep winning for the Giants. But his laughs had become fewer, his smile, once an infectious thing of sun-bursting warmth, had become thinner."

Over and above what was reported in the papers, there was an undercurrent to the Mays-Cepeda issue that remains very disturbing to Cepeda and other former Latin Giants. While not disputing the greatness of Mays, Cepeda wondered why there wasn't room for his confidence and cockiness, his belief in his abilities. Why were those qualities framed as a challenge to Mays? Most troubling of all was the edge to the stories back then. Reading them today, it seems as if Cepeda, the uppity Latin, was being put in his place.

Perhaps it was Cepeda himself, the type of person he was, who invited such problems. In the history of baseball up to that point, Cepeda represented a different breed. While even Clemente was negatively pegged by the press, the Giants star was more threatening. Clemente hit for average, stole bases, and played outfield like an artist. Cepeda swung the big stick. He swaggered. At six-two, 210 pounds, he walked around the Giants clubhouse with his shirt off, his back muscles bulging, a bat looking tiny in his powerful hands. He defiantly played pulsating salsa music full blast in the clubhouse. His face was chiseled and dark, his eyes seemed to flare. He didn't act like other Latin players.

"My first year, Orlando had this big ol' record player. A stereo, plus a big stack of records. And I had to tote all that stuff for him. He would say, 'Come on rook, come on rook.' " said Jim Ray Hart, who played third base for the Giants in the mid-1960s.[26] Said Felipe Alou: "Principally, Orlando was the main representative of the Latin American position. His music, his flamboyant style. Those were hereditary things. Orlando was the prototype Latin man. In him, there is represented everything you will find in a Latin man. And that was the problem between him and Dark."[27]

Cepeda admits today he was not blameless for the mess in the Giants clubhouse. Not running out that ball in Milwaukee was a big mistake. He also caused considerable controversy by refusing to move from first base to left field as futuré Hall of Famer Willie McCovey joined the team.

"I just wasn't ready mentally," Cepeda said in 1991. "I know I could have played left field if I put my mind to it, but I was only twenty-one years old and very sensitive. Friends and other players kept telling me I should demand to play first base. It was all pride with me. And ignorance."[28] Cepeda now regrets his lack of discretion with reporters, his willingness to blast away at any and all criticism. For all those headlines, he paid a heavy price—his peace of mind and reputation. A conquering hero when he arrived in San Francisco at twenty, he left amid tears, bitterness, and controversy at the age of twenty-eight.

Still, not all the trouble was of his making. Cepeda began complaining of chronic knee problems and was accused by his team of being a malingerer and a faker. Those accusations would prove false as his career was cut short by his failing knees. And today, whenever he plays in old-timers' games, Cepeda can no longer run.

But Cepeda's greatest problem may have been thinking he was on equal footing with Americans and behaving that way, an attitude his Latin teammates warned him about.

"First you have the white American, then you have the black American, then you have the Latin player who isn't from there and is only going to take away the job of the American," Pagan said of those years.[29]

In the 1960s, a time of great social upheaval in America, Cepeda stood apart from other players, including fellow Latins, because he wanted to be taken as he was—as a legitimate star. It was only later, when he made mistakes, that he found out how he was different.

Meanwhile, relations with other Latin Giants had begun to deteriorate as well. In a different manner than Cepeda, Alou was becoming a thorn in the side of the Giants front office. "I noticed this man staring at me and he came up saying he was a friend of [Giants owner] Horace Stoneham. He said, 'Horace likes you Latins quite a bit. He says you guys don't give him any problems, that you don't complain about negotiating your contracts,' " Alou said. "That was a great experience for me. . . . I never passed up an opportunity to learn and I took that as advice. From then on I became very difficult for the Giants." [30]

Weighted down by the feud between Dark and Cepeda, a lack of overall unity, and a lackluster 1963 season where the Giants finished 11 games behind the pennant-winning Dodgers, the whole situation began to unravel. At season's end, Alou was traded to the Milwaukee Braves. "They traded me soon after I began arguing over my contract," said Alou.

When the 1964 season opened, bad blood was evident, and it wasn't long before the situation reached an all-time low. In the summer of that year, Newsday columnist Isaacs quoted Dark making hideously racist remarks, blaming the Giants' failed potential on Latin and African-American players. Those remarks were devastating because, as Newsweek magazine wrote, the Giants were "more dependent on non white players than any other in the major leagues." The words attributed to Dark were, "We [the Giants] have trouble because we have so many Negroes and Spanish players on this team. They are just not able to perform up to the white player when it comes to mental alertness. . . . You can't make most Negroes and Spanish players have pride in their team that you can get from white players." [31]

Amid national attention, Dark said he was misquoted. And he wasn't without support. Dark had already been lauded by the NAACP for naming Mays as his captain when Jackie Robinson stepped forward to stand behind Dark. "I have found [Dark] to be a gentleman and, above all, unbiased," Robinson told *Newsweek*.

However, other sportswriters, such as Leonard Schecter, wrote: "Dark has expressed these opinions many times."[32] And despite Robinson's words of support, his statement didn't speak to the problems the Latin players had with Dark. Those issues were not about "black or white" but about culture and identity. Besides, the damage had been done. Soon there were reports that Dark had lost the confidence of owner Stoneham. The Giants once again came up short, finishing in fourth place. Dark was soon gone, and not long afterward, so were the bulk of all those talented Latin players. The end result of a wasted decade was the Giants as also-rans, possessors of the National League's best overall record of 902–704 but without a single championship to show for it.

In fairness, not all the Giants' problems were rooted in culture clashes. As an organization, they made many horrible trades, essentially giving away Hall of Fame pitcher Gaylord Perry, Cepeda, the Alou brothers, sluggers George Foster and Dave Kingman, and All-Stars Bobby Bonds, Gary Matthews, and Gary Maddux.

But the fact remains that the Giants were the leaders in Latin America at a time when Latin players were making an impact on the field like never before.

And what did they do? They let that advantage slip into the hands of their chief rival, the Dodgers. But more important are questions that will always remain unanswered, rendered moot by opportunities lost in the wind gusts of Candlestick Park.

Would baseball history be different if the team "more dependent on non white players than any in the major leagues" had won a world title or two? How many hardened stereotypes would have died? How many closed eyes would have been opened?

Instead, like the country they lived in, the Giants were divided in the most profound ways.

In baseball terms, those divisions harkened back to Pagan's words—white players first, blacks second, Latins third. In the 1960s and 1970s, it was hard to dispute that pecking order.

In 1973, Frank Deford wrote in *Sports Illustrated* of the escalating number of young Latin players being cast aside into poverty by major league baseball. Within a profile of Pirates' Latin scout Howie Haak, Deford wrote: "When a boy tempted by a few bucks, a plane ticket to the Estados Unidos and maybe a shiny new glove and shoes [Haak always throws them in] fails and returns home, he never plays baseball again. Two years ago [1971] 55 players were signed out of the Dominican Republic, 45 out of Puerto Rico, another 21 out of Venezuela and Panama. Most of them are back in hovels or jammed into New York tenements, hiding out [from the INS]. But they are not playing baseball anymore."

Like Miguel Tejada, Latin players came cheap, but the motivation for retaining and developing them didn't exist then as it does today. So hundreds were signed and chucked aside. Often, luck was all that saved a Latin prospect. In 1961, Tony Oliva—three-time batting champion for the Minnesota Twins—was released in his first spring training after signing for an obscene two hundred dollars. The Twins didn't think he could hit.

At the time he was scheduled to go back to Cuba, the island had been sealed off by the infamous Bay of Pigs invasion. Without a place to go, Oliva cooled his heels and then, on a whim, was sent to a Twins minor league team with no expectations. He started hitting—finishing the year with a .410 average. Amazed, the Twins reassessed, and in 1964, Oliva was American League Rookie of the Year and batting champion.

"My second chance, what saved me, was the Bay of Pigs," Oliva says today.[33]

By the mid-1970s, no one spoke out much about the treatment of Latin prospects because the one person who had the stature, authority, and inclination to do so—the player with the highest profile of any Latin major leaguer—had just died.

Now a part of baseball lore, Roberto Clemente perished on New Year's Eve 1972, in a plane crash while rushing food and supplies to earthquake-ravaged Nicaragua. Today, he is lionized, and deservedly so. His numbers spoke for themselves: 3,000 hits, a .317 lifetime batting average, 12 Gold Gloves, an NL MVP, 4 batting titles, 12 All-Star appearances, and an MVP award for the 1971 World Series. He led the Pirates to two world titles and was still great when he died at thirty-eight. Off the field, he was a model for youth, particularly Latin youth, dedicating his life to helping the disadvantaged.

And the way he died—on a mercy mission in the prime of life—created Clemente, the legend. Today, there is a statue of him outside Three Rivers Stadium in Pittsburgh. Among Latin players, his name is first. But without the complex man to speak for himself, the legend takes over, smoothing the edges, omitting strong words he spoke, making his memory palatable to those who once dismissed him.

Puerto Rico and Latin America have always loved Clemente and always will. But in the United States, his name was not embraced fully until after his death. "Had Clemente not died the way he died, he would have been like Marichal, respected in some areas, but forgotten in others," said Luis Mayoral, an old friend of Clemente's and now a member of the front office for the Texas Rangers.

"It was the way he died that was the key to his life."[34]

What makes Mayoral right? During his career, from 1955 to 1972, Clemente was portrayed much differently than he is remembered.

"Clemente is still too enigmatic and misses too many games to be the rock on which the team is built," wrote *The New York Times Magazine* in 1972—words the *Times* enlarged and ran next to a picture of Clemente's wife, Vera, and one of their sons. This was after Clemente's greatest triumph, his MVP performance in the 1971 World Series, in which he hit .414, hit 2 home runs, and played right field brilliantly. In the first Series played during prime time, Clemente seemed to jump through America's television screens, rounding the bases like a raging panther, on a level above all the others.

Yet there was always a caveat, a put-down in print, a withholding of recognition that rankled Clemente until the day he died.

A typical headline during his era was "Superstar frustrated by faint praise" or "Swat Star Clemente . . . an Angry man," or "It's Hard to Define Clemente's greatness."

A typical depiction was like this one, penned by famed writer Jimmy Cannon in 1970: "There is a strain of crankiness in Clemente's actions, a trace of petulance. It's a kind of smallness that you are aware of, but can't define."

Perhaps it was the statements Clemente made or the questions he asked. Like Jackie Robinson, Clemente was a crusader. He openly challenged the third-class status of Latins in baseball.

In his prime, he asked if America could declare the greatness of a foreigner in the American game.

This was a black Latin man in the 1960s and 1970s confronting predominantly white writers, asking: "Why do you make me sound like 'Me Tarzan, you Jane?' "[35]

This was a Latin player during the media blitz of the '71 Series who cracked, "[Hall of Famer] Frank Robinson is better than me. He's an American, that makes him best."[36]

Often, the responses were pointed jabs in the sports pages. After his Frank Robinson remark, Jerome Holtzman then of the *Chicago Sun-Times* wrote: "Stop the average fan on the street and he'll also tell you Clemente's an anti-social hypochondriac with a knack of finding ways to loaf." Holtzman then wrote how, on Roberto Clemente Night the year before, the man himself saved the game with a sliding catch. But even this was cast negatively.

"As he left the park, his knees wrapped in bloodied bandages, a fan walked up to him and said, 'I saw you showboating just because it was your night.' "

In fairness, not all of Clemente's press followed this trend. But a great deal of it did, and even sympathetic writers loved to poke fun at his "hypochondria." In 1966, the year he was named Most Valuable Player, *Sports Illustrated* ran a profile of Clemente with a drawing of him standing in his Pirates uniform, tiny letters marking his various strained body parts.

The New York Times Magazine wrote: "It is expected of ballplayers that they discuss their injuries and ailments, even minor ones, in grim understatements, prefaced by, 'I'm not making any excuses.' Clemente is utterly up front, not to say confessional, about anything that is bothering him—even if it is something minor, even if it is something uncanny. . . . Or maybe Clemente wants to be accorded the simple gee-whiz deference with which Mays and Aaron have been generally written up in recent years."

Clemente was never asked to do endorsements, never praised unconditionally until he was gone. Then, the accolades rained down from the very people who were offended by his words, threatened by his proud personality.

It was those qualities, and his talent, that made him so revered in Puerto Rico and throughout Latin America. There is now a sprawling baseball camp in San Juan bearing his name, dedicated to giving underprivileged youths a sanctuary. Run by his widow, Vera, the school has adopted Clemente's credo—it's just as important that kids be good citizens as good athletes.

A quarter century later, Latins old enough to remember can recite exactly where they were when they heard Clemente was dead.

He is their legend, the only legend of Latin baseball. Today, more than ever, that legacy begs the question: Can a Latin player achieve legendary status while he is alive, or does he have to die like Clemente first?

In 1998, while he and Mark McGwire surpassed baseball's hallowed single-season home run record, Sammy Sosa was asked if he felt angry that McGwire was garnering more attention than he was. Was it racial? Unlike Clemente, Sosa wouldn't bite.

But the question persisted. By the end of the season, something remarkable was happening: Sosa was garnering a level of acceptance Clemente wished for all Latins.

It's no coincidence Sosa wears number 21 on his back, the number of Roberto Clemente. It's a fitting tribute, linking the buried past of Latin players with a glowing present and promising future.

It's just too bad Zoilo Versalles didn't live to see it. If he had, maybe he would have finally reaped the benefits of doing something great, something even Clemente didn't do.

Though no one remembers it, Versalles was the first Latin player ever to be named Most Valuable Player in a season. A Cuban, Versalles enjoyed his best years with the Minnesota Twins in the early and mid-1960s. He was MVP in 1965, the key member of the Twins' pennant-winning season.

He was a shortstop, he wore glasses, was not handsome like Clemente, had acne, was gruff, and always had stormy relationships with managers and fellow players.

Even his name was different, unusual and easy to skip over on the list of MVPs, which includes Clemente in '66 and Cepeda in '67.

Indeed, when Versalles won his MVP, it was hardly noted that he was the first Spanish-speaking man to win baseball's highest individual honor.

Some say today that 1965 was an off-year for baseball because the fabled Yankees had collapsed and marquee players like the Twins' Harmon Killebrew had off-years. For his part, Versalles's numbers were quite unlike most MVPs'. He didn't lead the league in batting, not even cracking .280. He hit only 19 home runs—a lot for a shortstop then but not much for an MVP. He had only 77 RBI. But he wasn't paid to be a power hitter. He was a spark plug, a great fielder, earning his second Gold Glove that year. Versalles also led the league in at-bats, doubles, triples, and runs.

A testament to his unconventional ways, Versalles also led the league in strikeouts with 122. "People shouldn't forget Zoilo was responsible for us getting to the World Series,"[37] Oliva said. It was the first Series for the upstart Twins, who wouldn't go again for twenty-two years. In '65, they battled the favored Dodgers to a deciding seventh game in Minneapolis. Versalles hit a respectable .286, stroked eight hits, including a double, a triple, and a home run, and drove in four runs.

The Dodgers started Sandy Koufax, baseball's premier pitcher, in game seven and he was as dominant as ever—staking the Dodgers to a 2–0 lead.

But in the fifth inning, two Twins had reached base with one out when Versalles stepped to the plate.

A left-handed batter, Versalles was looking to slap the ball, to break Koufax's dominance before it was too late. And he got his pitch, blistering a screaming line drive down the third-base line that looked like a sure double or triple. He thought: tie score!

But it was not to be. Jim Gilliam, the Dodgers' third baseman, was playing unusually close to third considering Versalles hit left-handed, and he speared the liner in the webbing of his glove. The rally was over and the Twins were defeated. The Dodgers were champs. "Gilliam shouldn't have been standing where he was. If it had been a hit, who knows what would have happened," Oliva said.[38]

What should have been a joyous off-season for Versalles wasn't. The U.S. embargo of Cuba foiled a triumphant homecoming.

"He told me, 'With me as MVP and you the batting champion, they would have a parade for us throughout [Cuba],'" Oliva said.[39] At the time, Versalles said, "I feel that I have no home. I did not make a revolution [but] I am Cuban, it's snowing [in Minnesota] and no, I'm not happy."[40]

Versalles was tough and aggressive. In the language of baseball, he was a hard-ass, a barrio kid from Havana who, once off the field, was out of his element in 1960s America.

"He was street smart and he was baseball smart but away from the field he was always fighting a million wars," wrote Jerry Izenberg in 1973. While he was starring on the field, Versalles was tolerated. But when his production fell off, everything began to fall apart. He bounced to a number of teams. And he accurately foretold his future to Izenberg: "I am different. We, the Latins are different. If [an American] boy cannot make a play or throw he can go to his daddy, perhaps, and sell cars for him. But if I miss too many where can I go when they say good-bye [to me]. . . . I have no father with a business, no education. . . . I must, therefore, make the play."

When he couldn't make the plays, Versalles was through with baseball. Or rather, baseball was through with him. What followed were years of low-paying jobs in a box factory, cleaning airplane engines, working as a janitor and on a candy factory assembly line for five dollars an hour. "I even had to sell my house," he said in the 1980s. "No wonder people are committing crimes. There are lots of times I want to rob a bank."[41] But Versalles never did, he kept working and supporting his family. Needing money and angry with baseball, Versalles sold his MVP trophy and all of his awards to collectors. "People think I needed the money, but that was only a small part of it," he told sportswriter Bill Madden in 1984. "I felt that these things were given to me by people who wouldn't give me a job. I didn't want them around to remind me. Now, I think of my MVP trophy and I want to cry." By the early 1990s, Versalles was living alone, estranged from his family, in a tiny, unkempt apartment in Richfield, Minnesota. It was a short distance from the enormous Mall of America, which was also the site of old Metropolitan Stadium, where he had all his triumphs. In a telephone interview with the *Sacramento Bee* in 1993, Versalles was bitter: "If you are not blonde with blue eyes, no one will help you in this country."

Versalles later consented to a face-to-face interview at the urging of his friend, Oliva. But once the interview got started, he changed his mind. Sitting for a brief photo session, he said: "I have an appointment. I have to go. I have to go." He then rushed out, leaving two journalists standing in his apartment. Within weeks, his phone was disconnected. He would live this way for a time, while Latin players lacking his talent were making millions. Starting in the late 1970s, owners had begun aggressively recruiting in Latin America, and by the mid-1990s, there were scores of Latin players throughout the league.

But Versalles paid them no mind. No one remembered what he did, why should he pay attention? And then, in 1995, when he was only fifty-five, he died. He was found alone in his home. *The New York Times*, like other papers, finally cited his historical significance as the first Latin MVP. But it was too late. Having survived two heart attacks, Versalles's death was attributed to a hardening of the arteries.[42]

He was buried in June 9, 1995, just days before Miguel Odalis Tejada would play his first game in America as a prospect for the Oakland Athletics. Miguel is a shortstop just like Versalles. He is a poor kid from the streets just like Versalles. And he has the dreams Versalles once had—dreams shared by all the Latin men in major league baseball. No one could tell what lay ahead for Miguel as he arrived in America.

But he hadn't come alone. Many others had cleared a path for him.

7

LOS CAMINOS
DE LA VIDA
(The Paths of Life)

FROM THE MOMENT he set foot on U.S. soil in that spring of 1995, nineteen-year-old Miguel Odalis Tejada was heralded with the same indifference he received from his coaches at Campo Juan Marichal.

"He was a no-name," said J. P. Naumes, then a fourteen-year-old from Medford, Oregon, an avid baseball fan whose family housed Miguel in his first season of baseball in America. "He got a bonus of two thousand dollars. That's nothing." [1] In fact, Miguel wasn't supposed to go to Medford at all. The Athletics had planned to keep him with their absolute beginners, in an Arizona rookie league that represented the bottom of the totem pole in baseball development. The reason: They had their eye on another shortstop, Mark Christian Bellhorn of Auburn University. The team had used its second-round draft pick on Bellhorn and was busily negotiating his signing bonus and contract while Miguel practiced in Phoenix.

But as kids like Miguel broke into camp, raring to play their two-thousand-dollar hearts out, Bellhorn and eight other Americans drafted by the Athletics still hadn't signed. [2] Their hands forced by baseball economics, the Athletics put Miguel on a plane in the early morning hours of June thirteenth—a plane bound from Phoenix to Oakland. Once there, the kids were bused across the Nimitz Freeway to the Oakland Coliseum. Baseball was just coming back from the paralyzing strike that had canceled the World Series for the first time, and, in the Bay Area, had effectively destroyed fan interest in a losing team, shrinking from its championship years of the late 1980s and early '90s. Including Miguel and twenty-five other Southern Oregon A's holding freebie tickets, only 12,466 fans turned out for a game between the Athletics and the Chicago White Sox.[3] Nonetheless, Miguel was awestruck the first time he walked through the expansive stadium gate. While the Athletics no longer struck fear into opponents, they still had future Hall of Famers Mark McGwire, Rickey Henderson, and Dennis Eckersley. Much-traveled Dominican Geronimo Berroa had been acquired from the Florida Marlins, giving hope to Miguel by launching prodigious home runs into the wooden bleacher sections of the Coliseum. But of most interest to Miguel was Mike Bordick, who was in the middle of his third consecutive season at shortstop.

By this day Bordick was leading all American League shortstops in fielding and would hold that lead until the final week of the season, making only 6 errors through late September. So solid was Bordick that from June 7—six days before this night— to July 15, he would go 37 games without making an error.[4] Bordick was twenty-nine, in his prime, and Miguel studied him closely, noting that he was getting better and stronger with each year. At second base was Brent Gates, who was injured much of the 1994 season after playing well in '93. All these players seemed huge to Miguel, whose body was still filling out after a year of eating properly for the first time in his life. In fact, White Sox superstar Frank Thomas—all six-foot-five, 257 pounds of him—seemed like a monster. Never had Miguel seen anyone so large, so close up.

The plan that night was for Miguel and his teammates to board their bus for a long ride to Medford after the game. But the trip was delayed by an exciting, four-hour battle that went into extra innings and ended in the top of the tenth with a Thomas home run. The A's failed to score in the bottom half of the inning and the final score was a 7–6 White Sox victory. Miguel was tired as he exited the Coliseum, looking over his shoulder as both teams entered their respective clubhouses. Miguel vowed to himself that he would be back here, perhaps as soon as next season, though no one in the Athletics believed that could happen—not then, anyway. It was late afternoon when Miguel boarded the bus. The Oakland hills looked beautiful to him as he and his teammates pulled slowly out of the coliseum parking lot, going east on the Nimitz Freeway through downtown Oakland.

As Miguel sat, images of *Los Barrancones* commingled with the flickering lights of the fashionable suburb of El Cerrito. Soon the bus was shooting past the University Avenue exit leading to the heart of Berkeley and its community of neo-hippies, university students, think tanks, bookstores, and coffeeshops. Miguel was asleep by the time the bus crossed the Carquinez Bridge into communities born of a myriad of deltas connected to the Sacramento River, places like Suisun City, where Orlando Cepeda now lived an exemplary life. In a sense, this bus ride was a metaphor for Miguel's life in America—passing through, yet never really stopping to see, remember, or be a part of places that were very different from what he knew. Miguel was here to play baseball, nothing else mattered, and little else would be remembered—either by him or by the Americans who would be around him on and off the field. That night, he couldn't have noticed as the bus passed the turnoff to Highway 12, which leads to the spectacular Napa Valley and America's finest vineyards and vintages. He was dreaming by the time the bus connected with Interstate 5 in the state capital of Sacramento, where the final leg of this 370-mile trek began. At the time, lawmakers were struggling with a crippling recession that had violently turned public opinion against Latin immigrants, mostly from Mexico and Central America.

The remainder of the ride, through the northern reaches of California, occurred in darkness and silence and there was little stirring when, early the next morning, the bus pulled into Medford and the beginning of a new season. Though the kids were tired, there would be little time for rest. The first workout took place at noon that day at Miles Field, which holds slightly more than four thousand people.

This was the place where major league standouts Jose Canseco, Mike Bordick, Brent Gates, and Jason Giambi took their first steps as professionals with the Athletics. Along with simple necessity, sending Miguel to Medford was an experiment of sorts for the Athletics. They knew he had talent and potential but so had many other Dominican kids dispatched to the low-level Class A league in the Pacific Northwest. For most Dominicans, Medford had been like a way station to nowhere, a picturesque passing through a point twenty-seven miles north of the California/Oregon border.

The question for Miguel was: Would he excel or would he succumb to the groupies, beer parties, dispirited practices, and distant performances that felled so many previous Dominican prospects?

Upon his arrival, the local paper didn't give him much of a chance. "Once [Mark] Bellhorn comes to terms [with the Athletics] and is ready to return to the lineup, Tejada will probably return to Arizona."[5] The paper also quoted Oakland's minor league director, Keith Lieppman, as saying, "Normally, we like to keep the young kids in Arizona at least one year." But Lieppman also gave Medford fans a reason to think Miguel would be more than they expected.

Miguel "is a hard-hitting shortstop and we haven't seen too many of them over the years with the A's. He has good hands and arms and a good combination of tools," Lieppman said.

The Athletics had hope, but weren't certain what Miguel was "made of." Like all the rest of the Dominicans in their program, Miguel was unknown away from the baseball diamond. The Athletics don't delve into the home lives of their Dominican prospects. They had never been to *Los Barrancones*, knew little of Miguel's background, and wanted to keep it that way.

"If you begin to know too much about any one kid it begins to cloud your judgment. You don't want to make decisions based on feeling sorry for the kid. When you do that you're not doing the kid or the team any favors," Luis Martinez says.[6]

For his part, Miguel knew the rules. "All they know about you is baseball," he said. "So when I went to Medford I decided I wasn't going to be the kind of person who was always asking for help. When you do, the Americans speak badly of you. It's like you give them an excuse to criticize you and I wasn't going to do that."

He decided to speak English, even when he didn't know

the words and no matter how many mistakes he made. And early on, he made many.

THE ATHLETICS PLACED Miguel in the home of Pete and Bobbi Naumes, long-time Southern Oregon A's fans and members of one of the wealthiest families in Medford. But despite the disparity of wealth in the region, Medford people are down-to-earth. So much so that it's hard to distinguish doctors from lumberjacks on the basis of the cars they drive or the clothes they wear.

The Naumes family fit right in here, despite the fact that their family name is known around Medford by its company title: Naumes, Inc. Generating revenues between $55 million and $63 million a year, the family-owned business is made up of seven thousand acres of agricultural land in Oregon, Washington, and California. The Naumes family formed their company in 1946, but their roots in local history go much deeper. In 1910, Pete Naumes's great-grandfather by the same name kicked off a family tradition by winning a medal for the best box of Newton apples at an Oregon Horticultural Society meeting. From those humble beginnings the family business expanded to growing apples in the heart of the Cascades in Washington state and to growing apples and pears in California orchards just north of Sacramento, on land once owned by John Sutter, who owned the mill where gold was discovered in California.[7]

In southern Oregon's Rogue Valley, Naumes, Inc., employs 150 workers, many of whom tend the Naumes's prize pear harvests in and around Medford. Overall, the company has five hundred employees.

Though they are as down-to-earth as their community, the most direct contact the Naumeses had with any kind of Hispanics was with the Mexican farm workers tending their orchards and working their packing sheds near Miles Field, where Miguel hoped to make his reputation. The Naumeses loved baseball and loved taking their sons J.P. and Matt to games, where they sat in choice seats behind home plate. They would also open their home to A's players, a common practice at the Class A level, where players make only a few hundred dollars a week and need help defraying costs.

The year before, the Naumeses had played host to the Athletics' prized prospect, top draft choice Ben Grieve. But his arrival was far different. Before the season, the Grieves had called the Naumeses and were reassured by Bobbi that they were a "homespun family." [8] And when Grieve arrived, he was heralded as a future superstar by the press.

Miguel didn't know who he'd be staying with until he arrived in Medford. And, needless to say, Bobbi Naumes didn't have a conversation with Daniel Tejada about what his boy liked to eat. It was all trial and error, sweetly awkward moments when host and house guest stared blankly at each other, struggling to communicate, pointing and using exaggerated gestures to convey the simplest messages.

"I remember soon after he moved in Miguel wanted to cook something so he went down to the kitchen," Bobbi said. "Luckily my husband went down also because he found Miguel had stuck some food in the microwave, tin foil and all, and set the time at thirty minutes!" [9]

Though he put up a cheerful front, Miguel felt a great sadness upon arriving in Medford, a loneliness that far outweighed what he had experienced at Campo Juan Marichal. As a Latin immigrant, he missed the music, the people, the environment that had made him what he was.

Life around *Los Barrancones* had been an endless series of days in which camaraderie helped ease the sting of hunger and joblessness. When he was not playing baseball, Miguel loved to sit on a chair in front of his family's dwelling with his brothers, neighbors, and scores of friends. They would string an electrical cord to a dilapidated stereo and listen to music for hours at a time, moments that would foster a closeness, an ambiance endemic to Latin America. Poor or not, the people of *Los Barrancones* are like family.

Around his barrio, everyone knows Miguel and he knows everyone. He is Odalis, or Wau-Wah, or any number of other nicknames in a country where most everyone has a nickname. In fact, there are many people of *Los Barrancones* Miguel only knows by some moniker or another.

In Medford, Miguel found a community representative of America, or at least the America existing outside major urban areas.

Located 277 miles south of Portland and 385 miles north of

San Francisco, this expansive region makes for a scenic drive along Interstate 5 but isn't exactly known for its racial diversity. Of the 55,090 Medford residents, 94.8 percent are white, according to the U.S. Census. Only 5.1 percent of Medford's residents are listed as being of "Spanish origin," (or about 2,750 Hispanics). Most of those are Mexican farm laborers not known to be southern Oregon A's season ticket holders, or theatergoers at the nationally renowned Shakespeare Festival in nearby Ashland. Medford is a place where locals spend their free time fishing for salmon and steelhead in the nearby Rogue and Applegate rivers. Here Miguel was the oddest of oddities: a black man who was Latin as well.

Aside from a Spanish-speaking coach, the only other person Miguel could talk to was a Medford social worker named Jill Ramirez, an Anglo spouse of a Mexican-American transplant from northern California. Ramirez learned Spanish when she lived in Mexico City and through extensive travels through Latin America. Over time, her house became like a sanctuary to Miguel, and Ramirez a surrogate big sister.

It was against this backdrop that Miguel faced the task of succeeding on the baseball diamond. From the beginning, he tried to suppress his memories of home, to forget about what was at stake for him and his family. And he put up a good front, giving the impression that all was carefree and light with him. "He had a hundred-watt smile," Bobbi Naumes said.[10]

"He was always really cheerful and happy." It wasn't that Miguel was trying to be deceptive or dishonest. He was just having a difficult time reconciling who he really was with who he wanted to be. Here was Miguel, living among the Naumeses after having bathed in the streets of Bani as a child, shined shoes, and gone hungry. Though some, like Soto, would see his father's absences as abandonment, Miguel still forgives him, although he acknowledges he was orphaned for a time. "My father had to go away to work, because we didn't have any money," Miguel says. "So I would only see him once a month, sometimes less."

MIGUEL'S FIRST game as a professional in the United States was a Thursday night contest against the Boise (Idaho) Hawks, an Anaheim Angels affiliate. The Northwest League is often the first step for Athletics prospects, where they play a shortened season of seventy-six games. What is common to this league is forgiving fans tolerating the mistakes of players slowly discovering they have no future while playing alongside a tiny handful of future stars.

For Northwest fans, one of the kicks is discovering who those stars will be. The league is split into two divisions, southern and northern. In the northern division, except for the Boise Hawks, there are three teams from small communities in Washington state—the Spokane Indians, the Everett Aquasox, and the Yakima Bears. Respectively, they are affiliates of the Kansas City Royals, Seattle Mariners, and Los Angeles Dodgers.

In the southern division, there are the Southern Oregon A's of Medford and three other Oregon-based teams: the Salem-Keizer Volcanoes, the Eugene Emeralds and the Portland Rockies, affiliates of the San Francisco Giants, Atlanta Braves, and Colorado Rockies. In 1994, the folks of Medford were thrilled by Ben Grieve as he displayed a classic swing and an easy excellence, convincing A's fans he was bound for the majors. The 1995 edition didn't offer such tantalizing hints of the future—at least not at first. Returning to the A's squad was Manny DaSilva, a six-foot, 195-pound catcher who had led the Northwest League in doubles the year before and, at twenty-three, was pretty old for these parts.

Mike Moschetti was a shortstop out of La Mirada High School in California, who had been selected in the second round of the 1993 amateur draft but struggled in Medford, batting only .224. And soon, the team finally began adding its draft picks from that season, including Ryan Christensen and David Newhan, a pair of outfielders from Pepperdine University, Danny Ardoin, a catcher from McNeese State, and David Slemmer, a shortstop from Southwest Missouri State. This was not considered a particularly strong team by the organization, and they played that way once the season began—starting 1–7. As the team went, so went Miguel. He couldn't buy a hit, getting off to a miserable start. He was chasing bad pitches or hitting balls directly at people with gloves. In those first ten days, the pressure had clearly gotten to him and the few times he was questioned by reporters, he admitted he was pressing.

"The first few days I was here, I felt pressure," he told the

Medford Mail Tribune. Miguel still didn't have enough confidence in his English to speak alone to reporters, instead using A's coach Luini Aracena as an interpreter. It seemed the specter of Mark Bellhorn was always hanging over him, as it was widely assumed the Boston native and Auburn star would knock Miguel down a peg once he was signed. Certainly Miguel's early play made no one think that would be a wrong move.

But with no Bellhorn contract, Miguel played on—barely hitting as he silently rode the A's bus the length of Oregon and into Washington state, to Interstate 82 and downtown Yakima, where the A's would take on the Yakima Bears. While he was staying at the Days Inn in nearby Union Gap, word came on June 24 that Bellhorn had finally signed.

And then, in Yakima of all places, Miguel let everyone know who he was. At Yakima County Stadium, Miguel went 3 for 4, driving in four runs, scoring twice, and getting on base five times. The A's won 10–6, and, after the game, his manager said: "He's definitely got some big league potential."[11] He had gotten 4 other hits in the five-game series at Yakima, blasting his way through the Bellhorn signing weekend by going 7 for 16 while the A's took four straight to raise their record to 5–7. Miguel was happy as the team boarded their bus and elated when he heard even better news: Bellhorn was being sent two levels higher to Modesto, California, and the advanced Class A California League.

Locked in at short, Miguel relaxed and began playing as he knew he could. It was becoming clear that this boy had something in him, a strength and bravado that rose to challenges and obstacles, even when the obstacles were self-inflicted. In July, during a home game against the Portland Rockies, Miguel knew that the Athletics minor league director Keith Lieppman was in the stands. In a fast-moving pitchers' duel, the Rockies had runners in scoring position with two outs in the sixth inning when a playable grounder got past Miguel, allowing the first run of the game. Two plays later, the ball was hit in the exact same spot, and this time, Miguel made the play. But the A's lost the game 1–0 on Miguel's error.

Lieppman saw a kind of toughness in Miguel that he liked, the kind a scout yearns for. "That's showing a good mentality when he can come back and make the same play,"[12] Lieppman said. By this point, the Athletics were less and less worried about the internal policy they broke by sending Miguel to Medford. "It's sort of been our philosophy to put college seniors and some junior-college players here in this league and integrate high-school, junior-college, and Dominican players down in Arizona. Miguel is the first player we've sent through to Medford." [13] By July 26, Miguel had 4 home runs and, that night, he blasted number five—a two-run shot at Miles Field against the Everett Aquasox before 4,010 fans in Medford. Miguel was gaining momentum and confidence as the season went on, but there were still challenges. Early in the year, when a runner reached second base, Miguel would silently sneak behind the runner in thinly veiled pickoff attempts.

But more often than not, new catcher Danny Ardoin would launch moon beams into center field. Or Miguel would miss a sign, the play, and the ball, leaving himself standing disgustedly by the bag, looking young and foolish. For seven weeks it went like this, until a night in August when Medford faced the Eugene Emeralds, an Atlanta Braves affiliate. The Emeralds boasted two of the brightest lights in baseball's top organization of the 1990s: George Lombard, a swift outfielder and second in the Northwest League in stolen bases, and Glenn Williams, an eighteen-year-old phenom from Australia, who had signed with the Braves in 1993, the same year Miguel signed with the Athletics. Williams was a shortstop, though a much more valued one.

Indeed, Williams signed for the largest bonus in major league baseball at that point—$925,000[14]—even though his only experience was playing in Australia's obscure professional baseball league. Still, Williams was six-one and 185 pounds, and the Braves were wowed by his speed and figured that with training, he could be turned into a great ballplayer. Then, reality set in. By 1995, Williams had spent much time on the injured reserve and was in need of something to prove his worth.

In the top of the fifth against Medford, the Emeralds were leading 1–0 with one out, Lombard on second, and Williams at first. Once again, Miguel was trolling, his eyes alert, tapping his free hand into his glove as he rocked from side to side on the balls of his feet. Lombard was looking to bolster his stolen base reputation, creeping off the bag, looking for that extra inch, when Miguel shuffled forward, a split second too fast for Lombard, who, in an instant, found himself in no-man's land as Ardoin rocked and threw toward Miguel, who speared the ball and hurled it toward third to get Lombard by a wide margin. Williams moved up to second base on the play, where he stood with two outs and a notion to make something happen himself. The next day, the *Medford Mail Tribune* wrote: "Glenn Williams . . . apparently figured lightning doesn't strike twice in the same spot. He figured wrong." Ardoin said that Williams "took an aggressive lead and Miguel gave me the signal and I thought I could get him. I got the right pitch and the throw was right on the money." Tejada had gotten behind Williams when the young Australian wasn't looking. And by the time he retreated to the bag it was too late: His face, Miguel's glove, and Ardoin's throw met in a photo finish. Things wouldn't get any better for Williams, because while his bank account was healthy, he would suffer through injury-filled years in 1996 and 1997 while still toiling in Class A ball. In March of 1998, Alan Schwarz of *Baseball America* wrote: Williams "doesn't approach the prospect he once was. And even if the injury bug hadn't chomped on him, chances are he still wouldn't have played up to his bonus. Few ever do." Without a doubt, Miguel was playing up to his two thousand dollars.

By August 9, he was leading his team in every offensive category except batting average, and he punctuated that dominance with a blistering triple that would be the deciding blow in a 5–2 win. Miguel led the team with 7 homers when he pounded another against the Boise Hawks on August 25. In fact, things were going so well that even when he did the wrong thing it turned out right. On August 21 against Yakima, Miguel was standing on third when he thought he heard his manager tell him to steal home. Trouble was, his manager had said nothing of the kind.

But instead of holding his ground and playing it safe when the order clearly confused him, Miguel went for it, scoring easily. On the 26th, he stole home again—just like Minnie Minoso used to in the old days. Indeed, Miguel was becoming the latter-day Minoso of Medford. He was "flashy," he was exciting, he was "colorful." He was doing everything there was to do on the baseball field and he was doing it with a flourish, a style that was somewhere between what he had practiced in *Los Barran-*

cones and what he learned with the Athletics. "There was a game early in the season where I first noticed it," said Dan Kilgras, general manager of what are now called the Southern Oregon Timberjacks.[15] "Miguel was playing short, like he always did, and there was a ball hit hard in his direction, a ball that looked at first like it was going to be an easy out. Miguel had his legs planted in the ground, he was set to make the play, when suddenly the ball took a funny hop off the dirt. It began to go in a different direction, away from him and for a second I thought, Too bad. The ball is going to get behind him. But it didn't. He stood there planted in the ground and he didn't move his legs at all. He just caught the ball barehanded and threw to first for the out. I looked over at [a friend] and said, 'This kid is going to be tough.' "

Yet Miguel was also one of the least quoted players on the team and therefore one of the least known outside the tiny circle who spent significant amounts of time with him. Often, Miguel's feats were described by his manager Tony DeFrancesco or by Lieppman.

When Miguel spoke, it was always through the awkward filter of an interpreter. The pattern of Miguel's press clippings that year was a time-honored one in baseball writing—a Latin player does well, plays well, and yet the depth of his accomplishments stays out on the field, squelched in the clubhouse by a cumbersome, translated quotation or a reporter on deadline who walks right by the cubicle of the foreigner to the familiar kid from the States.

As they would be for much of his minor league career, Miguel's exploits, including his selection as an All-Star, were often summarized, while his teammates, Ardoin and others, were quoted most often. Miguel's life, his background, weren't even hinted at.

He was long gone from Medford by the time the local paper ran this short item on September 9: "Shortstop Miguel Tejada of the Southern Oregon A's Northwest League baseball team is listed as the NWL's No. 1 major league prospect by the NWL managers."

OVER THE COURSE of the '95 season, Miguel had been a silent wonder at short—a diving, flying, speeding acrobat, who would go home to the Naumes family after games, play Nintendo with

Matt or J. P. Naumes, listen to music, and periodically call his dad, sometimes crying on the phone when the loneliness became too great. His A's finished 33–43 that year, dead last in the Northwest League's southern division. During the course of the year, Miguel had been joined by Alex Rondon and Luis Silva, two genial Venezuelans, catcher and pitcher respectively, who had been demoted to Medford from the more advanced Class A team the Athletics ran in Grand Rapids, Michigan.

By the middle of the season, Miguel's loneliness was also eased somewhat by his friendship with Jill Ramirez, who had been opening her Medford home to Latin players on the A's for years. After a time, when he became more comfortable around her and her husband, Miguel had taken to asking Ramirez for the same favor. "It was sort of cute, he would ask me once every homestand if I could please cook him a Dominican meal. It seemed like he had strong family ties and a real need to keep his culture with him," Ramirez said.[16] "He would always be the instigator and would always ask if maybe he could invite a few other guys." Once, Miguel brought fifteen Latin players over to Ramirez's house—much to her amazement.

"Miguel would go over and see who was on the other team, any Latino who was over there, and invite them over. And they would all come over to our house and sit on the patio and talk and tell their stories. . . . When he was here in Medford, his lack of English is what hampered his real personality."

Ramirez, who works for a nonprofit agency assisting Mexican farm workers, had for years seen Dominican kids lose their way. While the Dominicans Ramirez came to know wanted to be in the United States, they had little understanding of how to handle themselves upon arriving in the Pacific Northwest.

"It's like every Dominican's dream to leave their country and come to the United States, and that seems so bizarre to grow up that way. We'd have other players stay with us so we'd be going to Safeway, ready to leave, and they'd be picking up chicks, or we'd go to Burger King and I'd have two clowns in the backseat trying to pick up the girl at the drive-through window. What I respected about Miguel is that he would never put you in that position. I've known a lot of players with talent that still don't know how to behave socially, they don't have it together, but he has that, that hunger to succeed. He doesn't have a high level of education but he was very respectful. He always seemed to be a really hard worker. I never saw him with the groupies around town."

Toward the end of the season, Miguel had tried to help a recent Dominican arrival. Helpis Sosa was a six-foot-three-inch, 180-pound pitcher who had a looming, slightly dangerous physical presence and a brooding attitude. Like Rondon and Silva, Sosa had been sent to Medford from West Michigan and wasn't happy about it. A demotion from one level to another in the minor leagues is never good news, particularly for marginal Latin players who always fear the dire consequences of being released.

Early on, Miguel asked Ramirez if he could invite Sosa to one of their parties, and she reluctantly agreed. She had already been put off by Sosa when she introduced herself to him at Miles Field but was willing to give him a second chance. With a house full of people, Sosa had spotted one of Ramirez's friends, a statuesque woman who was six feet tall. Ramirez said that Sosa marveled at the woman's height and then, in a loud voice, wondered in Spanish whether her height meant that she had a large vagina. Ramirez was horrified by the brazen nature of Sosa's statement, as was Miguel. "He was really upset, shocked at what Helpis had said, and dressed him down. But it seemed like he was more worried about me, like he was concerned that somehow my innocent ears had been offended by what Helpis said. He kept apologizing to me over and over." [17]

Soon thereafter, Sosa and an American player on the team were horsing around when things turned violent. Sosa, a strong kid from Santo Domingo, was—as they say—"the wrong person to mess with." He hit the American player flush on the jaw, breaking it and ending his season. Miguel saw the whole thing. The American player "tried to get up but he couldn't. He had been chewing tobacco and it was all oozing out of his mouth." Sosa was almost immediately released by the Athletics and he cried as Bobbi Naumes drove him to the airport.

He asked her to help him change his plane ticket, flying to Michigan instead of taking his scheduled route to Santo Domingo via Miami. Sosa had a girlfriend in Michigan, and that was where he would stay, instead of going back to his country. A year later he was living in West Michigan, his girlfriend having become his wife, expecting their first child and living a life of re-morse for his lost baseball career. He would spend endless hours hanging around his apartment on bitter cold Michigan days while his wife worked to support them both. The effect of the incident on Miguel was significant. "I was really upset be-cause I heard people around the park saying, 'Oh, Dominican people are bad, they are animals.' After that, I didn't go to the parties people had for the team. I just didn't want to go. So I would go home and listen to music." This suited J. P. Naumes just fine: It meant more time playing Ping-Pong or Nintendo with Miguel. "I used to wait up for him after all the games," he said.[18] Those games and a few other random memories are all the Naumeses recall of Miguel today. It's not that they didn't care for him when he was there, it's just that they didn't know him. He had been there, but in a way he hadn't—not com-pletely. And he had changed. Before he went to Medford, Ron Plaza and a few others were concerned about his cockiness and feared it might get in his way.

Plaza makes it a point to visit the Athletics minor league teams throughout the season to check in on kids, to reinforce one thing or another. But that season, health problems kept him away from Medford until the season was almost over. He won-dered what he would find when he got there. "He always knows I smoke out by the dugout so out he comes to see me. And right away I notice he's trying to say everything in English," Plaza said.[19]

"It's like he had grown up, he was a team player. He just knows how to fix things and he's got big confidence in himself. By that point, he was a star." By the time Miguel left Medford, the Athletics felt they truly had something. They sent him to Modesto—the highest of their three Class A teams—so he could take some swings in the California League playoffs. From there, they shipped him to Arizona for a fall league reserved for top prospects. By the time he went home to Bani in October, Miguel had been away for six months—by far his longest stint away from home.

As he always did in Bani, he worked out with Enrique Soto and prepared himself for the season that lay ahead. He needed to work out hard because in the pecking order of shortstops alone,

Miguel was still a million miles from Oakland: Mike Bordick had another solid year in 1995. At the minor league level, Miguel had three Dominicans in line ahead of him: Fausto Cruz, who had played both at Triple A and with the Oakland Athletics in 1995; Tony Batista, who had been the shortstop at Double A and was second on the Huntsville (Alabama) Stars in home runs and third in RBI; and Jose Castro, who had played with the Class A West Michigan Whitecaps, finishing third in the Midwest League in stolen bases. Also vying for Bordick's spot was Bellhorn, who had finished the '95 season at Class A Modesto. Some competition was already fading, like Mike Moschetti, who quit baseball before the 1996 season started. Others, like Arturo "Tabacco" Paulino, were starting to struggle, reassigned to other positions. Eddie Lara wasn't doing well either, but Juan Polanco put up solid numbers in the Arizona rookie league in 1995.

Meanwhile, competition came in other forms as well. Since signing Miguel in 1993, the Athletics had added two more coveted Latin prospects, high-caliber players who signaled a change in luck for the franchise in the Caribbean. Even as Miguel starred in Medford, a fellow *Banilejo* named Mario Encarnacion was destroying the Dominican summer league. The six-foot-two-inch 190 pounder hit .345, with 8 home runs, 79 hits, 11 doubles, 5 triples, and 44 RBI. By comparison, Miguel had hit .294 and had 18 homers, 64 hits, 9 doubles, 1 triple, and 62 RBI in the summer league. What the Athletics loved about Encarnacion was his body, which was already filling out even though he hadn't gone to the States yet.

At the end of the 1995 season, Encarnacion was only eighteen and was trying to become the first of his family to make it to the major leagues. Two older brothers—Richard and Victor—had both been released, by the Detroit Tigers and Athletics respectively. A big kid whose stern, serious demeanor became dewy and soft around his mom, Encarnacion already looked like a major league player in his uniform, particularly when he ran between the lines at his position in right field. Discovered by Enrique Soto and coveted by other teams, he had managed to squeeze ten thousand dollars out of the Athletics. The Athletics weren't used to spending that much money on a Dominican player, but were convinced Encarnacion was worth it.

Also generating increasing attention was Ramon Hernandez, a muscular, six-foot Venezuelan catcher who was almost exactly Miguel's age and was ruggedly handsome, so much so that he turned the heads of more than one girl while playing in the Rookie Arizona League in 1995. There, he hit an impressive .364 and was named league MVP. Hernandez led the league in batting, walks, on-base percentage, and slugging percentage and tied for the league lead in RBI.

The organization also loved the way he took charge of calling games and they loved his arm. And as 1995 gave way to 1996, Encarnacion and Hernandez joined Miguel in the top-ten list of Athletics prospects along with Ben Grieve and Mark Bellhorn. While younger, less-skilled Latin players began arriving at Campo Juan Marichal in March, Miguel was back in Bani—where he preferred to stay until it was time to leave for the United States. This year would be different from last year in that Miguel would be arriving in Arizona for a complete spring training and minor league season, unlike the shortened season of the year before.

And back in *Los Barrancones* he had set a goal of reaching the major leagues that year, just as he had promised himself the year before when he visited the Oakland Coliseum on his way to Medford. Spring has a way of doing that to young men in the Dominican. Once the winter league season is over and the championship team from the Dominican Republic competes in the annual Caribbean World Series, major league fever sweeps the island.

The emotions and well being of hundreds of boys rise and fall based on who gets picked for a complete spring and who is sent only to extended spring, which starts later in May and leads to shortened seasons in Arizona and Medford. By February of '96, those decisions were being made by the Athletics, sending some young men into despair. Jose Paulino was one of these boys, talented but frightened by his family's history in baseball. A cousin of "Tabacco," Paulino's uncle, Carlos Made, played briefly in the Athletics system before he was cast aside. And his older brother had been released by the Seattle Mariners, fleeing to New York like Made rather than returning to the Dominican.

Paulino was a six-foot-three-inch stringbean who weighed

1

Another prospect in a long line of Dominican ballplayers: Miguel Tejada, at home in Bani with his grandmother, Norinda Munoz Tejada.

Carlos de la Rosa uses a bamboo stick to hit a line drive during a stickball game in San Pedro de Macoris. The town is known for turning out some of the best shortstops ever to play major league ball.

2

In a filthy, graffiti-marked dugout, sitting on a cooler surrounded by discarded paper cups, this young Dominican prospect for the San Diego Padres dreams of leaving the island and making the *Grandes Ligas*.

Victor Uceta, one of Miguel's teammates on the Athletics summer league team, sidesteps the foul-smelling waste in the streets of Santo Domingo's Capotillo barrio.

3

4

Under conditions reminiscent of the military, young prospects are drilled six hours a day, six days a week at the Oakland Athletics baseball academy in the Dominican town of La Victoria. Here, five pitchers watch a bunting drill.

Some of the lucky few actually make it off the island and join the big league teams for spring training. After traveling all day and passing through three time zones, several Dominican prospects wait outside the Phoenix airport for their ride to the Oakland A's training site.

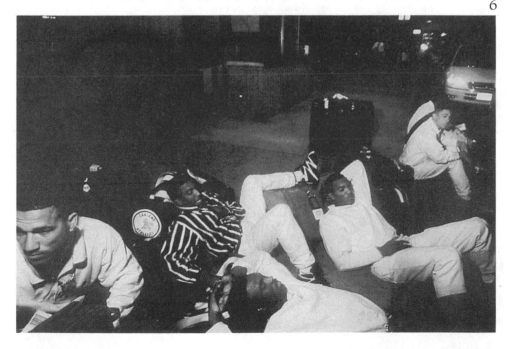

7

Life in the States can be very lonely: Oakland A's prospect Mario Encarnacion waits for one of his teammates at the Fashion Square Mall in Scottsdale, Arizona. Most of the Dominican ballplayers speak very little English and all of them find it difficult adapting to life in the United States.

Life on the ballfield isn't much better for the Dominicans. Huddled together at the far end of the dugout, most of the Dominicans consider themselves outsiders in a world dominated by privileged American kids.

8

Miguel Tejada (number 4) stretches before a 1996 game for the Class A
Modesto Athletics in the Oakland A's farm chain. Showing the confidence of
a player on the rise, Tejada wowed scouts with his spectacular defense, great
power, and awesome speed.

9

After Miguel Tejada was named to the California League All-Star team, his
sensational season was cut short when he broke his left thumb in a collision
with an opponent. Sidelined for a month, Tejada spent much of that time
watching television and wondering if he would ever play again.

10

11

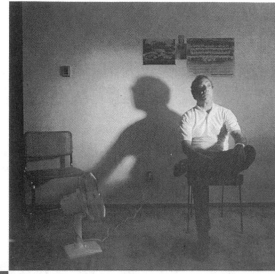

12

13

The pioneers of Latin baseball (*from top to bottom*): Chico Carrasquel outside his Chicago home, Zoilo Versalles two years before his death in 1995, and Roberto Clemente, memorialized in this statue in his homeland, Puerto Rico.

Not all Dominican ballplayers are as fortunate as Miguel Tejada. Those who aren't try to jump-start a new life in America. Here, former minor leaguers (*from left to right*) Robert Valera, Carlos Made, and Alexi Valera pass the time outside a beauty salon in the Bronx.

14

Even without their dreams of youth, many ex-prospects continue to play the game in the Pedrin Zorrilla Baseball League in Brooklyn, New York—one of the toughest semipro leagues in the state.

15

16

17

Above: Rounding second and heading toward third: In just his second major league game, Miguel Tejada tripled off Dodger ace Hideo Nomo.

Left: Tejada knows he has been given the chance of a lifetime. It is something he thinks about every time he hears the national anthem played.

Below: From shoeshine boy to hero: Tejada returns to the humble barrio where he grew up.

18

only 170 pounds. At nineteen years old, he had a rocket of an arm and had gone 12–0 in the summer league season in 1994, posting an amazing 0.67 ERA with 80 strikeouts in 107 innings. In 1995, in the Rookie Arizona League, Paulino was 9–2 with a 3.19 ERA and 72 strikeouts in 87 innings. He seemed certain to go to Class A ball somewhere but it was not to be. The Athletics told him he would not be going to spring training in March but in May—he'd have to pitch rookie league ball in Arizona again. The team was trying to make a point: Paulino was one of a group of boys who had caused damage at their hotel in Arizona. He had also created disciplinary problems on that rookie league team of '95. Impressive numbers or no, Paulino burned as other boys eagerly prepared for that early flight to Miami and beyond, while he stayed behind and went later with the kids and the rejects.

The twelfth of thirteen children in his family, Paulino sat and brooded, sulking in the stone bleachers at one of two baseball diamonds at Campo Juan Marichal. Under a blazing sun, he tried to make sense of what was happening to him: "When you are at this level, what are you going to do?" Paulino said.[20] "You can't do anything because you are nobody. They are the ones who know. They are the ones who decide whether it will be today, tomorrow, or the next day. You have to remain quiet, but it's hard when you know what you can do. I've said little things here and there but later I think, What am I going to do? I'm here."

Paulino is from the city of San Cristobal, just west of Santo Domingo and the place where Rafael Trujillo was assassinated while visiting his mistress in 1961. The Athletics signed him for two thousand dollars about a month after they signed Miguel, but the two were obviously going in opposite directions. Paulino had a strong streak to him, a kind of petulance the team was obviously trying to curb. "I'm not trained to do anything else but baseball. It's all I can do. My brother had gone over and pitched in rookie league in Arizona but they wanted him to come back and pitch in the summer league. He didn't want to so he went to New York and now he lives in Manhattan, working in a button factory. It was hard for my brother when he stopped playing baseball. My mother would tell me he didn't sound like the same person anymore. It seemed there was a sadness to him that didn't used to be there before. There are many men here who want to be professionals because the majority of people admire baseball players. Women, children, everyone. They see you walking down the street and shout out your name. They know you are someone, that you are someone who can earn money and help your country."[21]

Paulino then got up and walked onto the field to join other prospects as they stretched and cooled down at the end of a workout. Because some were going to the United States the next day, the coaches were trying to lighten the mood. One by one, all the players took turns telling jokes. In Latin America, jokes are elaborate ministories with characters and characterizations, some hilariously funny, depending on the teller.

You would never know it to see them in an American clubhouse, but these boys were uproariously witty, with razor sharp tongues and keen intellects. Although they all were competing for a few major league slots, there was an easy camaraderie among them, even though all knew poverty awaited those who didn't make it in the United States. On this day, those bound for the States—Tabacco, Jose and Freddie Soriano, Juan Dilone, Benito Baez, Jose Castro, Juan Perez, Juan Moreno—would tell their jokes to huge hoots and hollers. Then it came time for Eddie Lara. The boys fell silent as Eddie tentatively shuffled to the front of the group, his eyes twitching the way they always did, his luster as a shortstop obviously diminished since he had been supplanted by Miguel. While most of his teammates seemed to relish the chance to show off, Eddie froze—one hand on his hip, his head down. He stood silently as the others waited for him to say something, and after a few excruciatingly awkward moments, his teammates began to make fun of him. Several had joined the attack on the helpless, five-foot-nine-inch waif with the shaved head and the stunned expression when the Athletics coaches rescued him.

Soon, all the players were gorging themselves in the cafeteria, then rushing to pack their belongings as a bus arrived for dozens of boys too young or not good enough to go the States. One kid, a six-foot-one-inch Adonis named Jeison Arias, was readying to leave when Raymond Abreu and "Chago" Marichal called him into their office and closed the door. Another Enrique Soto prospect, a seventeen-year-old man-child, Jeison's strong body belied his age. He had broad shoulders, a strong chest, and strong legs. But his physical maturity was offset by a sweet-sounding voice that seemed halfway between puberty and adulthood. Jeison wasn't like most other Dominican prospects. He was a hot property and he knew it. The expansion Tampa Bay Devil Rays, who wouldn't play their first actual game until 1998, were already fanning out across the Dominican, throwing money around like never before. They were hot on the heels of Arias and had offered him thirty thousand dollars—an ungodly sum of money for a Dominican prospect in 1996. The Athletics were trying to counter, to put the heat on the kid and snare him before he signed with Tampa. Of course, they were trying to do it for fifteen thousand dollars, and on this day, Abreu and Marichal were pressuring Arias, telling him he would be crazy to sign with an expansion club. "I think I have a certain value," Arias said after emerging from Abreu's office.[22] As he talked, his chipped front teeth made him look like a twelve-year-old who just lost his baby teeth. Like Miguel, Arias had to negotiate by himself—he had no agent, and with only a nominal education, he was hardly prepared to represent himself in a professional negotiation with a major league team.

"Chago offered me ten thousand dollars and I told him no, that I couldn't because another team was offering me thirty thousand dollars. I said I appreciated his offer but if I took it the stupid person in our conversation would be me. He was offended and got angry. He started yelling at me, telling me that I was ungrateful. This is the first time in my life I've ever had to do anything like this. I didn't even have my mother and father to help me. Soto told me later that Chago was still offended, so I apologized to him. I told him that I was sorry, that I had never done this before, and asked him to please forgive me."

Nothing was decided on this day and Arias walked out of Abreu's office, joining other prospects on a complex stairwell as they waited to go home. All the boys were laughing and joking, and Arias fidgeted in his place, sitting up straight as he talked as if he were a giddy schoolboy. As he spoke he tilted his head to one side and smiled with the guileless charm of a boy not yet schooled in concealing his emotions. Arias couldn't know it then, but he was on the ground floor of a Latin wave that was starting to sweep the island, changing the rules of recruitment and offering a few boys like him money unheard of in the land of bargains. Arias's case wouldn't be the last time the Tampa Bay Devil Rays and other teams would make aggressive moves in the Dominican. Baseball was changing profoundly and it would not be long before those changes were felt. But they were still too subtle to be noticed on this day. And they had come too late for Eddie Lara, who sat close to Arias and listened as boys in much better positions strutted and bragged, safe in the knowledge that they were going to the United States.

The boys staying in the Dominican—boys like Lara— seemed smaller, more vulnerable, more invisible. Eddie was anxious as the time came to leave, and he seemed to want to hold on to something. He attempted to engage U.S.-bound players in mindless conversation. "It must be tough to play a whole season there," Lara said to pitcher Juan Perez, who never looked up at Eddie but seemed annoyed by his sweet-natured show of weakness. "Is it tough to play a whole season?" he asked. Perez sighed and snapped: "What do you think?" Other players sitting nearby stiffened and seemed uncomfortable, unforgiving of Eddie's plight. In the war of attrition, Eddie was losing, and the other boys seemed to distance themselves from him, disapprove of him, chide him, and not respect him.

Eddie's face was long, his head was down as a van drove him away from the complex on that humid day of March 6, 1996. American-bound players barely looked up as Eddie looked at them, expressionless from the van as it drove away, a trail of dust tailing behind as it passed the armed guard and chain-link fence that was quickly locked again. It was now late afternoon, a gorgeous time of day in the Dominican when the pulverizing sun becomes slightly less menacing and, if you're lucky, a Caribbean breeze softens the humidity as it blows through the palm trees. It was like that inside the Athletics complex, the kind of spectacular afternoon travel agents use to entice European and American tourists to the island. And once Abreu and his coaching staff left for the afternoon, shaking a few hands, offering a few wishes of good luck, the dozen or so boys bound for America scattered in different directions, alone with their thoughts. It was suddenly, uncommonly still, as a brilliant afternoon sun began to set.

• • •

NINETY MINUTES away in Bani, Miguel and Mario Encarnacion were enjoying the benefits of being the most touted Dominicans in the organization. The club had allowed them to go home for a few days before their big trip, while the other boys were back in La Victoria.

Encarnacion was where he could always be found, sitting in front of his house, attentive to whatever his mother needed. Compared to the stifling poverty of *Los Barrancones*, Encarnacion's mother's house was downright middle class: immaculate with its clean furniture, covered completely by plastic in the same way suburban Americans used to protect their furniture back in the 1960s. The house is painted in pastels, powder blue and flamingo pink, and lined with adobe tile. Curtains separate the bedrooms and a sixty-watt bulb lights the small living and dining quarters, leaving the rooms in various degrees of darkness once the sun sets. Three large trophy cases are filled with the spoils of Mario's baseball prowess, and pictures of Mario in his Athletics uniform are all over the house.

The home is next to an open field containing years worth of discarded trash, food wrappers, and mounds of rocks and discarded metal. All the windows and doors to the house are open at all times, and in the flickering light at dusk, a cool breeze blows through as Mario's ninety-year-old grandmother Carmela gently sways in one of four rocking chairs in the living room. It seems everyone in Mario's neighborhood passes through the house, walking in and out with the familiarity of family. "It's a sweet house," says twenty-eight-year-old Rodaisa Soto, a statuesque friend and neighbor of Mario's with long dark hair and coconut skin. In a tight blouse and tight black jeans, Rodaisa vaguely resembles Cher as a young woman, and on this day she was trying to get Mario's attention as he sat at the head of the dining-room table. Mario was filling out visa papers he would need for the next day's flight to Arizona.

At first, Mario acted sternly toward her subtle advances. When she leaned over him, he nervously tapped his Dominican passport against his mother's kitchen table. Rodaisa held her ground, touching Mario's arm as she spoke, her voice growing deeper with each sentence. Mario's arm twitched as they touched. But little by little, Mario seemed to soften, his scowl fading, his dark, handsome face breaking into a smile. Rodaisa coyly played with her flowing hair and Mario seemed taken by the perfume that rose from her bare shoulders. Finally, she got him to laugh, at which point she ran her hand over his tightly cropped hair. "She wants to be my girlfriend," Mario would say later. "But I don't want a girlfriend right now." Encarnacion's parents had separated when he was very small and the tall, strapping boy had been raised by his mom. Mario grew up in a house full of women, his mother, Porfiria, struggling mightily to support the family on the thirty-five dollars a week she earned making tomato sauce in a cannery. Whatever else they had, they had gotten from family members who lived in New York.

Mario had gone to school until he was about sixteen, quitting to concentrate on baseball and earning extra money by making window frames. His life had been far more structured and far less tumultuous than Miguel's so he had a confidence in himself that Miguel didn't. While Miguel didn't yet trust his emotions and was constantly fearful of doing or saying the wrong thing, Mario was more independent, more evolved, and less concerned with what others thought of him. When the Atlanta Braves, New York Mets, and Florida Marlins all offered him contracts, he held out for the best offer. "Atlanta offered me nine thousand dollars but I knew Oakland had an academy where I would be able to live and study English," Mario said. "Some American scouts told me it was too bad that I was born in the Dominican Republic because an American with my ability would have gotten a signing bonus of $1 million." [23] By this point, Mario was earning $350 a month with the Athletics. And, like Miguel, he had become the central figure of his family. Though Mario was only eighteen, all activity in his house swirled around him, while his older brothers Richard and Victor, both baseball rejects, shrank to the background. Richard seemed to skulk along the walls of the Encarnacion house, not doing much more than riding his motor scooter around Bani's crowded streets, while Victor seemed locked in adolescence, though he was two years older than Mario.

A few days before Mario left, the sun was setting when a voice was heard from twenty feet up in a fruit tree on Mario's block. Laughing giddily, there sat Victor, smiling widely with mango juice dripping from his chin. Mario didn't react one way or the other, never losing the stern look on his face. Though he believed deeply in himself, Mario conceded that fear and anger often ran through him as he prepared to go to the United States. Fear of the specter of America and his knowledge of how many Dominican prospects ended up. And anger that he knew—at least at first—he would be taking a big backseat to American players of lesser abilities but higher signing bonuses.

"I feel anger inside me and sometimes I don't know what to do," he said. "When I first went to the academy, I would miss my family so much, I would miss my mother and would begin to feel like a prisoner."[24] Behind the stylish dark sunglasses he likes to wear in boyish conceit, Mario can look menacing because of his stature and seriousness—the kind of Latin player who can easily be labeled temperamental or hotheaded in the states.

But in a moment he will easily smile in a way that reflects a tender soul and a sincere amiability. Ron Plaza and other Athletics instructors were growing to love his work habits and personality and—because of his size and potential to grow—even had him rated higher than Miguel before the 1996 season. To ready himself for the journey ahead, Mario had taken to borrowing psychology textbooks from a professor he knew in Bani, reading up on behavior, trying to spot deficiencies in his own character so he could be ready for the great north. He had taught himself to concentrate on the moment, as the Athletics preached, and he felt he mastered a particular art form.

"You have to know how to talk to gringos," Mario said. "We don't dominate English so it's logical that Latins would feel that it's not their game. I have accustomed myself to that. If, when I'm over there, the press and the public pursue me I would think that's great because it would show I am a good person. They would see me as an example. I am the great hope of my family, and you can also lift your nation through baseball. So I'm going to go over to fight for what is mine."[25] The last thing Mario did before he left that day was to arrange the installation of a telephone in his mother's house, the first ever. He would need it so he could regularly hear her voice. As he prepared himself to leave, his mother grew wistful. "There is going to be a big void when he is gone," she said.[26]

• • •

As Mario packed his things and his brothers prepared to drive him to La Victoria, Miguel was busily throwing his clothes into a bag at his home in *Los Barrancones*. Miguel's dad was proud of his son and his family looked on him with a kind of reverence. Indeed, all of *Los Barrancones* had seemingly been finding its way to the battered little dwelling where Miguel lived with an assortment of brothers, his dad, his grandmother—a frail, tiny little woman of eighty-three who is stoop-shouldered and walks gingerly about the barrio with an unlit piece of tobacco hanging from her lip.

By that spring it had been years since Miguel had seen his brother Juansito—the brother who had taught him how to play baseball but had left Bani for work in another town. In the cramped, tiny enclosure that was their home, Miguel had provided what little furniture there was. On a cramped dresser, next to the television set Miguel had purchased, was a plaque from the Rogue Valley Tire and Automotive Center, a keepsake for the Gold Glove Miguel was given in Medford. Next to it was the MVP trophy from the Southern Oregon Athletics. A watch Miguel had been given for playing in the Northwest League All-Star game was now on his father's wrist. And his brothers proudly wore an assortment of worn Southern Oregon A's hats Miguel had brought home, making them the envy of *Los Barrancones*. Miguel was spending twenty-six thousand pesos—or about two thousand dollars American—to refurbish a dwelling a few blocks away so his family wouldn't be crammed several to a room. Daniel Tejada was worried as his son prepared to leave. The superstitions that were a part of his life were becoming increasingly apparent as he looked upon his youngest son, who brought something he had never known: hope. Voodoo was a fact of life among the poorest people of the Dominican, brought across the border from Haiti. For years, Miguel's mother had been convinced that voodoo caused the death of one of Miguel's brothers before Miguel was born. Miguel's father was convinced voodoo played a hand in Juansito's leaving his family. And now, as Miguel prepared to leave for America, Daniel Tejada feared witchcraft would harm his youngest son.

It is said that if you collect a piece of a person's clothing and other belongings, you can take them to a witch who will conjure up all manner of bad luck, misfortune, and pain. Daniel

Tejada had spoken openly to his son of going to Haiti, to a witch who could counteract any bad luck anyone would send his way. Miguel shook his head, quietly laughing at the thought of him in Haiti on the eve of the greatest opportunity of his life. Daniel Tejada had told his son to be careful, to be wary of people who might cause him harm. He had even suggested that Miguel's seventeen-year-old girlfriend Alejandra could harm him if she ever became angry with him. "I know she wouldn't do that," Miguel said. "I really care for her and she really cares for me." Like Mario Encarnacion, Miguel had kept a distance between himself and any serious romantic attractions. He loved his girlfriend and even thought he might marry her if he became a major league star. But he had already decided he would not commit to anyone before that.

Miguel doted on Alejandra, treated her with an uncommon respect. Yet, in a manner that belied his youth, he kept her separate from the rest of his life. Miguel was a young Dominican man who was attractive to women and whose prospects were growing brighter every day. He compartmentalized a variety of relationships with a variety of women, keeping each separate from the others. When he was out and about, he was with one woman. When he was in Santo Domingo, he was with another.

But the girl from *Los Barrancones* was his *real* girlfriend, the one he intended to marry, the one he treated with respect, the one he tenderly held hands with, and the only one he planned a future with. Miguel behaved this way without openly talking about it and without flaunting it. Everything was controlled and beneath the surface with him. He busied himself with preparations, making sure things ran smoothly while he was gone. He thought of hiring a woman who could cook for his father. He wanted to put his younger siblings through school, to give them an education he didn't get. He wanted the other house to be finished so his family could live like human beings. He wanted to give them all the things that a father would normally give but that Daniel Tejada and thousands of poor Dominican men could never provide.

The sun had set on *Los Barrancones* and—because there were few street lights—much of the barrio was dark when Enrique Soto pulled up to take Miguel to La Victoria. It was growing late and Mario was already on his way. Quickly, Miguel kissed members of his family good-bye and off they went, Soto's shock absorbers tested to their limits by the potholes and unpaved streets of Miguel's barrio.

BACK AT LA VICTORIA, the complex was quieter than ever as the boys showered and prepared themselves for one last treat before embarking on a six-month journey of heated competition, of hopes being raised and dashed, of luck, loss, and lament. The boys were all quiet as they set out down the gravel road that leads into Campo Juan Marichal, the only noises generated by piercingly loud crickets, birds, and animals lurking in the underbrush outside the complex gates.

"We were all quiet that night, all lost in our own thoughts, because every time you go to the U.S. you think: Which one of us is going to make it? Which one of our friends will be released? Which one of us will be injured? Which one of us will have to give up his dream?" said Juan Dilone, who at twenty-two was the appointed leader of the Athletics Latin minor league prospects that year.[27] Dilone was probably the most educated of the Dominican prospects in the Athletics system and he came from the family with the most means.

Much more Americanized than any other Dominican player in the Athletics system, Dilone even had American slang down and would end many sentences with "Oh man, you have to be kidding me!" His appearance—six feet tall, neatly groomed hair, broad shoulders, a narrow waist, and a philosophical manner—gave him the look of a successful college senior. Dilone had his own reasons for feeling anxious this night. The year before, he had separated his shoulder on the first day of spring training while diving for a fly ball, causing him to miss the entire season. He was now desperate to prove himself in a year in which he would turn twenty-three—no longer a kid in a minor league system filled with kids. Walking with Dilone were Benito Baez, a crafty eighteen-year-old left-handed pitcher; Jose Castro, the former star shortstop now watching Miguel pass him by; Arturo "Tabacco" Paulino, whose 1995 batting average plummeted in his second season in the Rookie Arizona League; and Juan Perez, a gregarious twenty-three-year-old left-handed pitcher who was half Haitian, half Dominican, and had prepared for his career in baseball by cutting sugar cane near the coastal town of La Romana.

As they walked the mood turned lighthearted. The players made jokes to each other as they turned onto an exceedingly dark, two-lane rural highway. And it seems they laughed even louder as trucks and cars shot by, their headlights blinding, their steel frames only inches away. "The drivers here are crazy," shouted Perez with glee.

After a half mile, they reached the *colmado,* a roadside store. They took up stools in a patio section, walled off by metal bars and stacks of unsold Pepsi bottles. At first, the players sat stiffly, waiting while the proprietor searched for music he could play them on an ancient hi-fi. For the moment, all was still, as if the full weight of what was at stake hung over them, taking the very oxygen from their lungs.

Without warning, the music was cranked up to ear-splitting decibels—a wild mixture of reggae and Spanish rap. At first, the faces of the young men flickered sternly in the light shone by a sixty-watt bulb through a ceiling fan that, encased in cobwebs, looked as if it could be dislodged by its own movement. And then, behind them, a little barefoot girl wearing only dingy bikini briefs began moving to the music. She was joined by a boy. Another girl. Then an expectant mother who seemed barely out of her teens.

Soon the entire street was dancing, and bodies were throwing shadows on the walls of the *colmado.* They moved in perfect unison in a scene of sheer joy amid the tenements, the open trash fire, the dirt road, and the raw sewage. The young men smiled, their eyes glistening in the soft light. They bought a round of Presidente beer, they laughed, they shared a closeness that they knew would be in short supply starting the next day when everything would change, when everything would be about success, striving, and achieving. But for this night, they were happy because they could be themselves, Dominicans in their own country and the pride of their families. Just before 11:00 P.M., like the dutiful leader, Dilone got up and told everyone it was time to go back. As they neared the gates, Mario Encarnacion pulled up with his bag packed. He got out of his brother's car, and Victor Encarnacion smiled at his former Athletics teammates. Without a hint of jealousy he said: *"Buena suerte, señores."*

Good luck, gentlemen.

And then the older Encarnacion brothers were gone, driving back toward Bani. Before they got far, Soto drove past them going in the opposite direction. He dropped off Miguel and all the boys trudged toward the complex, knowing they had to get to sleep in order to rise by dawn, but too wired to retreat to their rooms just yet. Dilone remembered he was holding the keys to the cafeteria, and one of the others said, "Let's eat." Soon they were inside, cranking up a hot plate still containing heaping portions of Dominican-style chicken, white rice, and beans, called *habichuelas*. The players gorged themselves, taking seconds and thirds they wouldn't normally get on calibrated performance diets. Surrounded by the sounds of the night, the players piled their bones on their plates and washed everything down with papaya juice, teasing each other until they went to bed.

It was still dark when their driver, a man employed by the Athletics, loaded them onto the complex bus and off they went. As they passed the *colmado,* Dilone asked the driver to blare the horn—letting the owner know they were going to America. They sat mostly in silence as the bus bounced along the roads leading to Santo Domingo International Airport. The sun was just rising as they made their way into the American Airlines terminal and readied themselves for their flight. At the airport, they were somber and said little as they took their places in coach on a flight bound for Miami. Once there, most of them forgot to fill out their customs cards and were detained by an impatient agent who barked out instructions in rapid English.

"That's when it's the hardest," Tabacco said. "Like when a coach explains something and you don't understand what he is saying."[28] From Miami to Dallas, Dallas to Phoenix, the players began to droop, to grow increasingly silent. Their razor-sharp wits were abandoning them here. Suddenly they were introverted, shy, and tentative—newly arrived immigrants in America. Not carrying any money with him and fed nothing but snacks, Miguel was starving by the time the tiring group trudged through the enormous terminals at the Dallas–Fort Worth airport. Spying some of his teammates eating soft yogurt, Miguel shot an expression of total starvation. But when someone offered to buy Miguel his own yogurt, his face hardened and he declined. His immense pride was at work again. Roughly ten hours after leaving Santo Domingo—including airport delays and downtime between flights—the players finally arrived in

Phoenix late in the afternoon. They hauled their tattered luggage—misshapen suitcases and duffel bags—from baggage claim and trudged to the passenger loading zone to await their ride.

A spectacular Arizona sun was setting as the prospects craned their necks, watching for the Athletics van that would take them to their hotel. At first standing, arms crossed, in their cleanest jeans and cotton shirts, they waited and waited and waited. "Did they forget about us?" asked Tabacco. Soon, they put their bags at the curbside of the passenger loading zone and sat on them. Some of the players whipped out their address books, reentered the terminal and started calling girls they knew in town, hoping to snag a ride. No luck. One player called Fausto Cruz—a Dominican training at the Athletics major league complex—but he acted as if he couldn't be bothered, so he suggested they take a taxi. Spoken like a major leaguer with major league money.

Ninety minutes crawled by as the boys sat and waited.

Soon Javier Gutierrez, a twenty-year-old Venezuelan pitching prospect for the Seattle Mariners, walked toward the group and asked for help—his ride had also forgotten him.

Finally, the Athletics van arrived . . . two hours late. Taken to their hotel, the players ate their only meal at the local Coco's.

In a way, it was as if they were playing out some odd ritual for Latin players. In 1955—years before they were ever born—Orlando Cepeda had wandered lost in the streets of Kokomo, Indiana, where he was sent by the then–New York Giants to play minor league ball. Cepeda had traveled alone to Kokomo from Virginia, a black Latin man with no English skills in 1950s America. And when he had finally arrived late at night, there was no one to pick him up. As Cepeda was walking about town, completely lost, he was stopped by a policeman and all he could say in his fractured English was, "Kokomo Giants." Cepeda was escorted to the "black" side of town where he found a place to stay, connected with his team, and led the Midwest League in batting with an average of .390.

SHORTLY AFTER THEY ARRIVED in Arizona, the organization wanted to see a few of the Dominicans get a taste of competition against major leaguers. Miguel, Jose Castro, Freddie Soriano, and another player named David Francisco were shuttled a couple of miles away by distance, but a world away by level of competition, to Phoenix Municipal Stadium, where the big league team played.

Miguel had been in Phoenix for three days, and he began the game on the bench, sitting with the other Latin players in one corner of the Athletics dugout. The team had suffered through its third consecutive losing season in 1995 and had just gone through a change of ownership and a change in managers. Art Howe, formerly manager of the Houston Astros, was now at the helm, which was seen as a positive sign by the Latin end of the Athletics organization.

Privately, those who recruit and develop the Athletics' Latin players felt that former manager Tony La Russa, while one of the best in the business, was not keen on Latin players. Whether it was fair or not, that was the perception. And during La Russa's tenure—from 1986 to 1995—several Latin players had passed through Oakland, but none had ever really stuck. It was hoped that Art Howe—through his reputation as a level-headed teacher who liked young players—would develop more Latins for the Oakland roster. In reality, it didn't really matter to Miguel who was manager or where he was playing. He was excited just to be sitting in the dugout.

In this first game, Howe inserted Miguel in the fifth inning along with Soriano, Castro, and Francisco. Miguel handled a few balls routinely, nothing spectacular, and then he came to bat for the first time against major league competition. As he dug in, the public address system announced his arrival: "Now batting, shortstop, Jose Castro."

It took an inning before they realized that "Castro" was really Tejada. And by then, looking as if he was born to the game, Miguel had gone deep into the hole at short and thrown on the run to nail a baserunner—a difficult play that was applauded by the five thousand or so people in attendance.

Miguel had lifted a harmless fly to left in his first at-bat before getting a second turn, late in the game. As he stood in for his last at-bat, Miguel took a ball on his first pitch while the scoreboard flashed his name.

It was misspelled.

And then, on the next pitch, Miguel swung and lifted a

long, arching fly ball that soared high over the left fielder's head, over the wall and the Miller Genuine Light sign in left center field. There was a smattering of applause among the home fans, nothing too emotional for a lazy Arizona Sunday afternoon. And Miguel gave away nothing as he rounded the bases, smiling only slightly as he was congratulated by Freddie Soriano. After the game, while Athletics signed autographs, Miguel trotted past a group of kids shouting for him and entered the clubhouse. He got a thrill when Athletics superstar Mark McGwire congratulated him, yet he was smiling only tentatively a few moments later. There would be no celebration for him.

In the locker room, he quietly removed his uniform. Suddenly, he looked small, young. The other players went about their business. For a moment, he was a titan, but now, he was only a dreamer. He put away his clothes and, shoulders hunched, briskly walked to the showers.

Miguel had to hurry because the van would soon be taking the players back to their hotel. Soon after eating, Miguel returned to his hotel room—which he shared with two other players. He took off his clothes, wrapped himself in his bedsheets, and silently watched television until falling asleep. Juan Perez and a few others had already hooked up with their Arizona girlfriends and were seeing the Scottsdale sights. But Miguel rarely ventured out after dark. He was disappointed when word came through the grapevine that the Athletics would be sending him to the West Michigan Whitecaps in Grand Rapids. Miguel wanted to play in Modesto, in the tough California League.

What he didn't know was that the Athletics were beginning to reassess him. The flash he had shown in that first major league game continued, against both major league and minor league competition. Miguel's body had developed from its small, weak size into a powerhouse, as if he were a college running back. There was an explosion to his game, both at the plate and on the field. And it seemed every time he did something great, Sandy Alderson—then general manager—was watching. By the end of spring training it had been decided.

Miguel would continue his meteoric rise in Modesto. Jose Castro, once the star of the Dominican Summer League, would start another year in Grand Rapids. Castro, who was entering his third season of minor league ball, was bitterly disappointed at being passed on the evolutionary chart by Miguel. In the end, it was too much for him.

Instead of heading to Grand Rapids with Mario Encarnacion, Tabacco, Jose Soriano, Ramon Hernandez, Juan Moreno, Luis Silva, and Benito Baez, Castro fled to New York. The Athletics were then faced with two dilemmas: filling Castro's slot in Grand Rapids and somehow finding and retrieving a player with solid defensive ability but obvious attitude problems. While that was being sorted out, the Athletics decided to pull Eddie Lara off the scrap heap and send him to Grand Rapids, a development that sent Eddie into delirium.

He was still smiling when the West Michigan Whitecaps opened the season in near-freezing temperatures in Appleton, Wisconsin. Meanwhile, before he left for Modesto, Miguel implanted one more memory in the minds of Alderson, Plaza, and everyone else who was watching him in the final game of spring training—again against the Seattle Mariners. For the first time, Miguel faced the Mariners' hulking, ominous pitcher Randy Johnson—all six feet ten inches of him. And while he didn't get a hit off Johnson, Miguel made a phenomenal play that was picked up on highlight shows across the nation, including CNN, which named it its "Play of the Day."

A line drive was hit in Miguel's direction that looked to fly over his head until Miguel did a standing jump, achieved full extension of his body, and caught the ball in the webbing of his glove. He then nonchalantly flipped it to the second baseman. It all happened in an instant, the kind of reaction exhibited only by people born with a gift of rare athletic ability, the kind you can't teach and can develop only so far.

Enrique Soto liked to say that Miguel had the benefit of good coaching, but what grabs people's attention is a quality only God can provide. Miguel would say that God was with him when he went to Modesto, though he isn't a particularly religious person. Miguel believes but he is a realist. And when he arrived in Modesto, it was with more determination than ever. Once in town, Miguel took his place on a team quite unlike the Southern Oregon A's. This team had muscle, it had talent spread across many positions, and it had players who were going places. Ben Grieve was in the outfield for the 1996 version of the Modesto A's, a team steeped in tradition with the Oakland

Athletics. Mark McGwire played in Modesto, as did Jose Canseco and Rickey Henderson.

ALTHOUGH THE ATHLETICS have fallen on hard times, no franchise has won more World Championships in the last thirty years than the East Bay team of green and gold. Now, the organization was hoping that a nucleus for the future was growing in the middle of one of the richest agricultural valleys in America. While the image of California on the East Coast is of Hollywood, beaches, the Golden Gate Bridge, and earthquakes, this city of roughly 170,000 is closer to the real essence of California—a place fitting for a guy like Miguel, a place of soaring dreams and hard realities.

Modesto is a farming town, plain and simple. It is an integral part of a $17-billion-a year agricultural industry, California's biggest and most important. Modesto's symbol? An illuminated sign, in the shape of an arch across I Street, that proclaims: "Water, Wealth, Contentment, Health." Much of what is central to California history is here. The discovery of gold in 1849 brought hordes of crazed 49ers to the area, speeding the establishment of Stanislaus County in 1854.[29]

The first local irrigation canal was built in 1873, firmly establishing a region producing among the richest table fruits and vegetables on the planet. In 1915, Southern Pacific Railroad build a station on 9th Street, where it remains to this day. An hour and fifteen minutes south of Sacramento on Highway 99, Modesto is also in the middle of a region of enormous rural poverty, a region that—when measured north to Stockton and Sacramento—amounts to the second-highest concentration of medically uninsured people in America, the vast majority of whom are Mexican farm workers.

By the time Miguel arrived in Modesto in early April, the cold and Tule fog that blankets the region had given way to blossoming fruit and nut trees and seeding of summer fruits and vegetables. Freddie Soriano, Juan Dilone, and Juan Perez joined Miguel on a team that had other hot Athletics prospects, like D. T. Cromer, a twenty-five-year-old power hitter who was a former standout at the University of South Carolina, and David Newhan, who had played alongside Miguel in Medford and was poised for a big season.

The California League is one of the most competitive in all of minor league baseball, a ten-team circuit with clubs situated throughout established, second-tier communities such as Stockton, Visalia, Bakersfield, Rancho Cucamonga, Lancaster, San Bernardino, Lake Elsinore, and San Jose. The Oakland Athletics, San Francisco Giants, Milwaukee Brewers, California Angels, Seattle Mariners, Los Angeles Dodgers, and San Diego Padres are among the teams with a stake in the development of players from the San Joaquin Valley to Silicon Valley and the Inland Empire.

Miguel would be facing high heat from pitchers with exploding curveballs and wicked stuff—the likes of which he had never seen. He would be on a team with a strict, no-nonsense manager named Jim Colburn, who ran a tight ship and had a naturally suspicious nature, a serious man who would soon grow tired of participating in corny promotions like "Jim Colburn's Wacky Wednesdays." In fact, the entire 1996 season would be an intense, emotional ride played out against the homespun hokeyness of minor league ball in California.

On the Modesto team alone, clubhouse struggles would play out in full view of fans during one game in Bakersfield when Colburn got into a shouting match with Miguel Jimenez, a prospective pitcher and an American of Dominican ancestry. A short time after the screaming subsided, Bakersfield fans were dancing in unison between innings while chanting, "Heyyyy Macarena!!" Almost as soon as the season started, Freddie Soriano—the happiest, most lighthearted Dominican in the Athletics organization—shattered his ankle in two places while sliding into second base in a game at Lake Elsinore. The injury cast a pall across the team and ruined a budding, exciting double-play combination of Miguel at short and Soriano at second. As great a dancer as he was a ballplayer, Freddie's beaming, easy smile had lightened Miguel's serious mood. Their healthy relationship had helped them on the field, too. While Freddie took the league lead in stolen bases, Miguel was racking up RBI by bringing Freddie home on the slightest hit. So fast was Freddie that outfielders had to play singles with aggression, because with one careless lapse or bobble, Freddie would take an extra base or even sprint from first to home before the indecisive fielder knew what hit him.

At twenty-one when he went down with his injury, Freddie was another of Enrique Soto's discoveries from Bani, as was his half-brother Jose, who was playing in Grand Rapids. Freddie was the younger of the two Soriano boys, who were born four months apart in 1974 of the same father but different mothers. After he went down, Freddie had a hard time getting around and Miguel cared for him. Freddie's injury frightened Miguel to his soul, snapped him into realizing how fragile all their lives were in the United States.

"I play aggressively, really aggressively, and the same thing could easily happen to me. Then where would I be?" Miguel said in May of '96. Indeed, the injury was frightening to the other Dominican players because it was a serious foot injury that struck at the essence of a five-foot-nine-inch speedster who relied on his "wheels" to play and, therefore, to eat.

What if Miguel blew out his knee? What if he was struck in the temple by a pitch, clouding his vision? What if he shattered one of his hands and it hampered his swing or his ability to turn a double play? "You know what would happen to the Dominican if something like that happened?" Soto would say at such a question. "*Miseria.*"

Misery.

Miguel didn't have Ben Grieve's assurance that if he got injured at this stage in his career there would be a million-three to fall back on. So after some sleepless nights, Miguel steeled himself to do all that he could do: to play on at full throttle. And then something strange happened again, something that crystallized the capricious nature of baseball. When Freddie went down, the Athletics as an organization were faced with the same dilemma they confronted when Jose Castro bolted on the eve of the 1996 season. Now, the question was: Who would replace Freddie Soriano?

None other than Jose Castro.

Contacting Castro with the help of some of his Dominican friends, the Athletics enticed Castro to come back, and the twenty-one-year-old eagerly agreed now that he was able to go to Modesto. Plaza would say this angered some within the Athletics organization, who felt a "quitter" had been rewarded by getting what he wanted. But in reality, the team was stuck. They felt they couldn't stand pat with what they had in Modesto. It was still too early in the year for a high draft pick to bail them out, and even then, most draft picks don't start as high in the organization as Modesto.

They couldn't look to Medford, whose players were too low on the totem pole. And the crop in Grand Rapids—Arturo Paulino and Eddie Lara, among others—was thin.

The Athletics knew Castro was good enough to play second base for them—and soon he was. By this point Castro had trimmed the Afro he had sported back in '93 and adopted a close-cropped haircut, but he was still in possession of his cocky ways. The team Castro stepped into was launching moon shots in the dry California air, rattling rickety fences from Stockton to Rancho Cucamonga. Grieve was Grieve, as natural and fluid as any young kid could ever be. The six-four two-hundred-pounder with blond hair, a narrow face, and a slightly skinny frame could make wreaking havoc on the baseball field seem pacifist and nonviolent. He would swing that beautiful, picture-perfect swing from the left-hand side and the ball would sail higher and higher and be out of the ballpark before you realized how hard he had just hit it. He never seemed to struggle at what he did and reminded people of a young Will Clark before injuries and poor conditioning habits dulled Clark's game.

But Grieve wasn't brash, profane, and intolerant, as Clark was. In fact, if he was like anyone on the Modesto Athletics, he was like Miguel. Both were all business. Both were reserved and respectful. Neither was a partier. Neither seemed to feel the need to be the center of attention. In fact, the two seemed to strike up a genuine friendship. They would scream "Mother-Foy-Yay," at each other in a gentle lampoon of Miguel's English spliced with an obvious profanity. They would share the microphone at a team party, butchering the words to "La Bamba." They didn't hang out much together, but Miguel would say later that Grieve was the player he wanted to be like. "He never drinks, I never see him catting around with women when we're on the road, he works hard, he does a great job. That's why I want to be around him, he's a good example."

In a bad TV movie, Miguel and Grieve would be rivals, with Grieve portrayed as the spoiled white kid earning $1 million while Miguel would play the poor, black Dominican victim getting two thousand dollars. But Miguel had no hard feelings toward Grieve. Grieve didn't create the world of professional baseball they were both excelling in. The organizations that make up major league baseball and all the executives who rationalize a case like Miguel's are the ones who make this situation possible. Sandy Alderson is typical of baseball's defense of its bargain-basement practices in Latin America: "Let's say you have two hundred thousand dollars in signing bonus money for the year. Is society [in the Dominican] better off having you sign one or two kids for two hundred thousand dollars or a lot of kids for two hundred thousand dollars?"[30]

That rationale makes it seem that baseball teams are crusaders, providing a service to down-trodden, exploited Dominicans. The truth is that good things do come out of the opportunities availed to kids like Miguel, but those good things are generated through the heart and hustle of young Latins who put aside their fear and limitations. And, when they succeed, they generate far more than the investments baseball made on them.

Alderson's argument completely overlooks the kind of lives kids like Miguel live when they are toiling in the minor leagues. For Miguel, the 1996 season meant living in isolation, in a tiny farmhouse six miles south of Modesto in the agricultural community of Ceres. Dan Marchy, an avid Modesto A's fan, opened his home to Miguel and a revolving door of Dominicans, shared his food with them, cleaned his kitchen after they smoked the walls while cooking Dominican food, and cleaned up the messes they constantly left. While Marchy developed a deep friendship for Miguel and Freddie Soriano, during the day he had to work for a living.[31] So Miguel, Freddie, and then later Jose Castro, Juan Perez, and a big, husky catcher named Wilfredo Ventura, would be stranded in Marchy's farmhouse, which is surrounded by a ninety-acre alfalfa field. The house is south of the Tuolumne River, across the street from the local water treatment plant, and gets about as quiet as Campo Juan Marichal in the evenings, save for the rumbling eighteen-wheelers hauling loads of tomatoes and other produce to market. The town of Ceres was named in 1867 after the Greek goddess of agriculture, but it might as well have been Mars to Miguel and the other Dominicans.[32]

While American players on the Modesto A's availed themselves of any and all that existed in Modesto—and some even drove their own cars on off-day trips to San Francisco or Lake Tahoe—Miguel spent his days lying on a mattress thrown onto the floor of Marchy's family room, watching Spanish-language television, cooking rice and beans. Marchy's home is white and faded lime, more like a bungalow, with a tiny family room where the most important items are the television set, six autographed Modesto A's caps, and a framed, autographed jersey of former Sacramento King Mitch Richmond. There are two bedrooms, one bathroom, and a pantry that has been converted into a laundry room.

On most off days, Miguel, Perez, Castro, and Ventura took Marchy's kitchen chairs and hauled them out to the expansive front lawn. Just as they would back home, they placed a boom box on the grass, turned it full volume and sipped Bud Light, often drifting into their individual thoughts. Most of them were sending money home and, therefore, didn't have that much to spare. Even if they did, none had licenses to drive in the United States. And other players had no interest in coming to see them. Dilone said he went to Ceres once, took a look around, and promptly returned to Modesto. So the music played on and on in Ceres, while Miguel, Perez, and the others became a strange sight to passing truckers.

Miguel's favorite song was by a popular Dominican merengue artist named Alex Bueno. It is called "Los Caminos de la Vida." In the song, Bueno sings of a young man who begins a journey of discovery, finding nothing in his life as he imagined it. The song could be about Miguel, but he says it reminds him of his father. And though it bugged his friends somewhat, Miguel played it over and over again—never tiring of it. Then, the next day, he would go out and pulverize everything that stood in his path.

The 1996 season was a revelation for Miguel and the Athletics. They knew he was good, but in this season, he proved he could be great. "Maybe it was his steal of home in the first inning of the first game," wrote the *Modesto Bee* on May 21. "Perhaps it was the 10 home runs in the first 43 games, the way he turned singles into outs with his glove, the wide-eyed daring on the base paths, or the beat-me-if-you-can demeanor he takes to the field every night. At some point, the Modesto A's discovered the rare jewel that is their shortstop *Miguel Tejada*."[33]

One game in May stands out. Miguel and Castro were now the middle infield duo for the Modesto A's, and in one play, they showed what they could do: At the crack of the bat, Miguel raced toward second base to make a double play on a ball hit at a diving Castro. Stretching his five-foot-ten-inch frame as far as it would go, Castro stopped the ball from going past him into the outfield, but it started to roll away. Crawling on his knees Castro grabbed the ball and flung it like a Frisbee toward Miguel, who was now standing flat-footed on second base. Under normal circumstances, Miguel would have been gliding over second base, making the throw to first with the aid of his forward movement.

But as the ball rolled away from Castro, Miguel had to come to a dead stop as the runner from first barreled toward him. Now, with Castro's funky back-handed throw coming at him at knee level, Miguel had to make an instant decision: Do I catch the ball and get out of the way? Or do I try the double play and get clobbered? He did neither: He caught the ball inches from the ground with his bare hand and simultaneously shifted his body out of the way of the runner while whipping a bullet toward first for the double play. He seemed to do it all in one motion.

The players on the Modesto bench leaped in unison to their feet. Jim Colburn, not a man of whimsy, got a big, goofy grin on his face and shook his head while Miguel was mobbed by his teammates.

How well were things going for the kid from Bani?

Sandy Alderson was sitting in the stands, behind home plate, in what happened to be his first visit of the year to Modesto. "That may have been the best double play I've ever seen in my life," he said to someone sitting next to him. After the game, when told of Alderson's comments, Miguel and Castro broke into big grins and high-fived each other. Soon, they were back at Marchy's, sipping beer, watching television, and turning in for the night.

In the middle of the season, Miguel was selected to the California League All-Star team. He was well on his way at this point. But some of his Dominican friends—the ones who started out with him—weren't faring so well. Tabacco was having a horrible year in Grand Rapids, benched soon after the first week of the season, playing sporadically after that, and growing as gray as the Midwest skies that seemed to envelop his soul. Tabacco lived in the basement bedroom of a Grand Rapids family along with Mario Encarnacion.

Mario would try and cheer Tabacco up, calling him *"amigito"* or little friend and playing pool with him in their American home. Tabacco would bat only .221, with a paltry 2 home runs and 19 RBI. After the season, he would visit his uncle Carlos Made in New York, certain he was going to be released. Made would encourage him to keep playing, to not follow the tragic, well-worn path of Dominican players to New York.

Encarnacion also struggled mightily in Grand Rapids, inhibited by its early season cold and confounded by pitchers who—upon discovering his ease with high fastballs—began throwing him nothing but breaking stuff. Faced with pure junk, Mario began swinging wildly like a weekend hacker, looking downright foolish at times as the fluttering pitches and his jerking swings served to diffuse all the power he had inside him. In one game against the Lansing Lugnuts, Mario struck out three times in a row, growing more enraged with each failure.

After the last strikeout, he slammed his bat against a concrete support in the dugout and started up the tunnel toward West Michigan's dugout. But he decided to stop and pick a fight with the clubhouse door first, kicking the door jamb with his right foot so that it inadvertently closed, sealing him off in the clubhouse tunnel. No one dared open the door because from inside, a deep, primal scream exploded from Mario's insides, a shriek that sounded as if he were being mauled by a wild animal—a sound mixed in with his brutal pounding of the concrete walls connecting the dugout to a corridor leading up a stairwell to the showers.

When Mario came out, no one said a word to him. Mario had a horrible first half of the season and had to rally to finish with a batting average of .229 with 7 home runs and 43 RBI. In the clubhouse, he would seethe when American players turned off his merengue and replaced it with Alanis Morissette. The Dominican players kept to themselves in Grand Rapids as they did in Modesto. While Juan Dilone would go out with American players on road trips in California, the Dominicans of Grand Rapids rarely socialized with them, save for a few team functions.

Often Mario, Jose Soriano, Lara, Tabacco, Hernandez, and Benito Baez would sit in a row, leaning on each other, clearly separated from their American teammates on the Whitecaps bench. Once, as he sat with his hand bandaged after a game, Mario had struck up a conversation with Tabacco when he was interrupted by an American player who said: "Why don't you quit speaking that African shit." Mario glared at the player and then began speaking even louder. But not all of the Latins in Grand Rapids fared poorly.

Ramon Hernandez led the team with 12 home runs and 68 RBI. He would make the Midwest League All-Star team and was voted one of the top prospects in the league. Playing at Old Kent Park was not an ideal situation for hitters, with its spacious outfield and slow infield. A testament to this: Hernandez batted .283 on the road and .228 at home. But Eddie Lara still had the worst season of all. Thrilled to start in Grand Rapids, Lara even began the year as an early season hero, scoring the decisive run in a game between West Michigan and the Kane County Cougars, a Florida Marlins affiliate. After the game, Lara was beside himself with glee, gloating in a way that made you want to swat him across the head. But then, when he cut out the newspaper clipping and put it with his rumpled things, it became clear that Eddie was desperate to find a kind of acceptance, a sense of belonging to something that had been so lacking in his broken home in Bani. He had essentially been raised by his grandmother amid turmoil between his mother and father and now, as a pint-sized player, he was burdened by the health problems of both his mother and his grandmother.

He was sending money home to them and was already collecting battered baseball caps and other equipment he could take to his *compañeros* back home. In the very next series after his Kane County triumph, Lara's season began to unravel. Against Lansing, a Kansas City Royals affiliate, a Saturday night game went right down to the wire, tied in the bottom of the ninth. Lara—who had done nothing at the plate—booted a grounder hit his way, allowing the winning run to score. Lansing fans—who were just christening the sharp-looking Oldsmobile Park—screamed lustily as Eddie trudged toward the dugout. Tabacco tried to help, telling him he might as well forget about it as the entire team, except Eddie, headed for the showers.

Sitting alone in the dugout, with Bob Seger blaring over the PA system, Eddie put his head in his hands while swarming groups of fans participated in a postgame promotional event, a cash drop in which play money was dumped on the windy field and fans scurried after it in the hopes of collecting a prize. As Eddie gathered his things in the dugout, a young Lansing boy leaned over the railing and asked Eddie for a ball. Eddie gave the kid a thrill by handing him a bat instead. That act of kindness was just like him: He could be conceited and boorish and then turn around and do something like that. One day, he could play with intensity and win a game. The next, his mind would be elsewhere, costing the team a game. As the team prepared to leave that night, Eddie slipped on his Walkman and pulled the curtain of his window on the team bus. He would finish the '96 season batting .216 with no home runs and 16 RBI. West Michigan manager Mike Quade did guide the Whitecaps to a Midwest League championship that year, but by 1997, for a variety of reasons, the Athletics moved their operation from Grand Rapids to Visalia, California.

FOR HIS PART, Miguel was steaming toward a 30-home-run season with the Modesto A's—a kind of offensive showing few shortstops can produce. Then on a hot Friday night in Stockton on July 19, Miguel suffered his first injury. While making a double play, he collided with a runner, jamming his thumb on his glove hand. He had been playing so well up to that point the Athletics hated to pull him out of action. But X-rays proved they had no choice. Miguel had two small breaks at the tip of his left thumb and some damage to the joint. The prognosis: out four to six weeks, effectively ending his season. The organization was crestfallen. "They called me that night and then the nightmare began," said Keith Lieppman.[34] "I feel so bad for the kid."

Miguel tried to put on a brave face, but not being able to play deeply disturbed him. And while the team figured out what to do next, all Miguel could do was lie around Marchy's house with an oversized bandage on his left hand and the television remote control in his right. There was some talk he would go to Arizona for rehabilitation but he stayed put. Days blended into one another and Miguel felt more restless than ever. The A's were making a run at the playoffs, chasing their archrival San Jose Giants, and Miguel felt sick not being able to contribute.

He also felt that fear all Dominicans share—the fear of its being over before it starts, before the money comes, before he can be somebody. But after two weeks, his cast came off and he began working again. "I'm ready," he would say. It didn't take much convincing to get the Athletics to agree. And on August 10, just three weeks following his injury, Miguel returned faster than anyone imagined. But his timing was off, he wasn't launching homers the way he had, and one persistent problem remained: He was making errors, lots of errors. His problems came from both ends of the defensive spectrum—he would blow easy plays or try to make the impossible ones that led to the increasingly familiar E by his number. At a game played in mid-August at Bakersfield's Sam Lynn Ballpark, the best and worst of Miguel's game were on display. Playing against the Bakersfield Blaze, as the summer sun turned the sky lavender with streaks of rust and orange, Miguel hit a high chopper and gutted out the throw to first, getting on through a burst of speed and desire. But as he took the field again, he made the first of 3 errors by throwing high over the first baseman's head on a routine grounder. In the bottom of the second, Miguel snuck behind a Blaze baserunner and took a low throw while blocking second base—a great play that killed a Bakersfield rally. In the bottom of the seventh, he took a pivot from Castro while making what seemed to be a sure double play, but inexplicably dropped the ball. No error, but no double play. In the top of the eighth, he fought off pitch after pitch before finally doing what coaches love: hitting the ball to the opposite field for a single. "Damn, that kid uses the whole field," marveled Jeffrey Leonard, former San Francisco Giants All-Star, now an Athletics coach.

But then in the bottom of the eighth, Miguel booted a routine grounder. Error number two. In the top of the ninth, he crushed a fastball, sending it shooting off the Longs Drugs sign on the left-field wall, a blast so hard the Blaze were able to hold the speedy Miguel to a single. But back at short, he bobbled another easy grounder for another error. In all, he went 3–6 with 3 errors. After the game, Miguel calmly walked to a nearby Pizza Hut from his room at the thirty-dollar-a-night Regency Inn. Then, he, Castro, and Ventura watched ESPN for its baseball highlights and any movie they could find with women in bikinis.

The next morning, it was cartoons. By the end of August and nearing the end of the season, Miguel had a league high 44 errors. In one game against Visalia, Colburn moved him to third base in an effort to spare his psyche and stop the bleeding. The organization was concerned but not panicked. Young players make errors, particularly on minor league fields that are ragged and choppy. Stemming the tide of Miguel's errors was equated with polishing a fine stone. Miguel's rawness was still too much a part of his game, and it would be a major challenge for the coming year—there was no question Miguel was moving up in the organization.

The Athletics made the playoffs but were taken out quickly by the San Jose Giants. Castro, Perez, Ventura, and others were all sent home the next day. Miguel had to stay, however. For the second year, the team wanted him to play in their Arizona fall league. So for two weeks, Miguel sat around Marchy's house alone, stranded, with nothing to do but listen to his song all day and cook for himself. He didn't do much else while he was in central California. But while he was still there, it was announced that Miguel had been named the number-one prospect of the California League and its most exciting player. He was also named the best shortstop in the minors by *USA Today* and was selected to the All-Prospects team by Howe Sportsdata.

In addition, *The Sporting News* picked him as one of five "can't miss" prospects, writing: "He is the total package who can hit for power, average and steal bases. He should begin the next season at Class AA Huntsville, but don't be surprised if he is in Oakland before the end of the season."

Miguel returned home to a hero's welcome that year, mobbed by friends and family. It was really happening. He was really becoming a star. He had gotten attention the year before but this time, things were different—people at home looked at him differently. He was no longer just *Miguel*. And things became even more intense when he went off to the Dominican city of Santiago to play winter league ball. His team, the Aguilas, won the Dominican league championship and earned the right to represent the Dominican Republic in the Caribbean World Series.

Played in February 1997, the series was held in Hermosillo, Mexico, and Miguel was a starter on his country's squad—playing third base while Tony Batista, his Athletics teammate and Dominican League MVP, played short. The final game came down to a contest between the Dominicans and host-nation Mexico, a game in which Miguel scored the winning run. Returning home triumphantly, Miguel was now known throughout his country, and he was poised to make a run for the shortstop's job in Oakland. Mike Bordick, after playing solidly again in 1996, had bolted for the Baltimore Orioles and a hefty contract. Batista was next in line, but there was talk that Miguel was really well liked by the organization. He would have about a week in *Los Barrancones* before he joined that battle. He hoped to relax but that hope proved futile. Friends, neighbors, anyone who had known him at any time were coming to Miguel and, inevitably, asking him for things. That week he spent money he never had before with friends he never knew he had. On the Sunday before he was to leave, his father had arranged a special memorial for his mother—delaying it two months so Miguel could attend. As that day came and the preparations reached a fevered pitch, the full force of what his life had become hit Miguel. All he had to do was look at his siblings and see the pendants they wore with his likeness to know where he stood.

That morning, Miguel readied himself for the certain onslaught from people who meant well. He heard the music and the drums playing a short distance away, a signal that the memorial was in full swing. They were waiting for him. Fastening silver jewelry around his now-powerful neck, Miguel opened the curtain to face his people.

Despite the pressures, Miguel knew he was lucky—he was on the verge of his dream. He knew many others had been dumped by baseball. Unlike him, those young Latin men had no one calling out their names, nothing to do and no place to go.

Except America. New York City.

8

BASEBALL'S
LATIN BARRIO

THEY ARE DISCARDS and runaways, lost souls and drug dealers, petty thieves, day laborers, illegal immigrants, and, to a man, old before their time. They represent the underside of professional baseball—living, breathing relics whose only dream in life has either been stripped away, lost to intense competition, or squandered by youthful inexperience. Washed up, over the hill at twenty-one.

They can be found on countless street corners and alleyways of some of the most dangerous barrios in New York City—from 130th Street in Spanish Harlem, up eighty blocks through Washington Heights and the highest homicide rate in the city, to the tenements surrounding Yankee Stadium, across town in Brooklyn, and miles beyond. They are baseball's rejects, those tossed aside in the search for that one star, those unlucky enough or unskilled enough to face the nightmare haunting all Latin players: The nightmare of failure. They are the rule, while the players who make it to big leagues, the stars, the sudden millionaires, are the exceptions.

According to major league baseball, between 90 and 95 percent of all foreign-born players signed to professional contracts will not reach the holy grail of big league stardom but will be cut, released when their batting averages dip too low, when they fail to show adequate progress, when they get into trouble, if they have bad attitudes, if they have substance abuse problems, or if coaches take a liking to other players.[1] There are, after all, only twenty-six spots on each baseball team and hundreds of Americans and Latins vying for those spots. Only so many can play, only a very few will be stars. And so the battle of attrition is waged under the intense heat of Florida practice fields, in the bitter cold of a Western Michigan spring, in the stifling humidity of Huntsville, Alabama, in the purple smog of a Bakersfield sunset and on "San Diego Chicken Night" in Stockton, California. When the end comes, it will most likely occur at the Class A level—when teams have to make decisions with profound consequences for Spanish-speaking kids. In Class A, the emphasis is on instruction and evaluation, a time when teams are attempting to refine the raw gems, evaluate the budding stars, instruct the borderline starters, and separate the promising from the unfortunates simply filling out uniforms. To be promoted to Double A is to be sent where the "studs" go, the players with promise, the ones who have shown something while riding buses through the heartland of America and living in the homes of avid fans. There are no guarantees once Double A is reached, but it is a major victory of progress.

For the losers with Spanish surnames, defeat means they will be punched a one-way ticket home, their visas—the ones ensuring a legal stay in the United States—will be voided immediately, and they will have to face the prospect of returning home a failure. But make no mistake. A loss of pride is not what devastates the souls of baseball's Latin rejects. What truly hurts is a loss of hope, not being able to provide for their families, to feed their younger siblings, care for their elders, or buy something nice for their wives or girlfriends.

To the hundreds of Dominican players who suffer this fate every year, the word is always shattering but often expected. Players get an inkling the hammer is coming down after too many innings spent on the bench, too many weak grounders to third, too many throws pulling the first baseman off the bag and too many times seeing your best pitches sailing over the fence in left center.

Sometimes the bad news comes at the end of the season, at

home in the Dominican. Sometimes it comes during the season, somewhere in the United States.

When that happens, the scenario varies but often plays out this way: A player will collect his things, be given a plane ticket home, and be driven to the airport to prepare for a long, heartbreaking plane ride. But often, the rejected will have prepared for this moment with an alternative plan. Some will call a recently acquired American girlfriend, or a Dominican buddy, and a desperate scheme will take shape. The player will head for Santo Domingo, but when that plane stops in Miami or wherever else there is a connecting flight, he will slip out of an airport terminal and, more often than not, head for New York City—where the U.S. Census estimates there is a community of a half million Dominicans spread out across the city's five boroughs. That former player will then become an undocumented immigrant in the United States.

He will slip from plain sight, absorbed into a shadowy world of uncertainty and low-paying jobs, of fake documents and constant fear, of mind-numbing poverty and living for each paycheck. Nobody ever heard of the Dominican ballplayers living illegally in New York today and no one ever will unless they run afoul of the law. Short of that, they become invisible people, like ghosts earning the minimum wage. Government statisticians simply don't know how many illegal Dominican immigrants there are in New York City, just as no one knows for certain how many undocumented immigrants there are in all of America.

And no one knows for certain how many "illegals" major league baseball is generating every year. But they are out there and baseball knows it.

"There is no way we can prevent it," said Ron Plaza of the Athletics. "There is no way we can take a kid from someplace, send them directly to the Dominican Republic without him jumping off the plane into the ocean." [2]

Miguel Rodriguez, a consultant and sometimes spokesman for major league baseball, said all teams do their utmost to make sure released players are escorted to airports and given tickets for the Dominican capital of Santo Domingo. [3] But he also said that teams are limited in what they can do beyond putting players on airplanes.

In reality, baseball has never had to address this issue publicly up until now because it has stayed under wraps. "Illegal" immigration in the United States is one of the great muddles of modern times, inflammatory yet largely hidden from view of mainstream America. Those living the life of "illegals" will walk among everyday people from the bustling streets of Broadway to the farming communities of central California—unless they are busted in huge immigration stings in Los Angeles, are dredged from the filthy cargo holds of Chinese ships, or are hauled out of New York sweatshops and sent back to Santo Domingo.

Until that veil of secrecy is lifted, former Dominican ballplayers will look as if they were produced by the streets of New York, down to their streetwise attitudes and their Nike sweat pants. The newest arrivals will cling to the game for a time, playing ball in semipro leagues filled with major league castoffs, men once the property of major league baseball but now toiling for teams sponsored by travel agencies, meat markets, and grocery stores. They will play in Central Park, in Washington Heights, in Brooklyn and the Bronx, directly across the street from Yankee Stadium. But after a time, they will quit, their once-hard bodies having grown softer, the reflexes they hoped would lead to millions betraying them on lazy Saturday afternoons. Once that happens, it's time to face whatever their lives will bring. But silently, they will keep coming—more and more each year.

"I could go walking down the street and I could grab a person from each corner who has played minor league or major league baseball," said Clemente Sosa, a New York City police officer who resides in Washington Heights, the former neighborhood of Henry Kissinger and now the heart of New York's Dominican community.

"Most of them have talent; it's just that they come here and they mess up—with drugs or with anything. Most of them aren't bad guys, they just have to survive."[4]

Most are like Jose Santana.

Released by the Houston Astros in 1995, Santana found himself mopping floors in a Brooklyn bodega, all the while frantically placing calls to an American agent who once filled his head with dollar signs but couldn't be bothered once the Astros had dumped him. At five-ten and 160 pounds, Santana still looked like a professional after he had been released, particularly when he donned a borrowed uniform and played with scores of Dominican men like him in a Brooklyn semipro league considered one of the best in the city. Born and raised in the famed community of San Pedro de Macoris, the Dominican town that has produced dozens of major leaguers, such as superstar Sammy Sosa, Santana played in the minor leagues for four seasons, never making it out of Class A ball.

Arriving in the United States in 1991, Santana bounced around from Kissimmee, Florida, to Asheville, North Carolina, Osceola, Florida, and Davenport, Iowa. "I thought I had everything," said Santana, who has two cousins who were released by the San Francisco Giants and also fled to New York. "I went from being a prospect to being released." In reality, Santana's story is not that black and white. He had talent, there is no question about that. But in the white-hot arena of minor league baseball, he faced huge obstacles from his first day. "The same year the Astros signed me [for two thousand dollars] they signed a draft pick and paid him a lot of money and I had to play behind him. So I couldn't play every day. I only had something like 66 at-bats. They signed him for something like three hundred thousand dollars. But we became friends and sometimes he would pretend like he was hurt so I could have the opportunity to play. I treated him well and he treated me well. The only thing he had that I didn't have was the money." Santana also didn't have the language when he arrived in the United States, and he struggled with his confidence while trying to stand out on the field.[5]

He came back in 1992 but his chances began to diminish when he turned his right knee in spring training, restricting his movement on the field. He would bat a miserable .198. The next year, he was sent to play in North Carolina and managed to lift his average forty points in a higher-caliber league, but it was still only .238. He wouldn't bat that high again. He would have knee surgery in 1995 and finish out his aborted career in Iowa before being cut loose for good at the end of the season.

"The scout who signed me was the one who gave me the news. He told me that they were going to release me because I hadn't done a good job defensively. I didn't say anything. I stayed quiet. I had a few weeks left on my visa and so I came to

New York to try and get a contract. I wasn't going to stay stuck over there in Santo Domingo without any options because there is just no life back there. So I came back here because I want to develop. I know I have the ability to play baseball."[6]

But in the process of looking for that elusive chance, Santana discovered the harsh secret of life as an undocumented immigrant in the 1990s. By staying in the United States, he essentially traded one form of misery for another.

This is because while it is true that he had no options waiting for him back home, there were very few to be found in New York. And what he stepped into was a world for which he had little preparation. The word among Dominican ballplayers is that if you don't reach the major leagues, New York is like a "second" major leagues, a city where money can be earned and mailed home via certified checks. But what Santana found instead was that of the half million Dominicans living in New York City, nearly 20 percent are unemployed. Twenty-nine percent of Dominican households are on welfare, twice the city's overall rate. And nearly 50 percent of Dominican households live in poverty, which is also double the city's rate.[7]

Dominicans are considered the fastest growing immigrant group in New York by the U.S. Census Bureau. In comparison to others, the Dominican community is still relatively new to the United States, and, like all new immigrants, they are still at the bottom trying to claw their way up. The 1990s version of the bottom for Santana was mopping floors, stocking grocery counters, and sweeping stockrooms in a Brooklyn corner store. Each day, while being tortured by thoughts of time slipping him by while other, younger stars were practicing hard somewhere, Santana would whittle away the hours lifting crates of Midnight Dragon, a potent malt liquor that is a hot item among the drinking crowd in Brooklyn's Dominican neighborhoods. He would have loved to have worked out every day but he had to survive now by mopping up the floor or sweeping the front stoop. Not a drinker or a smoker, Santana was shocked at first when he saw people congregating on the corner near the store, cracking open a can of Midnight Dragon and downing a few before noon amid street strewn with trash and broken bottles. Standing in the doorway, on a street littered with empty beer cans and stripped and stolen cars, his mind and spirit would drift away to conflicting thoughts of success, failure, and memories that scraped his heart. He would see himself as a star somewhere in major league baseball, he would see the faces of his two cousins—Andres and Angel Santana, both of whom were released by the San Francisco Giants despite showing potential—and he would see the image of his mother, *Luz Divina*, Divine Light.

"I think of my mother most of all," Santana said. "She is in her seventies now and she is all alone. I've always tried to be good to her, to be close to her. Maybe someday God will bless me for that.[8]

Before moving to Washington Heights in 1997, Santana lived in a cramped room over the store where he worked, his only diversion being the calls he placed to his mother on Sundays and his dream of the game, the one he clung to by playing on weekends before handfuls of people at a Brooklyn park. Spanish-speaking people go to Brooklyn and spend every sunlit weekend from spring to Indian summer watching a fusion of American and Latin baseball, a melding of two worlds where Old Glory is flanked by the flags of Puerto Rico and the Dominican Republic. Where kids ride their bikes to the park on the grounds of a public school and lean on the chain-link fence, watching men like Santana take their at-bats. On hard bleachers painted green, women and older men watch under tarps to shade spectators from the sun, while younger men stand around the backstop and participate in rapid-fire trash talking done entirely in Spanish.

The identities of almost all the players are tied to their former lives as major league prospects. "You see that guy over there," one man says. "He could have been a major leaguer but he was done in by his vices." The man is pointing at Elvin Paulino, a stocky Dominican who once hit 24 home runs in Double A and was even invited to major league spring training by the Colorado Rockies before being undone by his drinking. Standing off to one side of Paulino is Tony McDonald, who is older than the others and was a former minor league star who had the misfortune of playing third base in the Philadelphia Phillies organization at the same time Hall of Famer Mike Schmidt was in his prime. Today, McDonald works in a warehouse.

Playing on another team is Jorge Moreno, a Detroit Tigers castoff. Next to him is Luis Santos, dumped by the Los Angeles

Dodgers. The list goes on and on. As teams congregate before games, the men readying themselves for battle look like what they are—weekend warriors. Many have slight paunches, their uniforms tighter than they would like to admit. There is a PA announcer and a color commentator, both of whom speak the language of baseball in Spanish at high decibels, but no one seems to mind. At the same time, an alternating mixture of salsa and merengue plays at all times, while vendors cook fried pork, plantains, rice, and beans. The stands are always full, and because of the circumstances that brought the players there, the games are always tinged with sadness. But when the first pitch is thrown, the heat of competition takes hold and baseball, *estilo Latino,* goes on display. Games become beautiful, error-filled, spirited. Bonehead plays will be followed by brilliant ones. Here, a batter can laugh when he's swung hard and missed at a crafty breaking ball. Acknowledging the pitcher, spectators will whistle and laugh also, appreciative of solid play.

Still sporting a rock-solid twenty-eight-inch waist and a tight, defined upper body, Santana still had moments of inspiration when he would move effortlessly toward the deepest part of the infield, backhand a ground ball and fire it to first for an out. It was during these plays that his dream seemed to have some justification behind it. But when he ran on extra-base hits, he seemed to have a hitch in his stride, not enough to deter him in Brooklyn, but enough to make him slower than the powerful jackrabbits who have become the standard in the big leagues. In this way, Santana represents the saddest aspect of baseball— the Latin player whose mind and heart are willing, but whose body isn't up to the task.

He is quick, but not fast. His arm is strong, but not a cannon. He hits well, but is not a constant threat. Put it all together with a twitchy knee and a failure to communicate and you have a man who mops floors for two hundred dollars a week. A man who, after nine innings, will be back in his barrio stocking Midnight Dragon. Over the years, thousands of Dominicans fled repression and economic hardship to find new lives in New York City—an exodus that began to gain momentum in the mid-1960s, after the assassination of Rafael Trujillo and the U.S. invasion of the Dominican in 1965. Ballplayers are just a small part of that chain of migration.

Once in the city, they will have children, they will work low-wage jobs, they will stay on their side of town, and they will move through formerly Italian, Irish, and Jewish neighborhoods that now look and sound like downtown Santo Domingo. To walk down Broadway north of 135th Street is to see windows filled with religious artifacts, a blending of Christian saints and African deities, the smell of sweet pork and the sounds of merengue, *Rock en Español* and Afro-Cuban rhythms. Rows of boys, their pants baggy, their baseball caps pulled down low over their eyes, will stand in doorways, looking hard or looking away. Men will drink beer in front of bodegas and women will push their baby carriages into corner markets. The farther north on the island of Manhattan you go, the deeper you get into areas notorious for drugs and violence—areas decimated by the explosion of crack cocaine and unemployment. In 1992, there were ninety-eight homicides in Washington Heights.[9] As in the rest of New York, violent crimes have decreased significantly, but there were still forty people murdered in Washington Heights in 1996. Across the river, in the Bronx, it's more of the same.

Indeed, to take a walk around the area where the cathedral of major league baseball sits—the site of Yankee Stadium—is to be transported to the heart of the Dominican Republic. Their presence, their lives, their struggles are the results—whether intended or unintended—of U.S. military invasion and economic domination. The dream of the United States, of earning dollars, is so strong in the Dominican Republic that it has been transported to New York City, a whole way of life shipped as if by air mail to a new destination.

Baseball players like Santana are part of that arrangement. They knew what the risks were when they left the island, but they figured it was worth it. It's only after all hope for a career in baseball is gone that they realize America is not what they were told it would be—at least not for them. "When you're back home they paint a different picture of this country of a place of beautiful birds," said Jose Moreno, who spend a few seasons in the Detroit Tigers system before being released after the 1994 season. "But when you get here it's another story. You have to come here and experience it to believe it. If you don't support yourself, you die. In the Dominican, everybody says you can find everything here, but it's not true. It's a lie. You have to kill yourself to get what you want and then you could lose it in a minute by somebody jumping you and taking it away from you." [10] Playing in the Tigers system for four years between 1991 and 1994, Moreno scarcely played, and when he did, his coaches weren't impressed. Today, he irons clothes in a Brooklyn garment factory, working alongside his brother. Yet he is one of the lucky ones. He has been able to stay out of trouble, to avoid the drug trade that swallows young Dominican men every year.

In 1997, Ignacio Rodriguez, a former minor leaguer in the Montreal Expos system, was gunned down in a drug-related shooting near the corner of 148th Street and Amsterdam Avenue. [11] To the undying sadness of those who live there, Washington Heights is known throughout New York as a wholesale drug community.

In 1992, the rest of America heard about Washington Heights when massive rioting was triggered in its streets after police gunned down drug lord Kiko Garcia. Its reputation set in stone after the Garcia riots, the neighborhood was later described by the *New Republic* as "the crack capital of New York and perhaps the country."

The article continued: "In the early '90s, Washington Heights was a giant, open-air drug mart. Customers drove over the George Washington Bridge and lined up to buy drugs, as if at a McDonalds's take out window. Drug gangs slaughtered one another over control of tiny slivers of territory."

A marginal Chicago Cubs prospect who lasted one summer league season in 1987 and one Arizona spring training, Victor Martinez was seduced by this world. Martinez's life in the tiny Dominican town of Moca had given him no preparation for what he would encounter in New York after being let go by the Cubs. He was just another immigrant, not even remembered by his old team.

A check of the Cubs records shows that Martinez did in fact play in the Cubs' Dominican summer league camp in his hometown. Spring training got him to the United States and he took care of the rest. "What I found here was an atmosphere of corruption," Martinez said. "What hurts me now is that the Cubs didn't release me. I hurt my hand and I was afraid they were going to release me so I left. Things are so difficult back there that once you've lived as a ballplayer and you go from the highest point, you just can't go back to the lowest point.

"So the first time I got here, my cousins and I went to a disco and we stayed out all night. I had never seen the sunrise until that day and when I came out I thought, Oh, my god. Where have I ended up?"[12] Before very long, Martinez was selling drugs, carrying a pistol at all times, and spending his entire life looking over his shoulder. "When I got here I got into that life because that is a way that you can make a lot of money fast. You don't need your papers and if you have luck, you can make money. I was afraid. There are lots of people who say they aren't afraid in that life but I'll say that I was afraid. You get in because you don't have any money. And here you have to have money. There is no other way. So they get in for that reason."

A self-described has-been, Martinez bears the scars of his failed baseball career. His sinewy six-foot, 160-pound frame has fleshed out by forty pounds since his early twenties, leaving him with a paunchy, bearlike figure. His reflexes have been slowed by inactivity and sitting behind the wheel of the taxi he now drives for money. And his deep brown eyes now bear the world-weary quality of someone who has lived life on the edge, someone who has periodically sold drugs and has faced death with a gun pointed at his head.

"You begin selling drugs because you get hungry and you notice that others are making money. So you get in," Martinez said. "That is life here. I stood that for six years. I had a lot of luck. There were times when I came so close to being arrested. I just thank God that I wasn't. But my soul hurt, not because of the money that I made, but because of my family. I'm married. I have children, and I didn't want to be arrested or have anyone say, 'Look, your father is in jail.' "

The closest he came to death was when he was held up at gunpoint one night in Washington Heights, the robber stealing a wad of cash and tying him to a fencepost after pressing the steel of a revolver against his temple. Even though Martinez is no longer earning his money by selling drugs, he still longs for what he lost. "I would always think I would play baseball and so my heart hurts today because I don't. If I had a chance to give everything I had for that life I would gladly give it because I liked it so much. Baseball is my life. My best days were all those days I played from the time I was small to the last time I played as a professional." [13]

Baseball is so much a part of Martinez that when his son was born in the early 1990s, he chose a name directly from the box scores. "I always really liked the name of [former New York Met] Gregg Jefferies so I named my son Jeffery. It's a good name for a ballplayer."

Now past thirty, Martinez doesn't play baseball any longer, choosing softball instead. Though he's been invited to play semipro ball, he doesn't want to keep at something he knows will never be his. So he drives his cab in uptown Manhattan, servicing a clientele that is almost 100 percent Dominican. Martinez isn't proud of the life he led and, in fact, New York's Dominican community has been working to change its image—not an easy thing to do when so much anguish plays out in close proximity to the media capital of America.

Over the last five years, the headlines relating to New York's Dominican borrios have come nonstop. In 1994, *Newsday* wrote, "In 1983, there were fewer than 100,000 Dominicans in Washington Heights, now there are more than 350,000. Crime has risen sharply, especially since crack cocaine hit in 1985. Homicides went from 57 in 1987 to 122 in 1991, topping every other precinct in the city. In 1992, there were 98—also the highest in New York. Since 1985, more than 400 young Dominicans from one town—San Francisco de Macoris—have been killed in the United States."

Also in 1994, thirty New York police officers working out of Washington Heights were charged with running a virtual crime ring of grand larceny and narcotics conspiracy. There were reports in the media that even as the corruption scandal was exploding, other cops were referring to the Washington Heights community as "Dumb-inicans" and "Domos." The assumption was that "Dominicans are all lowlifes and drug dealers," as *Newsday* wrote in April 1994. Lost in all the crime statistics and the headlines are the people in the community itself. "We have over sixty-six thousand young people under the age of eighteen, that is more than a lot of other communities have in population, and until recently we didn't have a single youth program for them," said Moises Perez, of Alianza Dominicana, the largest service group for the Dominican community of New York. [14]

"At the same time, schools were and continue to be the most overcrowded. So we had the most overcrowded schools, no youth programs, the highest unemployment rate for young people in the city, no role models of other young people who have graduated high school. What is there for them to do? There are fewer jobs now. That to me is the crux of it. In the 1970s New York lost its manufacturing base completely, which was the backbone of the employment pool, and precisely when the jobs became scarce the Dominicans began to spread out across the city."

So in the city that symbolizes the hope of immigrants and immigration in America, the newest arrivals stagnate—trapped without the safety nets of jobs and security that past immigrants could rely on. For such a people, baseball is the great hope, the arena where so many formerly poor, young kids have excelled. In New York, every time Manny Ramirez of the Cleveland Indians hits a home run, some young kid in Washington Heights takes comfort because Ramirez is a homeboy, a native son.

However, these dreams are about used up for the most recent arrivals—baseball's Dominican rejects. In 1996 and 1997, Santana continued trying to play and was even picked up by an independent baseball league in upstate New York. But his time was running out. He was approaching the realization that Tony McDonald had come to years before. Like Santana, McDonald is from San Pedro de Macoris. And between 1977 and 1982, he played in the Philadelphia Phillies minor league system, putting up the kind of numbers that would attract a shot at the big leagues. But he never got his chance.

In 1980, in Double A with the Phillies team in Reading, Pennsylvania, he hit .309 and hit in 136 games. In 1981 and 1982 he played in Triple A for the Phillies and played well enough to get the call—but Mike Schmidt was powering his way to a Hall of Fame career, leaving no room for McDonald.

McDonald was signed by the Phillies for fifty-five hundred dollars, which was more than they paid for two other Dominican prospects they also signed in the late 1970s—George Bell and Julio Franco. "We had the same kind of years in the minor leagues. I maintained the same numbers as them," McDonald said.[15] Indeed, when Franco played at Reading the year after McDonald, he batted .301, eight points lower than McDonald. The Phillies liked McDonald, and, in fact, years later his old minor league manager still remembers him fondly. "Tony is one of my favorite people," said long-time baseball man Ron Clark.[16]

Both Bell and Franco would go on to stardom and millions. Bell would win the American League MVP in 1987. Franco would be the American League batting champion in 1991. McDonald would be released by the Phillies after the 1982 season and, Clark's feelings notwithstanding, would never get a substantive call from another team.

"I played well enough to get a contract but I didn't have the luck. There was just no room on the team for anyone from the minor leagues. They had Mike Schmidt, [Gold Glove shortstop] Larry Bowa, and [Gold Glove second baseman] Manny Trillo. A rookie just couldn't break into that lineup."[17]

After playing in Mexico for a time, McDonald moved to New York where he works in a warehouse forty hours a week. "In the end, I did get frustrated. I knew I could make it. Later it affected me. I would see players with less ability who made it in the big leagues."

Yet today he has no bitterness for the way his life turned out, even though no teams made him any offers when the Phillies let him go. "I don't complain about my life. I did what I had to do, I gave it what I had. After I was released, I approached some teams, but they weren't interested any more. You have to have luck for everything in life. Attitude and luck are two major things you need. I am happy because in my case, it wasn't anything that I did wrong. It wasn't because of my personality. It was just a twist of fate, something that happens in life. I don't wish for things I don't have. I'm another type of person, I am proud of what I have gotten for myself. I came here looking for work and not looking for something in the streets."

Disturbed by the reputation Dominicans have in New York, McDonald—a husband and father—offers his own life as a counterpoint of all the headlines. "I have lots of friends who have been prospects and ended up in jail. They didn't have the same luck as me. There is lots of talent on the streets of New York, you see them and they are good but they are done. There are lots who have good jobs. The majority of us have good jobs, we find a job some place in a company and we work. There are lots of Latins working."

As McDonald talked, Santana's team was playing in a tight

game whose winner would advance in the playoffs of the Brooklyn league. The loser would be eliminated. Although he played well, Santana made a throwing error that nearly tied the game. A teammate in center field badly overran a routine fly ball and the run scored anyway. Suddenly the skies grew black—the remnants of a hurricane that had pounded North Carolina—as Santana's team lost the game just as a blistering rain began to fall.

Fans scattered to their cars even as pulsating salsa music from an old PA system continued to play. On the ride home, Santana and two of his teammates talked of the loss and how if only some key players had showed up, they would have won.

One of them, a former minor league rising star named Elvin Paulino, was particularly missed. Dick Balderson, vice-president of the Colorado Rockies, described Paulino as having had "major league power."[18] And Paulino was on the verge of making the Rockies when he was thrown off the team for drinking in 1993. Paulino admits today that he "screwed up" and is now playing semipro ball in an attempt to make a comeback at twenty-eight. But as he did when he was a professional, he let his team down when they most needed him. He didn't show up for the game.

"That happens a lot on Sunday games. Guys go out the night before and then they don't show up to play," Santana said. "I'm not going to do that. I'm going to keep working. I'm going to keep trying until I get my chance."

As the rain continued to fall, Santana said, "I just need one chance. Just one."

Later that evening, across town in Washington Heights, Victor Martinez was driving his taxi when he happened on a friend—Luis Santos, who was released by the Los Angeles Dodgers in 1988.

Santos, at age thirty, and the twenty-eight-year-old Martinez used to believe as Santana did that they still had a chance to make the major leagues. But there is no room in their lives for that anymore. On this night, in a somber drizzle, Santos was feeling good—he had downed several Coronas. "I was better than [Dodgers' right fielder] Raul Mondesi!" Santos shouted, slurring his words beneath his white baseball cap in the front seat of Martinez's cab. "I could play with all those guys!"

Rafael Avila, the Dodgers' top Latin scout, said of Santos: "He had the tools, but for some reason he couldn't put it all together." When asked if he thought Santos stood a chance when he first left the island, Avila said, "Not really." [19]

In the state he was in, Santos would never believe that. Stopping himself for a moment, he said, "You see those guys in the big leagues and you just have to envy them. What I wouldn't give to be up there with them. What I wouldn't give."

Martinez was silent as Santos spoke. He had stopped laughing at his friend. "That's why I don't like to go to games or talk about baseball. It just embitters my life. It hurts my soul to think about it."

Suddenly, Santos shouted, "Let's get out of here. I'm tired of talking about this."

The two men looked at each other for a moment and Martinez started his car. As the rain fell harder on New York, the George Washington Bridge cast a beautiful reflection on the Hudson River.

In an instant, Martinez's cab was gone. They were headed nowhere in particular.

9

GRANDES LIGAS

THE SUN WAS SETTING on *Los Barrancones* when Miguel left his mother's memorial. He had to get away. And he had two words on his lips:

Grandes Ligas.

Big leagues.

The thought of making the Big Leagues was a twenty-four-hour obsession for Miguel.

Three nights before his flight to America for spring training, the emotion amounted to a heavy load. Miguel just wanted to escape, to get away. So he pulled thirty Dominican pesos from his pocket—about two American dollars—and took off with a three-man crew of barrio admirers tagging along to amuse him.

These were Miguel's "boys," and some carried revolvers, silver-plated handguns stuffed into the crotches of their tight-fitting jeans.

They were a merry gang of hangers-on, some unemployed, some earning money by charging a few pesos for rides into town on their Honda motor scooters. It hardly seemed worth the effort, yet there they would park, at the end of dusty streets in groups of five, snapping into action the minute someone needed a ride.

Gangly and rough, Miguel's boys sped over the open field separating *Los Barrancones* from the rest of Bani, seeming to know every pothole and ditch, slowing down in a heartbeat and then gunning it again. Miguel coolly hung on to a beefy friend during the ride, adeptly balancing himself on the rear seat while keeping his hands in his lap.

After navigating the field, the group turned onto paved streets until reaching the tree-lined main square of Bani, the plaza, where Miguel and his pals hailed a cab for a six-mile drive to the ocean.

It's an instructive drive, demonstrating that young men need not look far for drug money. Standing out in an outrageous way, a sudden burst of in-your-face wealth in a sea of tin shacks, are gated, Caribbean mansions with tiled driveways, white-painted wrought-iron gates, immaculate carports, and spotless BMWs parked side by side. Boys like Miguel view these places with wide eyes and knowing smiles. "You see the homes," Miguel would say as a young man. *"El Medio* paid for those houses." Roughly translated, *"El Medio"* is what Dominicans call life in the underworld. *Medio*—or middle—meaning life somewhere between good and evil, between what you hope for and what life gives you. Venture into *El Medio*, the Dominicans say, and "only God knows what you will find."

Miguel knows many men in *El Medio*. Where he is from, the temptation is great. Luckily, he can play baseball and go dancing without looking over his shoulder.

Arriving at one of Bani's open-air clubs, sweet merengue is playing. Young people here dance for hours at a time, drinking in the smell of the Caribbean, which is easy to do since the clubs were built along a rugged stretch of the sea—lending a soothing contrast to the music and a natural aphrodisiac to already sensual surroundings.

There are two types of men here: baseball players and non–baseball players, and it's easy to tell them apart. The ballplayers are the taller ones, bulked up by American food, stylized in Versace shades, Guess Jeans, and the ever-present Nike swoosh. Some men wear the logos on black baseball caps that go well with skin-tight knit shirts and expensive jewelry, like a gold chain or watch. These men have chiseled features, use expensive hair conditioners, and stand in groups. They are completely unlike everyone else here.

Miguel's boys seem ecstatic just to be there, festive as they stuff greasy fried bananas into their mouths and listen to one mournful merengue song after another. As they jabbered on, Miguel struck up a conversation with a pair of beautiful women, still just teenagers, but here obviously to enjoy themselves.

There came a song he liked, and Miguel danced with a gorgeous, dark-skinned woman with full lips and smooth, bare legs—a radiant girl wearing an alluring blouse cut low to reveal a supple, full bosom and the white-chocolate flesh of her toned waist and abdomen. The woman was assured in her sexuality, her face and breasts moist from the Bani afternoon.

The people of the Caribbean seem to wear their perspiration like clothing and this girl was stunning in her sweat, which, mixed with perfume, drew Miguel in like a magnet. The song they danced to was about leaving: leaving a lover, leaving the island, losing one's self.

Miguel was a good dancer, confident as he held the small of her back, bold as he pressed his upper body against hers. He looked powerful in a black cotton shirt painted across his defined biceps and washboard stomach. His body was rock-solid and his American-bought clothes hung perfectly, as if he were a blue jeans model selling image and attitude to the youth of the world. In 1993, before Miguel signed his first professional contract, he was skinny and ragged, his hair rough, his features coarse and ill-defined.

Now his hair was perfectly cut, his skin treated with moisturizers and a cologne called *Cool Water,* which he bought while shopping alone in Modesto's Vintage Fair Mall. On that day, with his baseball cap turned backward, Miguel had tried to bargain with a bemused sales clerk with big hair and gaudy jewelry—an unlikely meeting of middle America and the Third World.

Back in the Dominican, he had meticulously dabbed the fragrance on himself, careful not to waste any, and set out for the music and the sea—to a place he couldn't have gone just two years before. While there were other ballplayers standing around on this day, Miguel was special: He was going to the *Grandes Ligas.*

At the end of the song, Miguel and his partner returned to their metal table with metal chairs and the girl smiled seductively as she sat next to him, deferring to his every word and wish.

When he wanted to dance, they danced. When he wanted to sit, they sat. When he wanted to eat, they ate—in this case, heaping platters of fried chicken cut in small chunks and speared with toothpicks, which the boys used to pick their teeth while washing it all down with big bottles of Presidente.

But while others drank and drank, Miguel only tasted his beer in little sips, nursing a glass for hours without refilling it. The most active thing he did was order rounds and pull dollar bills out of his pocket. The group would stay and visit until it was dark and leave only when Miguel said so. The girl he had danced with tried to extract some kind of commitment, a telephone call, some future meeting, but Miguel promised nothing. And then he was driven away.

He slept late the next morning, a Monday, two days before he and Geronimo Berroa, Tony Batista, and Jose Herrera—the Athletics' Dominican major leaguers—were scheduled to fly, first class, to Phoenix. By the time Miguel woke up, the rest of his family and *Los Barrancones* had been stirring for hours. Pushing through the soiled curtain that was his bedroom door, Miguel wrapped a towel over his shirtless back, grabbed a bottle of Head and Shoulders and walked past his elderly grandmother, who was tending to boiling pots on the Tejadas' battered stove.

In the backyard, among the chickens, pigs, and dogs, Miguel's uniform from the Dominican national baseball team hung next to a rainbow of colored T-shirts and underwear on a rickety clothes line. Miguel had worn his favorite number 4, as he always did, during the series. He also wore it for the Aguilas, his Dominican winter league team, which played in the second-largest Dominican city, Santiago—an inland metropolis, far from Bani in the northwest corner of the island. A testament to the rarefied heights he was reaching, Miguel hadn't been the star on that Aguilas team—not by a long shot. While Miguel's average hovered around .260 and his brilliance emerged in fits and spurts, his Athletics teammate and Dominican friend Tony Batista was destroying the league. It was Batista, and not Tejada, who was the shortstop on the Aguilas. Batista batted .320, was selected league MVP, and was named to *Baseball America's* All–Winter League team, a collection of stars from all the Caribbean leagues, including major league All-Stars Ivan Rodriguez of the Texas Rangers and Robby Alomar of the Baltimore Orioles.

Batista, a sleepy-eyed shortstop who was nineteen months older than Miguel and hailed from the resort city of Puerto Plata, had already reached the big leagues with the Athletics, batting an impressive .298, with 6 home runs and 25 RBI in 74 games at the tail end of the 1996 season. A six-footer at 190 pounds, Batista was significantly bigger than Miguel, had an explosive bat, and played a smooth game at short in contrast to Miguel's aggression. Batista was an established prospect when Miguel was failing his sixty-yard sprint tests at "La Normal." Batista had kept a watchful eye on Tejada ever since, expressing siblinglike annoyance at Miguel's early, foolish boasting, but later realizing the young player could not be dismissed.

"When Miguel was still just starting out, [Batista] would say, 'We better watch out for this kid. He's really hungry,' " said Luis Martinez, the Athletics Dominican coach who had known both since they were boys.[1] With Mike Bordick gone to bigger money in Baltimore, fellow Dominican shortstop Fausto Cruz traded to Detroit, and Mark Bellhorn still too green, Batista emerged as the leading candidate for Oakland's starting shortstop job and Miguel's greatest obstacle. For Miguel's part, he had built a case for himself by finishing strongly in the winter league and by doing what he always did: making plays people remembered.

At the conclusion of the winter season, Miguel was named as having made the best play of the season—an impossible, acrobatic, one-handed stab of a soft liner along the third-base line that Miguel fielded barehanded and threw across his body while flying through the air. The play garnered him a bonus equivalent to seven hundred American dollars.

He also starred in the Caribbean World Series in Mexico. After winning the title game, Miguel allowed himself the luxury of sampling the Mexican nightlife before returning home with souvenirs for everyone and a dirty uniform to be washed by *abuelita*—grandma.

Adjacent to the line where his number 4 hung was a common outdoor shower where the Tejadas bathed behind the cover of a rusting metal enclosure that looked like a battered old car door. With song birds chirping in the trees overhead, Miguel turned on a garden hose that shot ice-cold water on his sculpted body. As he bathed, family members and neighbors passed in and out of the backyard, going about their business on a typical day. Inside the rusted metal encasement where Miguel washed off yesterday's grime was a foul-smelling open hole. There is no mistaking what it is: the Tejadas used the hole when they had to relieve themselves.

Meanwhile, around the corner and down the street, work continued on the home Miguel was building with his baseball money. He had eagerly described it to American friends and coaches in Modesto, conjuring in their minds American definitions of a "home." But it is unlikely those people would believe their eyes if they saw the dwelling, which was slightly larger than the one where the Tejadas lived then.

Showered and dressed, Miguel went to check the progress of construction, which was being done by men from *Los Barrancones*. By this point, the foundation and outer shell were completed, but workers were still plastering the walls, electrical wiring was still unconnected, two-by-fours were strewn about and concrete had not been poured over dirt floors. The new house made Daniel Tejada very happy, and he spent most of his time working and watching others work. Already, the address of the home was etched in yellow paint—in honor of the Oakland Athletics. As is the custom in Latin America, the maiden name of Miguel's mother's was included—Martinez. When adding that detail, workers painted the letter Z in the shape of a baseball bat. But what made Daniel Tejada proudest of all was the room for Miguel. At that stage of construction, it was windowless with no flooring and about the size of a storage room. However, it did have one special feature: an open corridor leading out of the house, a secret exit Miguel could use to escape in case danger ever came calling.

"That's in case anyone ever got in the house who we didn't want, Miguel could escape without being seen," Daniel Tejada said. "It's so dangerous today, I think there has to be a way for Miguel to get away." Even though Miguel hadn't reached the riches of the *Grandes Ligas*, the Tejadas already had more money than anyone around based on Miguel's earnings as a minor leaguer. To Daniel Tejada's way of thinking, that reality could bring danger. He thought for a moment and then his face brightened. "This is where Miguel will live from now on." Such a statement was indicative of how the world of Miguel's dad left him no understanding or point of reference for the riches awaiting his son. He simply had no idea.

A man who wore tattered cotton dress shirts, Goodwill pants, and thongs on his deeply callused feet, Daniel Tejada oversaw the construction of "Miguel's house" as a way of showing his son how much he cared for him. It was all he could give. And despite the nature of his childhood, Miguel responded to his father's love in kind and would carry the sound of his dad's voice to the United States in two days.

But he was already having doubts about living in this house.

His experience in Modesto had opened his eyes to the possibilities. And the overwhelming reaction his return drew in *Los Barrancones* made him reassess long-held ideas. "I definitely want to live in my country and I want to stay in Bani, but I don't know if I can live here after I reach the *Grandes Ligas*. I can't relax here anymore. Sometimes I think I can relax more in the United States."

Miguel was certainly ready to go. He went to the ballpark in Bani for a few last workouts with a sense of purpose usually reserved for autumn pennant drives.

When he took the grassless infield, young players cleared a path for him. Next to their skinny frames, Miguel looked powerful wearing his Athletics cap, a spotless white T-shirt, snow-white major league pants, and brand-new Nike baseball shoes. When Miguel was ready, groups of boys who had been practicing anonymously were pushed to one side while a park caretaker dutifully watered down the patch of dirt between second and third. They were preparing the field for a big leaguer.

Miguel then signaled he was ready to take a few grounders. To practice *rolling*, as the Latins called it.

With the dirt wet, dozens of balls Miguel had brought for Soto would now bounce somewhat honestly off the ragged, rocky surface. After a time, Miguel came to bat and suddenly, the hundred or so players and gawkers gathered under a hot sun stopped what they were doing.

Miguel was standing in against a big kid, a six-footer, who was considered a hot pitching prospect. Rearing back, the kid fired a fastball as Miguel nonchalantly dropped his bat and studied a strike as it shot by.

Nodding, Miguel quickly dug in for real. And when the young pitcher reared back and fired even harder, Miguel was in perfect synch with the pitch.

He crushed it, sending it sailing high over the left-field wall, 340 feet away.

As he rounded the bases, an audible buzz went up from those gathered around, an electricity normally reserved for packed major league ballparks.

"*Diablo*," screamed more than one.

Rounding third, Miguel stutter-stepped like a mad chicken and grinned maniacally as he crossed the plate. The pitcher stood straight as an arrow, trying not to look too embarrassed. Standing off to one side was Jeison Arias, the big kid the Athletics had been pursuing the year before. Arias was preparing to attend spring training for the first time—as a member of the Tampa Bay Devil Rays. When the Athletics wouldn't go as high as fifteen thousand dollars, he took the thirty thousand dollars the Devil Rays had offered him.

After a while, Miguel gathered his things, signaling he was ready to go. Soto left practice in the hands of one of his assistants while he and Miguel, his prized pupil, piled into his car—with a dozen young boys trailing after them. Many asked Soto for money, and those he was trying to encourage got a few bills. Those who weren't working hard, he amusingly scolded. Pulling away as a few boys pedaled alongside the car on their bikes, Soto put on his favorite Julio Iglesias tape, looked at the boys, and turned to Miguel with a fatherly expression: "Miguel, remember when that was you?"

Miguel nodded slightly, expressionless as he pulled his Athletics cap over his eyes and settled in for the ninety-minute drive to Campo Juan Marichal. Miguel planned to pick up his visa from Abreu, go home and prepare for the seven o'clock flight the next morning. Slumping in the front seat, Miguel was upbeat, the tension of the last few days seemingly gone.

Entering Santo Domingo, he and Soto stopped to eat American food—fried chicken and French fries. Soto told him again how, if he just maintained his work ethic, his talent would make him a star.

Soto seemed just as excited as Miguel, a find who would not only become his first prospect to reach the majors, but his first star. Some American scouts retire on less than that.

Soto was dressed the same way he always was, a T-shirt, sweat pants, and Nike sneakers—his paunch a little bigger, his hair a little thinner than the year before. As they pulled into the gates of the complex and were motioned through by the guard, Soto and Miguel were quiet. Toward the back, the dormitory was bustling. The latest crop of minor league players were preparing to leave—but not until March. A February trip was for major leaguers only. Inside the dorm, on an upper bunk, lay Arturo "Tabacco" Paulino, still smarting from a trying year in Grand Rapids. It was unclear where he would go in 1997 and he was somber as he read in his underwear, having just showered and eaten following a workout. Though he knew Miguel was on the grounds, Tabacco didn't rouse himself from his bunk.

Meanwhile, Miguel stepped into Abreu's immaculate office to discuss business while Soto retreated to a cool, tree-lined spot on the grounds where coaches go to gossip in privacy, their words heard only by field mice, birds and other creatures lurking around the complex. Along with supervising an expansion of the Athletics program, which saw them sign just under one hundred prospects to new contracts in 1997, it was Abreu's job to deal with visas for foreign players.

Miguel was prepared to be given his final instructions.

But what he got instead was one of the biggest disappointments of his young life.

He would not be leaving tomorrow with the major leaguers. His visa hadn't arrived.

"Did [Geronimo] Berroa's visa get here?" Miguel asked. Abreu said yes. "How about [Tony] Batista?" Abreu answered yes. The only one that hadn't arrived was Miguel's.

"I don't know when yours will come. They didn't say," said Abreu. "We're going to have to keep checking. I'll let you know." Miguel sat silently for a moment, before getting up and leaving.

Soto was nowhere to be found and it was getting dark.

Hungry again and momentarily disoriented, Miguel went into the cafeteria and was served a plate of food. He ate with the groundskeepers. Then he and Soto began the ninety-minute drive home. "When I make it to the major leagues, I'm going to buy a car. A red sports car," Miguel said to Soto.

"You can't do that, Miguel," Soto responded. "That's the first thing that Dominicans do wrong. You spend all that money, you wreck the car because you don't know how to drive, or you become a target for someone who wants to steal from you. You have to be smart, Miguel."

Miguel said nothing as Soto continued talking, warning him of the women who would throw themselves at him, the vultures who would try to steal his money. "Remember, Miguel. A lot of people are depending on you. Your family, everyone. You're useful to a lot of people."

Miguel would only look out the window for the remainder of the drive, silently watching darkened palm trees, thatched huts, and jungle brush shoot by in the dark. What would he tell his family now?

The next day, under beautiful blue skies, all the Dominicans on the Athletics boarded the airliner Miguel should have been on. While these players didn't get noticed much, another did—Sammy Sosa. Having hit 40 home runs in 1996, even though he missed the last month of the season with an injury, Sosa had signed a gigantic, $40-million contract, making him one of the highest-paid players in baseball. And on this day, a year before he would make baseball history, Sosa looked regal in an expensive suit with gold jewelery, resplendent in his first-class seat.

Back home, Miguel sat and waited. Almost every day of his absence, the *San Francisco Chronicle* or *Sacramento Bee* published items about how the "shortstop of the future" was due any day. But for two weeks that day did not come. In that time, Grieve was the subject of glowing stories about youthful potential, while Miguel cooled his heels, religiously working out in Bani while Soto encouraged him to stay focused.

SINCE BASEBALL BEGAN importing Latins in significant numbers, players have been at the mercy of bureaucratic snafus between their governments and U.S. embassies in Latin America. A few years before Miguel signed, a Venezuelan player named Marcos Armas couldn't get his paperwork and remained in his country, while then-manager Tony La Russa did a slow burn in Arizona. Armas had other problems with the club, but his visa hold-up didn't help, and soon player and team parted company. Miguel's case was not part of a recent phenomenon.

"I arrived late for spring training in my rookie year. My rookie year! Can you imagine that?" said Felipe Alou, of his own personal visa problems.[2] "Our visas always arrived late and so we would get to spring training late and they would accuse us of lying. And today, Dominican boys are always accused of lying on their visas but this has always been a problem. We would go to the embassy and our visa would not have been processed. Or there would be an error in the spelling of the name. Any number of things. And so you would always be starting from behind."

As it turns out, the U.S. State Department and Dominican immigration officials had misplaced Miguel's visa papers, Abreu would say later. Luckily, in his case, no one was blaming him or accusing him of any wrongdoing. After one week had gone by, Athletics manager Art Howe was asked about Miguel by Pedro Gomez, then the Athletics beat writer for the *Sacramento Bee*. Howe said: "It's a shame. It's not his fault." When Miguel finally got on a plane bound for Phoenix, he went just as he had the year before—with the minor leaguers—although once he got there, he was shuttled over to the Airport Hilton, where the players from the *Grandes Ligas* were staying. The next day, with barely a moment to practice, he was inserted into a split-squad game against the San Diego Padres—he went 0–2, though, as he usually did, Miguel made an impression.

"How about that," said Athletics infield coach, Ron Washington. "He stepped right off the plane and gave us some damn good at-bats. He wasn't intimidated at all."[3]

IN THE RAREFIED AIR of the *Grandes Ligas*, the slightest hitch in timing, the most minuscule quirk in rhythm, can mean the difference between a .200 hitter and a .300 hitter. It wasn't that Miguel was playing badly, it's just that his dominant game, the attention-grabbing quality that excited everyone, was not yet on display. In a long season, days and weeks of performances like these are part of the game. But in the compressed time of spring training, where unproven players have a finite number of games to make an impression, a lag like the kind Miguel was experiencing results in one thing: reassignment to the minor leagues.

Miguel was working hard, working out the bugs of what amounted to three weeks of inactivity since the Caribbean World Series in Mexico. His hard sessions in Bani meant nothing here.

In that first week in Phoenix, stretching and running with millionaires Jose Canseco and Mark McGwire, Miguel was silent, respectful, and observant. He was trying hard to do the right thing, to say the right thing.

He was leaning heavily on Batista and another Dominican infielder, named Rafael Bournigal, a slight, steady utility guy who had knocked around the Dodgers system for eight years before the Athletics signed him as a free agent before the 1996 season. Bournigal was unlike most Dominican players. With very fair skin, an American high-school diploma, and a degree from Florida State University, he came from a family where his father had been a well-known baseball broadcaster in the Dominican. And he also lived in Florida during the off-season. Known as a gentleman in baseball circles and beloved by clubhouse attendants for giving sizable tips, Bournigal knew his way around the league and the Athletics organization, and Miguel was rarely away from his side.

What concerned Bournigal most about his young pupil was his total lack of guile and his tenuous grasp of English—a deadly combination when operating around the mostly white-bread crew of writers working the baseball beat. Except for Gomez of the *Sacramento Bee,* no other writer coming in contact with Miguel that spring of 1997 spoke Spanish fluently. "And the problem is, they ask you questions indirectly, they speak in off-hand, indirect terms, and it's easy to misunderstand a question and answer the wrong way. It's really easy for someone like Miguel to be misunderstood," Bournigal said. It was only March, but Bournigal couldn't know how prophetic his words were—that very issue would rear its head later.

Up until that point, the press coverage of Miguel had been in keeping with the press coverage of most Latin players through the years. Except for a few superficial references to life back home, all that ever came across was what happened on the field. And at every level, there were always other American players the beat writers would go to for that much-sought-after quotation. Indeed, no one writing about Miguel could have imagined the journey that had led him to locker rooms in Medford, Modesto, and now here.

Now that he was around the big leagues, his name in the pages of the big dailies, scrutiny would increase among a group of writers who knew little of the Latin experience in baseball. So while on one level it was only right for Miguel to be approached like any other player, given his status in the organization, the truth was he wasn't like every other player. And it was this gray reality that spooked Bournigal the most, made him work harder at schooling Miguel to be careful, to be aware, and to watch his words. Many Dominicans in recent years and many Latins over the years have come across badly in print, and Bournigal wanted to protect Miguel from that as much as he possibly could.

Finally in camp, his jersey hanging in a major league–size locker, Miguel noticed that his modest jeans, cotton shirts, and Nikes looked shabby and soiled next to the tailored suits, expensive sports jackets, and Italian shoes worn by the big leaguers. On the field, he was attracting a lot of attention for the first time, which came with its own challenges. In the 1997 Athletics media guide, in the player development section where the team lists all its minor leaguers, there was a picture of Grieve standing next to Miguel—an obvious signal by the team that these were their two prime hopes for the future. For the first time, big league fans who knew who Miguel was were calling out his name, asking for his autograph. People he had never met before, baseball people of some importance, were sidling up to him to shake his hand, patting him on the back. Shortly after he arrived, he was approached by Bill Rigney, a Bay Area institution, the inaugural manager of the San Francisco Giants and a fixture in the Athletics organization since 1982. Silver-haired and spry in his white sun hat with the wide brim and oversized glasses, "Rig" took Miguel's hand in his and said: "Hello, young fella. I've heard a lot about you."

"Yeah," Miguel replied, not as a question, but a declarative statement.

Rigney then gave Miguel the standard baseball pep talk, with Miguel nodding, but it was hard to tell what he understood and what he didn't. Bournigal was there, and as soon as Rigney was out of earshot, Bournigal gave Miguel the rundown on who he was and how he needed to remember him.

To a member of the Athletics staff, Rigney then said, "Miguel Tejada. Remember that name."

Taking his place in the outfield for stretching exercises, Miguel found himself in conversation with Jose Canseco, the former AL MVP, All-Star, and media bad boy, who was back in Oakland after a five-year absence, trying to regain his past glory. Possessing one of the most formidable bodies in baseball, with huge biceps and enormous neck muscles, Canseco dwarfed Miguel, who suddenly looked like a waif from *Los Barrancones* again.

The rich superstar and the kid talked and talked for some time.

Later, Miguel would say: "He [Canseco] was trying to talk me into changing my agent. He said he was starting a company of some kind that represented players and he asked me if I wanted to be represented by his company."

Miguel left it at that, fostering the assumption that the millionaire superstar, one of the most high-profile Latin players ever, would have some sway with Miguel.

He didn't.

"I told him no," Miguel said. "I told him I was happy with my agent."

Miguel's agent had been recommended to him by the Athletics, and in reality he couldn't know how good he was because Miguel wouldn't begin making real money until he was in the Majors. But Miguel thought his agent was a nice guy, so he said no. Turning down someone like Canseco was no big deal to Miguel. The entire encounter didn't seem to make an impression one way or another. At the end of practice that day, he was far more concerned with changing and seeking out his old minor league friends from the Athletics at the Scottsdale mall. But as he was leaving Phoenix Municipal Stadium, he stopped dead in his tracks, whirled around, and called out after a pair of ballpark maintenance workers who were driving by. Miguel's mood had changed in seconds from friendly to deadly serious.

"Did you say something to me?" he shouted out at the workers, who had stopped their motorized gardener's cart at the sound of Miguel's raised voice.

"What?" said one of them in return, over the rattling of his engine.

"I said did you say something to me?"

The two workers, who appeared to be Hispanic, looked long and hard at Miguel before answering, and though their expressions weren't menacing, they weren't exactly friendly either. For one unsettling moment, it appeared that one of Oakland's key players of the future was about to slug it out with two guys probably not making much more than the minimum wage. But the bravado-filled silence was broken by one of the workers who said, "No, I didn't say anything."

It was clear Miguel wasn't afraid of or intimidated by anyone. Not Jose Canseco and not two guys he thought might have insulted him. Yet it was that very pride that took a blow a short time later, when he made a beeline for the food court of Scottsdale's mall, spotted Tabacco and Eddie Lara in line, and was stunned when they were cool to him, when they didn't return his enthusiasm, when they didn't smile, and when they were noncommittal at his suggestion of doing something later. He stayed around them for a short time, standing stiffly in the food line, but then he left and headed back to the Airport Hilton, where the big leaguers were. He went to his room—*his* room, not one he shared with two other guys—watched TV, flipping channels madly with the remote control, just as he had on those exceedingly boring days in Ceres when his friend and host Dan Marchy was working.

Miguel was floating between two baseball worlds now, not fitting in either. He was younger, far less wealthy, and far less worldly than the players he had watched on television and now shared a clubhouse with. And his old buddies, the kids he had passed on a dizzying ride up the ladder, were too insecure in their own situations to share in his excitement. *¿Yo qué voy a hacer?* Miguel said, *What am I to do?*" "What am I to do if they feel that way? I can't concern myself with that, I have to keep moving forward. They would do the same thing if they were in my place."

For eleven days, Miguel lived this way: suiting up for major league games in which he played well but was still working out the kinks. Then going home alone to watch television in his room.

And then on a Sunday as he was getting ready at the big league park, he was told that he was being reassigned to the minor leagues—to Double A Huntsville. Once given the news, Miguel found himself alone in the Athletics clubhouse, left to collect his things in silence and head back to the minor league facility.

Canseco, McGwire, and the rest of the Athletics were already out practicing for what would be a horrible regular season.

In reality, Miguel's making the Athletics was a long shot, though some said he stood a chance if he made a big impression. It wouldn't have been the first time in baseball history such a long shot came through. But missing two weeks of big league work ended that possibility. On the other hand, it wasn't as if Miguel was going to purgatory. Only the best of the best prospects go to Double A, especially the Southern League, with its fire-throwing hurlers and stud hitters. Miguel would get pushed where he was going, there was no question of that. But he would have loved to have taken a shot at changing people's minds.

The competitor in him sorely missed that. From the time he was in Medford, when Keith Lieppman had told the *Medford Daily Mail*, "This kid loves a challenge," Miguel had advanced that reputation wholeheartedly. The reason he loved a challenge was that his whole life had been a challenge, surviving had been a challenge, eating had been a challenge, his mother's death had been a challenge, being abandoned at thirteen was a challenge.

Compared to those things, latching on to the Athletics when they really didn't want him and then shooting through the minor leagues was just part of who he was. And because of who he was, what he lamented most about this truncated spring was losing out on twelve hundred dollars in major league meal money the Athletics would have paid him for those two weeks he missed.

His family could have used it.

For their part, the Athletics were happy. "He's got a bright future," said Howe, the day Miguel was reassigned. "He has a very accurate arm, great speed and baseball instincts. I think in a year or two we'll have a rose ready to blossom. He's in the bud stage right now."[4]

In 1996, when he was starring in Modesto, the Athletics had begun to receive inquiries about Miguel from other big league teams. Grieve's name also came up often. But the team wasn't interested.[5] And going into the 1997 season, they rated Miguel as their number-one prospect, with Grieve at number two. While Grieve had a higher overall batting average than Miguel, the organization rated Miguel higher because he was faster, had a stronger arm, and had greater defensive potential. Grieve's bat was his meal ticket, and he swung as few his age could ever hope to, but Miguel had a deeper game. In baseball parlance, Miguel was a "five-tool" player, someone who could hit for average, hit for power, run, and play great defense, and he had a great arm. So in April 1997, he and Grieve headed to Huntsville with great fanfare. In northern Alabama, near the Tennessee border and just west of the Appalachians, Huntsville is a community of 166,000 with a rich southern heritage.

As with Modesto, many great Athletics players have come through here, but unlike Modesto the staple of this place isn't produce, it's aerospace. Attracted by cheap land, the U.S. Army first changed the essence of this former cotton mill town when it built formidable structures to manufacture chemical weapons during World War II. As a result, Huntsville evolved into "Rocket City," the place where America's first rocket was built.[6] Since then, Huntsville-based aeronautics teams have been integral to NASA's space program. Indeed, Huntsville scientists were key players when America put the first men on the moon.

The result: This small Alabama town saw its population increase tenfold in forty years, bringing with it a surge in the local median income to the highest anywhere in the American South—$29,400. According to locals, so many scientists and engineers moved here over the years that less than half the local workforce is native to Alabama. Quite a recent history for a place that was the first capital of Alabama, where the secession movement took hold, and where Leroy Pope Walker—first secretary of war for Confederate leader Jefferson Davis—was born.

It was Walker, history books tell us, who issued the telegram order for southern troops to fire on Fort Sumter, triggering the Civil War.

Huntsville is one hundred miles south of Nashville and one hundred miles north of Birmingham. It is a long-time Southern League city where baseball is played in a humidity familiar to Miguel's Dominican upbringing. The strong ten-team circuit consists of teams strung across three states, with some of the best prospects in baseball.

The Huntsville Stars alone were loaded with Grieve and D. T. Cromer—who had been the MVP of the California League in 1996. Juan Encarnacion, no relation to Mario, but a power-house outfielder in the Detroit Tigers system, would launch rockets for the Jacksonville (Florida) Suns. Kerry Wood, a hard-throwing right-hander in the Chicago Cubs system, would confound hitters for the Orlando (Florida) Rays. Another Southern League star was Kris Benson, the first player selected in the 1996 amateur draft, who played as a Pittsburgh Pirates prospect with the Carolina Mudcats.

The season underway, Miguel passed through Memphis, Knoxville, and Chattanooga, Tennessee. He played in Greenville, North Carolina. He rode the bus into Florida, ate fast food in Jacksonville and Orlando. Then he swung back toward home base in Huntsville, passing through Mobile—the birthplace of Henry Aaron and Willie McCovey.

Miguel started the season slow, unlike his blazing start in Modesto, and seethed with barely controlled frustration as early May saw him still batting eighth in the order while barely cracking .200. Wood and Benson were representative of a level of intensity far and away superior to the leagues Miguel had known. Each step, each game was a difficult one and yet his manager, Mike Quade, came to figure that this Dominican boy had it all in him—all he needed was a little mileage.

"It's youth," Quade said of Miguel's early struggles. "He still doesn't know his strike zone as well as he should and I know he's frustrated. But it'll come. He's not going to disappoint anyone." [7]

Miguel was still only twenty, but it was easy to forget that, to get caught up in the excitement of a developing player who projects a special quality, makes you think he makes plays that you've never seen before. But even as Miguel struggled in the South, major league baseball was becoming more Latin than ever.

On opening day '97, there were fifty-eight Dominican players on major league rosters, twenty-eight from Puerto Rico, twenty from Venezuela, eight from Mexico, six from Cuba, five from Panama, and one each from Colombia and Nicaragua.[8]

In the Southern League, Dominican Juan Encarnacion was a phenomenal talent, who would hit .323 with 26 home runs and 90 RBI. Juan Melo, also of Bani and a San Diego Padres prospect playing for the Mobile (Alabama) Bay Bears, was on his way to becoming one of the top prospects in his organization. And virtually every league in the minor league circuit, from Rookie League to Triple A, was being dominated by Dominicans and other Latin players.

Some said kids like Miguel were filling slots that Americans weren't interested in any longer, that young Americans were being diverted, lured instead to basketball or football. Others said expansion to thirty teams had diluted an already tepid domestic talent pool.

But the greatest reason baseball was becoming such a Latin game could be found in Huntsville, Alabama, in mid-May.

In the span of two weeks in May, on the eve of his twenty-first birthday on May 25, Miguel hit 8 home runs and pushed his RBI total to 31. By June, he and the rest of the Stars were lighting up the Southern League. By late June he had 57 RBI. *Baseball America* listed Miguel as the number-six prospect in all of organized baseball, and he had exceeded 71 RBI by late July. Following his progress from day one, Lieppman was in Huntsville often now, checking on Miguel and Grieve. Miguel still could be a wild jumble of excellence and carelessness. He was blasting home runs but he was still making routine errors. The adjustments the Athletics sought in his game were elemental and subtle. Miguel was a natural performer, and he would blaze after balls that weren't his, cutting off a third baseman who was in better position. Or he would try to fly through the air while making a hard throw to first, instead of planting his feet and using his major league arm.

As Quade said, his mistakes were mistakes of youth. And then he would hit another home run, steal a base, drive in three and four runs in a game. Against Jacksonville one August night, he made twelve plays, spearing a line drive, barehanding a ball on the run and hurling it in time for an out, going deep in the hole time after time. By early August, he had passed the 20-home-run mark—a level that, if attained in the big leagues, would make him a rich man. As the Stars steamed toward the playoffs, they did so without Grieve—who was promoted to Triple A Edmonton in July after hitting .328 with 24 home runs and 108 RBI. Before a doubleheader on August 26, Miguel was hitting .275 with 22 home runs and 97 RBI. He was assured of cracking the 100-RBI plateau and was aiming to use the final days to ratchet up his average to .300.

It appeared the Athletics had a plan. Miguel would finish out the year and playoffs in Huntsville and be brought up to Oakland in September. The team wasn't thinking of activating him as a major leaguer, just having him work out with the big club to get a feel for the surroundings.

Everything seemed set, and then the Athletics hosted an afternoon game against the New York Yankees, a miserable, humiliating distillation of their season of woe, in which the Yankees pounded out 22 hits in an 18-run drubbing of the last-place Athletics. Soon after the season began, the team had gone straight into the toilet, undone in many ways. The A's had virtually no pitching, its starting rotation an ever-shifting collection of guys whose best skill was backing up third base. The team's ace, Aaron Small, won nine games. Mark McGwire was gone to the St. Louis Cardinals, traded when it became obvious he would leave town as soon as his contract was up. Canseco had been a bust, Berroa was gone, third baseman Scott Brosius had a horrendous year, there was no catcher to speak of, the infield was porous, the outfield was a mess, and the relief corps was atrocious, save for veteran Billy Taylor.

There were pockets of light, such as first baseman Jason Giambi and second baseman Scott Speizio—but not much else. And then there was Tony Batista. Miguel's best friend on the Athletics—despite their built-in rivalry—had seen all his promise go up in smoke. Having won the starting shortstop job for Opening Day, he was made a leadoff man when Howe had no recourse, but his bat had gone into hibernation in '97, and he crashed into a wall that only he could see. And as the Athletics began to go south by early May, exposed as a minor league team masquerading in major league uniforms, Batista was sent back to Edmonton to regain his shattered confidence.

The Athletics brought him back, but only because they didn't have much else. Alderson and his assistant Billy Beane—both smart baseball men—knew a stinking team when they saw one and, once McGwire was traded in late summer, had decided to start from zero with their farm system leading the way. That meant their interests were better served if Miguel and Grieve stayed put in the minors, learned all they could, and came on strong when they were ready.

In the meantime, the Athletics would take their licks. And that they did. By the Yankee game on August 26, they were heading for a 97-loss season and the worst attendance record in baseball. On a beautiful Indian summer afternoon, only fourteen thousand people watched the Yankees slaughter their A's. Batista was the casualty. With one out remaining, bad luck struck Batista again when he got caught in a rundown between first and second bases during a double play. As Batista tried to evade the tag for the final out, he stopped short and felt his left quadriceps twang like a guitar string. With pain shooting up and down his leg, Batista was unceremoniously tagged out to end the game.

In the trainer's room afterward, his leg tightened and resisted pressure. Batista couldn't run, stop on a dime, accelerate, or do any of the things he was paid to do. So he was placed on the fifteen-day disabled list and the decision makers in Oakland had yet another problem to add to their list.

Who would play short?

Bournigal, his Achilles sore and aching, was unavailable. Tilson Brito, a skinny Dominican utility guy, was also hurt and not very desirable anyway. Nobody in Edmonton provided inspiration. No time to make a trade.

All of a sudden, the phone rang in Mike Quade's office: Get the kid on a plane, Quade was told. Miguel was needed in Oakland.

Grandes Ligas.

The words shot through Miguel's mind as he flashed that "hundred-watt" smile of his. Miguel was in the land of Elvis, in between games of a twinight doubleheader between the Stars and the Memphis Chicks. He had played in the first game, colliding with teammate Dave Newhan on a play at second in which the legs of both men rattled hard against one another, leaving a welt and increasing soreness on Miguel's left knee. But Miguel didn't care. Quade told him to sit for the second game and he did, smiling the whole time, shaking his head, fidgeting, barely sitting still. Afterward, he raced to the team's motel, threw his things into a bag, and had a sleepless night before leaving at dawn for Oakland. Miguel had tried to reach his father long distance before he left Memphis, but the phone lines in the Dominican failed him. He stopped trying when he realized he might miss his plane.

It would be a week before they finally talked.

MIGUEL ARRIVED at the Coliseum at 2:30 P.M. on Wednesday, August 27, coming directly from Oakland Airport. Five hours before the game, there were no other players around when he surveyed the clubhouse, with its spotless green carpet and large cubicles with perfectly hung uniforms, all exactly in the same position—facing outward, with number and name in full view.

A cubicle had been set aside toward the back of the clubhouse for Miguel. Above it read: "Tejada 4."

On his new jersey, the number looked huge beneath his name. In the minor leagues, Miguel had never worn a jersey with his name on it—minor league teams generally don't stitch them because of tight budgets and the constant player movement. Moreover, the jerseys Miguel wore in Huntsville, Modesto, and Medford, looked like what they were—minor league uniforms. So when he took his major league jersey in his hand for the first time, the Athletics home whites were the brightest he had ever seen. The green and gold lettering on front and back were perfect.

At that moment, Miguel couldn't help himself—he smiled broadly, his normally serious eyes perfectly gleeful. There were no older players around to mock him, to chide him for acting like a boy, for being less than a man, less than a professional.

That would come later.

For now, he hadn't even noticed how hungry he was or how tired he was. He still hadn't eaten and had barely slept by the time he dumped his duffel bag on his assigned stool and tried on his new gear. For ninety minutes, he was virtually alone, save for the clubhouse employees scurrying around to make sure he had everything he needed. After trying his jersey, pants, socks, and spikes, he waited for other players to arrive. And when they did, Miguel was stunned at the sight of Batista. *"Tony no esta bien,"* he would say later in a deeply somber voice.

Tony is not well.

Batting barely over .200, being demoted to the minors early in the season, coming back to more failure, feeling the disapproval of his organization—all of it was sitting on Batista's chest like a boulder. It was amazing to see how promise could fade so completely in the game of baseball. But in reality, it was to be Batista's first full major league season and he obviously still had confidence problems to sort out. He wasn't much older than Miguel, really, although it had always seemed that way back on the island. Now, with Miguel standing before him in full Athletics uniform, Batista's last shreds of hope for this season went out the clubhouse door. It wouldn't be long before he emotionally forfeited his job to the young understudy. An off year was bad enough. But an off year finished with an injury creates a level of vulnerability that will frighten a player like Batista—a player not yet established. While Miguel felt for Batista he couldn't concern himself too much. He had to play. This was his chance and there would be someone—maybe even Batista—waiting to push him aside if he faltered.

So as older players were still milling about, Miguel got dressed and walked down the expansive tunnel leading to the field at the Oakland Coliseum. It was a luminous Bay Area afternoon, with a slight breeze and temperatures in the mid-seventies. With three hours before the 7:35 P.M. game, the first groups of fans began trickling into the stadium to hunt for autographs. As coach Ron Washington hit grounders at him, Miguel's legs seemed anchored and he strained to make his feet move. He tried to suppress the anxiety welling inside him, but he couldn't deny to himself how nervous he was. Really nervous. As he grunted beneath his breath on each grounder, the stands were filling up with one of the larger crowds to watch an Athletics game all season.

Most of them were wearing Yankee blue, a reflection of the many transplanted New Yorkers in northern California and the woeful state of the Athletics. There was also a huge contingent of Japanese and New York media at the game to witness another attempt by the Yankees to transform Japanese pitcher Hideki Irabu into a major league star. Going into the game, Irabu was 4–2 with a bloated ERA of 6.40 and had already been sent down to the minor leagues after being pulverized by major league hitting. By the time he reached Oakland, Irabu was perceived as a $12-million disaster, though it was still too early to render judgment. Mercurial owner George Steinbrenner had chosen to invest considerable money in Irabu after refusing to shell out the cash for Jimmy Key and John Wetteland—pitchers who helped the Yankees win a World Championship in 1996.

Missing the first half of the season as the Yankees bid for his services, Irabu had been rushed through a minor league stint during which he dominated young players on the way up. But after an initial, impressive victory against the Detroit Tigers, the bottom fell out. Irabu's mid-nineties fastball was fast all right, but it had little movement and was being drilled consistently. And when Irabu struggled to throw his breaking ball for strikes, he began getting used to whipping his neck around to watch long home runs. With each home run the New York media ravaged him and Steinbrenner, while the Yankees fell a little farther behind the Baltimore Orioles.

It was in this atmosphere that the huge New York/Japanese media throng descended on the Oakland Coliseum. Needless to say, Miguel was hardly the center of attention.

The few fans there to support the Athletics were aware of his debut, as was the Bay Area press, but interest in him played second billing to the New York Yankees. In fact, once the game was underway, anyone listening on radio would have had a difficult time knowing the contest was taking place in northern California. The most recognition Miguel received was from a single fan who shouted to him as he was stretching his bum leg on the field before the game. "Miguel, Miguel, do you remember me? I'm from Modesto. I used to talk to you in Modesto."

Not good with names, Miguel had no idea who it was and was too preoccupied to care. In fact, save for a few exceptions, he seemed like one of the few players who seemed preoccupied at all.

A young team that was constantly changing faces—Miguel

was the forty-sixth player to wear the green and gold in 1997—the Athletics were playing out the string of remaining games. And on this day, they clearly lacked the businesslike intensity of the Yankees. Indeed, these were two teams going in opposite directions. The Yankees still had a chance to catch the Orioles, while the Athletics were a band of kids, a few veterans, some castoffs, and a coaching squad struggling to keep them together.

Miguel, for one, didn't need to be motivated. Told to practice his swing before the game, he made his way over to a stationary tee where he whacked ball after ball to solidify his swing. He was one of the last players to leave the field and thirty minutes later one of the first ready for pregame introductions and the national anthem.

As a violinist named Dick Bright plowed through the Star Spangled Banner, Miguel stood alone down the left field line. And soon, he was in his position taking grounders while the Athletics starting pitcher Andrew Lorraine warmed up. By this point, his heart was racing. While by New York standards the crowd of 18,079 was meager, for Miguel it was huge, one of the biggest he had ever seen. Back home, *Los Barrancones* was alive with excitement, crowded around the television of a Tejada family friend, watching the game on a Yankees station that reaches the island. Miguel's agent had managed to get through to his dad and Daniel Tejada did the rest, spreading the word until "the entire barrio was going crazy," Miguel would say later.

At exactly 7:37 P.M. (PST), Miguel's major league career began with him poised in a deep crouch, his glove and throwing hands out and open, and his eyes fixed on Yankee leadoff hitter Derek Jeter. Miguel didn't even stand in the infield—his feet instead planted at the edge of the outfield grass.

On the Athletics telecast, announcer Greg Papa wondered if this meant Miguel was a little nervous. He was, but this was how he usually played, confident in his ability to cover a lot of ground. Then, Papa told Northern California viewers, "Miguel Tejada is here, let the future begin."

The Yankees were retired quietly and Miguel raced to the dugout with his new teammates while—to the wild cheering of fans—Irabu took the mound for the defending World Champions. The Yankees desperately needed Irabu to realize his potential. At six feet tall with a round face and the body of a pro bowler, Irabu didn't inspire awe as he took his warmups. In fact, concealed from the media, there was an intense desire on the part of opponents like the Athletics to crush him, to prove American superiority in the American game. One Athletics coach would later say, "Guys focus in even harder when they see this guy from Japan come over here with people saying he is going to dominate. It's like they go up an extra level. Like they're saying, 'Okay, motherfucker. You may have scared them hitters in Japan with that fastball but you ain't going to scare anyone here.' Yeah, he has a good fastball. He throws hard. But major league hitters are a different breed. It don't matter if you throw 190 mph. They aren't going to be scared.

"And if you throw that weak breaking ball like he throws, they're going to fucking kill it. You just can't come over here like that and expect to dominate. It don't happen that way. This motherfucker is the major leagues."

Irabu made quick work of leadoff hitter Jason McDonald. He then faced Mark Bellhorn, now playing third and recently promoted to the big leagues himself. Bellhorn was walked by Irabu and then promptly picked off. But then Dave Magadan, a journeyman outfielder and one of the few veterans on the club, singled sharply to right. Another journeyman player, Matt Stairs, followed. Irabu was mixing his straight fastball with a split-fingered pitch he was trying to perfect. Matt Stairs had 22 home runs when he stepped in against Irabu. And he had 23 two pitches later when he deposited one of Irabu's split-fingers into the right-field stands to give the Athletics a 2–0 lead. Miguel sat intently at the far end of the bench, near the bat rack, as Stairs rounded the bases. Because of his youth, Miguel would bat last this night—the ninth spot normally reserved for the weakest hitter on the club or for unproven rookies like him.

There were still several batters in front of him. But after Jason Giambi doubled, Brent Mayne walked, and Scott Spiezio singled, the score was suddenly 3–0 and Irabu was in a pitcher's nightmare, facing the prospect of getting pulled without completing a single inning. For Irabu, this would represent a new low. With center fielder Ernie Young next at bat, Yankees pitching coach Mel Stottlemyre and catcher Joe Girardi walked to the mound in an effort to calm their pitcher down.

As he had done in previous games, Irabu lost his temper

with each setback, cursing at Stairs's homer and breaking the cardinal rule of all pitchers by showing he was rattled. Miguel was now standing in the on-deck circle, simply trying to take it all in. Mayne was at third and Spiezio was at first. Irabu tried to jam Young with an inside pitch but Young hit a little grounder that no Yankee could get to in time for an infield hit.

And now Miguel Odalis Tejada would come up for his first major league at-bat against the defending World Champions, facing their most ballyhooed pitcher with the bases loaded and two outs.

As he walked to the plate, he crossed himself with his right hand, kicked at the dirt, and dug in against Irabu. Dan Marchy of Modesto had made the ninety-minute drive and was sitting in the stands smiling from ear to ear as Miguel took his stance. As always, he held his bat high with his left elbow almost up to his chin and his right elbow pointed skyward. Irabu's strategy was transparent. He threw a fastball low and away, hoping the kid would chase it. He didn't. Announcer Papa said, "I said at the beginning of this month that if Tejada shows some discipline both offensively and defensively he would be here."

Citing Miguel's Achilles' heel and foreshadowing a threat to his future, Papa then said, "He has occasionally gone out of the strike zone a little bit [with his swing]."

A second fastball was again low and away and all of a sudden Miguel was in a position hitters dream of: a 2-and-0 count with the bases loaded. Miguel stepped out of the batter's box to take a swing while Girardi ran out to talk to Irabu again. By this point, the Japanese "Nolan Ryan" had thrown 36 pitches and was hanging by a thread when Miguel stepped back into the batter's box. Irabu had no command of his pitches. His breaking balls simply weren't working. He was pitching as if he had no confidence in them at all. He was behind in the count and was only able to do one thing: throw the ball hard.

Here it comes, Miguel told himself. Fastball. It's going to be a fastball. Irabu went into his motion and heaved one as hard as he could. Miguel was right. It was a fastball and from behind home plate it looked as if it would be a perfect strike. Miguel's thick legs and muscular back seemed to whip in one perfect, fluid motion and he let loose a swing that made the Japanese media inhale in unison. The ball jumped off Miguel's bat with the unmistakable crack that makes crowds jump to their feet. From the broadcast booth, Papa screamed, "Oh, Miguel!"

If this were Hollywood, the ball would have sailed into the left-field stands for a grand slam in Miguel's first major league at-bat. His story would have been the first one featured on that evening's SportsCenter show on ESPN. His name would have come before the score in every game story written for the next day's New York tabloids. He would have become a trivia question.

But in real life, in a life where nothing is ever certain, there would be no Hollywood ending tonight. Miguel had gotten his pitch. It was right there for him to crush for a grand slam, but he was too anxious. He swung too early. He hit the ball off the end of the bat and after making everyone at the ballpark scream, Yankee left fielder Chad Curtis simply shifted his feet and caught the ball for the final out of the inning. Like everyone else, Curtis was momentarily fooled and began backtracking before he stopped and ran forward to catch Miguel's deceptive stroke.

Irabu had survived momentarily. And Miguel had learned a lesson of instincts—of how you can be betrayed by them. Being aggressive, being bold, playing full out all the time was what had gotten him off the island. He had always been able to count on his instincts, to rely on them for all the answers. But the baseball he was playing now was a baseball of deception, of subtleties, of precision, in which certain situations require that emotions be kept in check.

"You can see right now Miguel is a little juiced up," Billy Beane said as he watched the game from the broadcast booth. "He hit the ball off the end of the bat when he was ahead in the count. . . . Miguel has a tendency to get a little too excited. . . . That's one of the reasons we wanted to get him up here. To see how he would respond to playing in the bigger stadiums. To playing day in and day out at this level. Only time will tell."

Miguel would contend with this lesson again. It would dog his every moment on the field as he tried to make a lasting impression.

"It was my pitch," he would say later. "I thought I had hit it out."

With that moment gone, there was still a game to be played, and the way the Athletics were playing, no lead they held was safe—least of all on this night. The lead was threatened when third baseman Charlie Hayes hit a roller to Athletics second baseman Scott Spiezio. Yankee right fielder Paul O'Neill was on first and barreling toward Miguel as Spiezio speared the grounder and seemed to hesitate in throwing the ball to second base. But Miguel, his feet planted on the bag, finally caught the ball in the webbing of his glove as O'Neill headed for his legs. And at the last possible moment, he moved to one side and let O'Neill fly by him as he flung the ball toward first base to record the double play. It wasn't pretty, but it got the A's out of the inning.

"He never had a good grip on the ball and it almost popped out of his hand as he threw it," Papa said. "He had us all fluttering a bit as he turned it."

Miguel was a picture of unrefined brilliance—his every move played as if he were on the edge of a cliff. A short time later, when he covered second on a stolen base attempt, the catcher's throw careened off his glove as he tried to make a sweeping tag of the runner. Again, his timing was off just slightly because he was overanxious. Yet he never took his head out of the game.

In the fourth inning when he came up for the second time, Miguel followed Ernie Young's home run with a shot to the outfield that again looked like trouble but died before it was caught by Bernie Williams in center. Again, he was ahead in the count, and again, he swung too soon, squandering a chance to hammer the hapless Irabu some more. With Miguel still running toward the Athletics dugout after his out, Yankees manager Joe Torre was already walking toward Irabu. He had seen enough—Miguel's smash being the last straw. With the Yankees trailing now 5–3, Torre sent Irabu to the showers and called on one of his veterans, left-hander Kenny Rogers, to finish the job. Meanwhile, the many New York fans in attendance booed lustily, having only seen three and one-third innings from Irabu, whose ERA was now a skyhigh 7.07.

The score was Athletics 6, Yankees 4, when Miguel came to bat again in the bottom of the fifth. The Yankees had already figured him out. Having easily handled Irabu's 90-mph-plus fastball, Rogers would come at the kid with nothing but off-speed pitches. Unlike Irabu, the veteran left-hander had confidence on this night, a departure from the rest of his time in New York. Rogers showed Miguel a nasty curve, one that started up at his head and broke downward like a falling missile. Spiezio was on first, it was already 9:45 P.M., and Miguel was mystified as another big curveball went right past him for strike two.

He was barely able to foul off another curve when an even better one ate him alive, his bat flailing wildly as he swung at the third strike. On this at-bat, Miguel looked completely overmatched, his record for the evening now 0-for-3 and his average still stagnant at .000. Miguel knew the word was out on him. He would be thrown breaking balls until he proved he could hit them. By the seventh, he had no hits, and few balls had been hit in his direction until Charlie Hayes of the Yankees hit a grounder to his left, one that Miguel seemed sure to field and turn into an out.

But inexplicably, the ball rolled under his glove and into center field. Miguel seemed to get to the ball in plenty of time, but somehow he couldn't make the play. He would be lectured later for not getting his glove down. He would fail again at the plate in the bottom of the seventh, an 0–4 night. All in all, it would appear to be a horrible debut, until the ninth when the Yankees were threatening once again with one out and a runner on. The ball was hit to second base where Spiezio fielded it and threw unsteadily to Miguel, who caught the slightly errant play, held his ground before a charging runner, and completed an explosive, acrobatic double play—the Yankee threat was ended. Miguel raced back to the dugout to a loud ovation, seemingly shaking away all his butterflies.

He hoped to have another chance to finally get a hit, but center fielder Jason McDonald broke a tie game with an in-the-park home run ending the game in the bottom of the ninth. Afterward, Miguel served himself a plate of ribs and, in his underwear, signed a major league contract paying him the minimum $150,000 a year.

IT HADN'T BEEN PRETTY, and he went 0–5, but he was in the majors. Talking to reporters afterward, he was asked what his goals were now that he was in the big leagues. In his mind, in Spanish, he thought: My goal is to be the shortstop for the next ten years. What came out in English was: "I'm going to be the A's shortstop for ten years, maybe more." Across the country, readers of *USA Today* read: "SS Miguel Tejada, who should get much playing time in the final weeks of the season, isn't lacking in confidence. 'I'm going to be the A's shortstop for 10 years, maybe more,' said Tejada, 0-for-5 in his debut Wednesday."

Arriving in Los Angeles the next day for a two-game set against the Dodgers, Bournigal picked up the paper to see his worst fears realized. Reading it, Bournigal thought: Miguel, a rookie who has done nothing, is making a prediction like that.

In the hypersensitive world of big league clubhouses, Bournigal knew this wasn't good. Miguel could get a reputation, the kind that will make him easy prey for printed digs like the one in *USA Today*. It's one thing to be an established player and say things like that, but a kid like Miguel?

Outside baseball, such a concern might seem overblown. But Miguel took flak the minute he arrived at Dodger Stadium for an interleague game. The "ten-year" comment stuck in people's minds. You just don't play in the big leagues for ten years, it's not that easy. Miguel was upset and stuck close to Bournigal. "I told you, you have to be careful what you say," Bournigal said. "It's easy to be misunderstood." Bournigal did a lot of explaining that day.

On top of that, Miguel had to face Hideo Nomo, the other famed Japanese hurler. In 1995, Nomo had been the NL Rookie of the Year and still could confound hitters with his strange, freeze-frame pitching motion, in which he threw his arms over his head, stopped, turned his back and arched his leg, stopped, and then threw at 90-mph-plus. Batting ninth, Miguel didn't come up until the top of the third. The first time Nomo wound up in that wild motion of his, Miguel decided to let a fastball go by for a strike. Nomo then threw a ball. Toeing the rubber, Nomo wound up again and fired another fastball low. This time Miguel swung, cracking one down the right-field line where fellow Dominican Raul Mondesi gave chase. Miguel flew around first base and instinctively looked toward Ron Washington to see if he had the green light to try for third—he did. Churning around second, Miguel gritted his teeth and gave it the gas knowing Mondesi had the strongest arm in baseball. And sure enough, playing like a true Dominican, Mondesi launched a bomb toward third and actually made the play closer than it should have been.

Miguel had his first hit in the *Grandes Ligas.* A triple.

The Athletics retrieved the ball and gave it to him at the end of the game, a 7–1 Athletics loss. Returning to his hotel suite in the Sheraton Grande, on 3rd and Figeroua streets in downtown Los Angeles, Miguel trudged through a sweeping atrium with an enormous oil painting called "In the Absence of Paradise." Turning on the lights to his room, Miguel was awestruck after his first hit and, admiring the lights of Los Angeles, said, "Man, what would my father think if he saw this."

Miguel was feeling sentimental on this night and even allowed himself to think about his life and what he'd been through—something he rarely does. He cracked open a can of Heineken from the hotel minibar, leaned back on his king-size bed, and was enveloped by the smell of lilacs in a room of warm rosewood furniture and stylish, contemporary art. As he always does, Miguel turned in soon after the game. He fell asleep with the television on and missed himself on ESPN.

The next day, he awakened with a mission.

He needed clothes.

And with the money to buy them he set about to find the "Latino section of town." When the concierge asked him if he could be a little more specific, Miguel said that some ballplayers told him of a Latino clothing store. The Anglo man had no idea what Miguel was talking about. But luckily for him, the Mexican bellhop did—he pointed Miguel to the corner of Santee Street and Olympic Boulevard, the garment district of L.A., and soon Miguel was walking the streets with blaring boom boxes playing before open store fronts. Mexican shopkeepers spoke to Miguel in Spanish while showing him the kind of clothes a young man would wear to a disco. Soon, Miguel pulled out a pair of hundred-dollar bills to buy three shirts and two pairs of pants. Clutching his new purchases over his shoulder Miguel suddenly craved Latin food. So against his better judgment, he entered a hole in the wall where they serve "fast Mexican food." He ordered a big plate of meat with rice and beans, eating sheepishly and appearing self-conscious.

He soon explained why: "If the players on the team saw me

eating in a place like this, they would really give me a hard time," he said. "They would say, 'What are you doing eating here?' "

Miguel went back to his hotel to prepare for that night's game, no longer thinking of clothing but of the exploding curves and wicked changeups he had faced in his first two games. Ismael Valdes, the heralded Mexican hurler, would be Miguel's opponent that night. Since Miguel had drilled Nomo's fastball for a triple the night before, Valdes fed Miguel a steady diet of breaking balls, frustrating him until Miguel dug in for his at-bat in the sixth. It was then that Valdes tried to go inside on Miguel and fired a fastball that flew at Miguel's head. Rocking backward, barely able to get his hand up, he blocked the path of the ball but got drilled on his forearm. Walking to first, Miguel's arm throbbed but he refused to give himself away. He didn't score, but that beaning had angered him. Not the kind of anger that would make him drop his bat and fight. The kind of anger that would make him want to do something on the field.

Valdes was gone by the time Miguel came up in the eighth with no one on. Left-hander Scott Radinsky was pitching. The Dodgers were up 3–2 when Radinsky quickly got two strikes on Miguel. After a ball, he was waiting for Radinsky to come after him. He did, but with a low fastball near knee level.

Miguel's likeness was on the Jumbotron in left field, wearing a beaming smile that expressed just how he felt when he swung and golfed a long fly ball that flew in a straight line toward left field. It was his first major league home run.

With the ball landing in the left-field bleachers, Miguel flew around the bases. But as he neared home, he reached into his jersey, pulled out the eagle-shaped necklace he always wore and pressed it to his lips.

Pointing it skyward, he looked up as well—a tribute to his mother.

In the next half innning, the homer was replayed on the Jumbotron, a little snippet of film that froze as Miguel crossed the plate, his eyes looking to the heavens. The image hung for a moment, then faded to black before giving way to an ad.

It was just another moment to Dodger fans but that it happened at all, considering Miguel's roots, was a small miracle. But Miguel wasn't through. In the 10th inning of a tied game,

Miguel came up again with runners in scoring position. He blasted a single to right, putting the Athletics up 4–3. Miguel was the hero of the moment. But he played for the 1997 Athletics, a team that found new ways to lose every day. And in this one, T. J. Mathews, the pitcher the Athletics got for Mark McGwire, blew the lead, the game, and Miguel's performance.

Dressing in silence afterward, Miguel was questioned by reporters. This time he was certain to make no declarative statements, though he did explain that when Valdes hit him he "felt emotion."

The Athletics would go on to Denver and then return for a home series against San Francisco. In between Giants games was a day off, and Miguel used the time to shop for family members, descending on an outlet store in the East Bay community of San Leandro where he would buy five hundred dollars worth of dress shoes for himself and boxes of discounted sneakers for his family. He would go to another mall and buy more skin-tight clothing and inexpensive jewelry.

He was unfazed at having made his first error as a big leaguer the night before. He pulled out his address book and dialed Marchy's number in Modesto, where Tabacco was staying for the 1997 season. "¡Estoy en la gloria!" he crowed through the phone.

I am in my glory!

He told Tabacco of the clothes he had bought, of the food he had eaten, of the hotels he had slept in, and of the ballparks and pitchers he had seen. Hanging up, all seemed forgiven from their moment of tension in Arizona. Miguel then noticed that his red light was flashing on his phone and checking messages he heard a familiar voice on the other end. "Mother-Foy-Yay!!" It was Ben Grieve.

Grieve had been brought up exactly one week after Miguel after tearing up the Pacific Coast League. Once they connected, Grieve came up to Miguel's room and the two greeted each other warmly. "How much did you pay for that jacket, Miguel, ten dollars?" Grieve asked. "Hey Ben, you're not going to believe the pitching up here," Tejada replied. At that point, Grieve was all ears, and Miguel excitedly explained to him how tough the pitchers were in the big leagues. "They throw all breaking balls."

Grieve paused for a moment and said: "Well, don't swing."

Miguel then corrected himself. "No, Ben. They throw them for strikes."

"Ohhhh."

After a few moments, Grieve smiled amiably and said: "Hey, so you're going to be the A's shortstop for ten years, huh?" Miguel's faced turned sour and he gave a disgusted wave. "Man," Grieve said. "I think that way, but I would never say it to a reporter. Never."

Interviewed by the Athletics broadcast team the next day, Grieve spoke of being happy to be where he was, of trying his best, and of respecting the veterans on the team. The announcers were charmed, and Grieve followed it up by lashing 3 doubles for 6 RBI against the Giants, a phenomenal performance that drew nationwide attention.

Grieve was on his way, and for a time, Miguel held up his end, too—batting .270 in his first 15 games with 9 RBI. The highlight of that run came on September 10, during an afternoon game, when Miguel blasted a three-run homer off Pat Hentgen of the Toronto Blue Jays—the 1996 winner of the American League Cy Young Award. But as always, Miguel was alone in his room again after that game, celebrating on his own. And soon, he would feel totally alone on the field.

Falling into a horrible slump, he would barely hit again after the Hentgen triumph. During one stretch, he would go 0–22, flailing wildly at breaking balls, reaching and lurching for off-speed pitches, frustrating Athletics coaches with his overly anxious batting style. As the season came to a close, Miguel's batting average plummeted, and going into a final weekend series against the Seattle Mariners, he was hitting only .202. Howe decided enough was enough, and sat Miguel most of the last week to keep his average from dipping below .200. Miguel was philosophical about his slump. "Those things happen sometimes in baseball."

And after the final game at Seattle's Kingdome, he rode away from the stadium with Grieve, both of them annoyed at the hordes of autograph seekers who dogged their every step until they reached their vehicle.

"You know, when I go home, I'm going to have all these people asking me for balls or autographs. You know it's going to happen," Grieve said.

Miguel considered Grieve's comment and answered: "Yeah but Ben, when I go home I'm going to have all these people saying, 'Miguel, can I have some money? Miguel, can I have some shoes? Miguel, can I have some food.' "

The two rode together in silence the rest of the way into downtown Seattle. Under perpetually gray skies they said their good-byes and left—Grieve for Texas, Miguel for *Los Barrancones.*

With him were eight huge duffel bags packed with twenty to thirty pair of baseball spikes, eighteen bats, twenty-seven balls, scores of shirts, pants, and other baseball gear, and stacks of wristbands in plastic wrappers. Before the season was over, Miguel had gone from stall to stall, collecting shoes, hats, and whatever other baseball things his teammates could spare— they were constantly getting all new gear anyway, Miguel thought. He would give much of it to Soto.

For his brothers, Miguel took home a Sega Genesis game and also transported three portable CD players, twenty-eight caps, canisters of Right Guard aerosol and Wizard Morning Rain air freshener for his new house. Miguel would need two cabs to get it all to Seattle's airport and the help of an amazed porter. Miguel didn't want to fly back to Oakland first on his way home, he wanted to leave that night and he did—on a red-eye with Batista and Tilson Brito. Batista was somber and bitter on the ride home, telling all who would listen that Miguel was "the man" now and that he was history. Miguel didn't respond one way or the other. He had dressed to the nines in a white suit, somewhat reminiscent of *Miami Vice,* and another one of those tight black shirts. It didn't matter to Miguel that his new clothes would get wrinkled on the ten-hour flight home, he wanted to look good when he arrived

The group flew together to New York, where they went their separate ways, and Miguel found himself talking to a young man who was a Pittsburgh Pirates prospect from Santo Domingo. A lady sitting next to them overheard their conversation and asked Miguel what level he was playing at.

"*Grandes Ligas, doña.*

"You've heard of *Grandes Ligas,* haven't you?"

Miguel traveled the rest of the way alone. Soto was waiting for him at the airport. As he had done in Seattle, Miguel hired an extra cab to follow him all the way back to Bani—at a cost of fifty dollars. He and Soto chatted easily on the ride, Soto told him not to worry about the slump and Miguel felt right at home. Driving through Bani's street's he grew suddenly nervous and fidgeted in his seat as Soto began the last bumpy part of the ride, turning down a packed alley that led into *Los Barrancones*.

It was a sight to see: the entire street, jammed with people who had waited for hours, Miguel's neighbors running after Soto's car as Miguel rolled down the window screaming, "*¡Mi gente! Mi gente!*"

My people, My people.

Dozens rushed up to Miguel as he climbed out of Soto's car, others seemed nervous and tentative. Miguel struck a profound contrast with the people of his barrio in his new clothes and dress shoes. He embraced his shirtless father and was surrounded by the people he had always known.

He walked from house to house, shaking hands like a presidential candidate. And while dozens of people milled about, they now kept their distance, leaving room between them and the big leaguer. It was the biggest day ever in *Los Barrancones*.

The excitement didn't subside for a few weeks, until Miguel left for another winter league season. It was then that Miguel learned that Soto and the Athletics had parted company—a dispute over signing bonuses. Soto always wants the most for his players, and after a time, that ran at cross purposes with the Athletics, Abreu said. So forevermore, Soto would recommend players to the team but he wouldn't be on their payroll.

Miguel felt this parting on a personal level but he did and said nothing. It was business. Another season in Santiago resulted in another league championship and another title in the Caribbean World Series, in which he hit a home run against Mexico in the final game. During the off-season, Batista left the Athletics—claimed in an expansion draft by the new Arizona Diamondbacks. As insurance, the team signed journeyman shortstop Kurt Abbott to a one-year contract, in case Miguel needed another year to get ready.

But there would be no visa problems this year. Miguel would arrive on time in Arizona in February 1998. He would fly first-class to Phoenix and ready himself to compete against Abbott, a competition that was scuttled almost immediately when Abbott jammed his wrist. So on the first game of spring training,

Miguel was the starting shortstop. And this year, things were different. Miguel was hitting, blasting a 3-run homer off Orel Hershiser of the San Francisco Giants in a game in which he had 6 RBI.

His play at short was solid. He was refining his game and the press was noticing. Steve Kettmann of the *San Francisco Chronicle*, wrote, "Miguel Tejada's eyes have a burning, ornery quality that tells you he will never be satisfied until he is an All Star. But Tejada, 21, has learned patience. The way he sees it, he is going to be turning heads in big league ballparks sooner or later."

By the middle of spring training he was leading the team in RBI and batting over .300. While the team had planned to use Abbott as the starter, his wrist wasn't healing, and Miguel was filling the gap.

"He just keeps doing the job," said Howe, who said he had made up his mind the year before about keeping Miguel in Triple A for another year.[9] Miguel was riding a wave of Latin players growing stronger since the 1997 World Series when, for the first time, Spanish-speaking men were the key to a World Championship. Indeed, when Edgar Renteria of Colombia knocked in the winning run for the Florida Marlins and Livan Hernandez of Cuba was named Series MVP, it was a big step toward erasing the memory of the Washington Senators and of an English-only San Francisco Giants clubhouse.

The bottom line in baseball is winning, and there could be no denying who won when Renteria got his fateful hit off the Cleveland Indians. If the Indians had won, the likely MVP would have been Sandy Alomar, Jr., of Puerto Rico. Even the coverage in the press changed, a shift exemplified in the words of Claire Smith of *The New York Times:* "How delirious is the fever throughout Latin America when it comes to *beisbol?* While the addresses of this year's World Series participants read Cleveland and Miami, the sights, the sound, the flavors are rising up from the Americas south of the United States."

Soon after the '97 season, Pedro Martinez, a Dominican, signed the richest contract in the history of baseball—$12 million a year. Cuban Orlando "El Duque" Hernandez signed for $6 million with the New York Yankees. The brother of World Series MVP Livan Hernandez, El Duque made headlines and helped the Yanks to a World Series, shutting out the Cleveland Indians in a crucial playoff game.

The world Miguel was about to enter was different from the one he had joined less than five years before. At the start of the 1998 season, it was his picture that graced the cover of the Athletics media guide. And the confidence he felt at the end of the 1997 season, despite his slump, was born of a feeling that has grown within him year after year. Sportswriters saw it in his "ornery eyes."

Miguel began to taste his dream in 1998, leading the Athletics with 14 RBI in spring training.

But then, fate stepped in again.

On a freak play on March 21, while trying to field a grounder, Miguel jammed the middle finger of his glove and felt a small pop. The Athletics held him out for a game, had him X-rayed, and were deeply disappointed to find he had another hairline fracture. He'd be out for at least three weeks.

Opening Day was one week away.

And when the Athletics faced Pedro Martinez and the Boston Red Sox before a national audience, Miguel was stranded in Arizona, rehabbing his hand. He had again been named the Athletics' number-one prospect. *Baseball America* had once again selected him the best shortstop in minor league baseball.

But it didn't matter. He had cried that night of his injury, knowing his dream of major league stardom would be delayed just a little longer.

"This is my saddest day in baseball," he told the *San Francisco Chronicle*.

It would take a while, but his resolve hardened. He threw himself into his rehabilitation. A few days later he said: "I'll be back. I'm know I'm going to make it. I know I'm going to be the one."

He wouldn't be alone. By Opening Day '98, a new crop of rookie leaguers were in Arizona and Florida. Meanwhile, every team in baseball was training prospects back in the Dominican. And with Sammy Sosa leading the way, the profile of Latin players grew even greater, cementing the obvious: that this is the Golden Age of Latin players in baseball, the era when they will finally take their rightful place in the game.

Miguel was no longer just a dreamer. His was the face of a new future.

And so it goes on, in barrios like *Los Barrancones*, determined boys playing baseball every day. They are Dominican and Puerto Rican, Venezuelan and Colombian, Panamanian and Cuban, Mexican and Nicaraguan. They are out there and they are part of one story—a story that begins when those boys pick up a stick, dig their toes into the scalding dirt, and stand ready for their pitch. In an instant, their dreams and the ball will come hurtling at them. So with hope and resolve, and with all their hearts, they will swing as hard as they can.

EPILOGUE

MIGUEL TEJADA achieved his dream in 1998. On May 29, while the Athletics were in Kansas City, Miguel got the call to rejoin the team. He had missed six weeks of action following the injury to his hand, a period of time that was extended when he removed his splint too soon and began taking batting and infield practice.

The Athletics had been frustrated and mystified when X-rays kept showing little progress. Then they realized Miguel was practicing before his hand had truly healed. By May 29, he was raring to go and showed it: He hit 2 doubles and and 3 RBI in that first weekend series.

While the Athletics had hoped to play Miguel in Triple A for all or part of 1998, his path was cleared when journeyman infielder Kurt Abbott lost the confidence of the organization by making 11 errors in 28 games.

Soon Abbott was gone and Miguel was officially named the starting shortstop of the Oakland Athletics at the tender age of twenty-two. His ascent had been swift and he threw himself into the competition. Now, there was no doubt that he belonged, that he was a big leaguer. But he still had a way to go.

In one game against Detroit, Miguel lashed 2 home runs.

On some plays, he looked like a wizard, making the highlight reels of ESPN with an eye-popping catch or throw. "He throws at Mach speed," said Athletics first baseman, Jason Giambi. But experienced pitchers still frustrated Miguel, handcuffing him with off-speed pitches. And while he was making fewer errors, they were still a problem.

Meanwhile, the Athletics were in total rebuilding mode, starting a pack of twenty-something-Generation-X players where twenty-seven-year-old Giambi was one of the older starters on the team. Ben Grieve would do as he has always done—make everything look easy. Starting fast, Grieve was undoubtedly the top rookie in the American League and was rewarded for it. After hitting .288 with 18 home runs and 89 RBI, Grieve was voted American League Rookie of the Year.

The Athletics finished last again, 74–88. After the season, Sandy Alderson left the club to take a top job under Baseball Commissioner Bud Selig. Art Howe was signed on to continue as manager, and the team was committed to staying in Oakland for at least three more years and began preparing itself for the spring of 1999.

The influence of Latin players and of the Athletics Dominican operations will be felt in 1999. For the first time ever, six Latins are invited to play in their major league Spring Training. Miguel will be joined by Ramon Hernandez and Mario Encarnacion, who had great years at Double A Huntsville; Jose Ortiz, a shortstop who was drawing raves for his speed and skill; Luis Vizcaino, a pitcher who not only is from Bani, but grew up a short distance from Miguel in *Los Barrancones;* and Juan Perez, the half-Dominican, half-Haitian lefty who finished 1998 in Triple A.

The rest of Miguel's group haven't fared so well. Arturo "Tabacco" Paulino was released by the Athletics in 1998. So was Jose Soriano and Juan Polanco. It's hard to believe now that all were rated above Miguel at one time. Juan Dilone had also been cut loose by the Athletics and was picked up the San Francisco Giants organization. The future of Jose Castro, another former rising star, was up in the air as 1998 came to a close. Club officials said they weren't sure what they would do with Castro after he hit only .163 in Double A Huntsville.

But one kid did manage to hang on for another day. Eddie

Lara opened some eyes in 1998 by hitting over .280 at Class A Visalia and was still with the team.

And Miguel? From late May until the end of the '98 season, he hit .233 with 11 home runs and 45 RBIs with the Athletics. He lived in a luxury apartment complex near the Oakland Coliseum. He bought a fancy sports car. He took a mountain of baseball cleats and clothes back to Enrique Soto and his family.

He hadn't torn up the league like Grieve had, but he showed that stardom in him. Whether he does or doesn't ever reach that potential, his life is a victory. He had gotten out of *Los Barrancones* and has a bright, limitless future ahead of him.

And he had stayed true to himself, to the kind of decent person his mother wanted him to be. No matter what happens from this moment forward, no one can ever take that away from him.

Buena suerte, Miguel.

—MARCOS BRETÓN and JOSÉ LUIS VILLEGAS
Sacramento, California, December 1998

NOTES

CHAPTER TWO

1. Interview with Sandy Alderson, March 17, 1996.
2. Source: Major League Baseball.
3. Interview with Mario Soto, July 5, 1993.
4. Pedro Gomez, "Mondesi Was in Team's Camp," *Sacramento Bee,* June 13, 1997, p.C6
5. Interview with George Bell, June 17, 1993.
6. Interview with Julio Franco, May 12, 1993.
7. James D. Cockroft, *Latinos in Beisbol: The Hispanic Experience in the Americas* (New York: Franklin Watts, 1996), p. 159.
8. Press conference at Qualcomm Stadium, San Diego, September 15, 1998.
9. Interview with Tony Oliva, June 10, 1993.
10. Interview with Alderson.
11. Interview with Dick Balderson, September 20, 1996.
12. Milton Jamail, "Government Quota Creates Bottleneck for Players," *Baseball America,* March 15, 1998, p. 12.
13. Source: Major League Baseball.
14. Interview with Alex Rodriguez, March 12, 1996.
15. William Brubaker, "Hey Kid, Wanna Be a Star?—Latin Players Scouted for the United States Big Leagues," *Sports Illustrated,* July 13, 1981, pp. 64–66.
16. Tom Weir, "Hispanics' Big League Breakthrough," *USA Today,* September 29, 1997, p. 1.
17. Milton Jamail, "Extension of Draft Closed Door on Open Market," *USA Today,* August 15, 1991, p. 51.
18. Milton Jamail, "Astros Led Expedition into Talent-rich Country," *USA Today,* August 15, 1991, p. 52.
19. Ibid.

20. Alan M. Klein, *Sugarball: The American Game, the Dominican Dream* (New Haven, CT: Yale University Press, 1991), p. 64.
21. Ibid., p. 65.
22. Interview with Luis Rosa, June 25, 1993.
23. Interview with Rosa.
24. Larry Ronter, "Dominican Sex Scandal Mars Big League Dreams," *The New York Times*, December 11, 1997, p. A1.
25. Klein, p. 54.
26. Interview with Bill Murray, executive director of Baseball Operations, August 19, 1993.
27. Interview with Alderson.
28. Interview with Billy Harford, September 25, 1996.
29. Interview with Enrique Soto, September 30, 1998.
30. Interview with Balderson.
31. Interview with Felipe Alou, July 20, 1993.
32. Interview with Mario Soto.
33. "Martinez Sees Green in Red Sox," Associated Press, November 11, 1997.
34. Interview with Alou.
35. Interview with Juan Marichal, July 2, 1993.
36. Robert Peterson, *Only the Ball Was White: A History of Legendary Black Players and All-Black Professional Teams* (Old Tappan, NJ: Prentice-Hall, 1970), pp. 263–302.
37. Ibid.
38. Interview with Alou.
39. Interview with Marichal.

CHAPTER THREE

1. Klein, p. 56.
2. Interview with Ron Plaza, Sept. 23, 1996.

CHAPTER FOUR

1. Source: Oakland Athletics.
2. Interview with Ron Plaza, March 20, 1998.
3. Interview with Luis Martinez, March 14, 1998.
4. Interview with Plaza, 1998.
5. Interview with Hector Rodriguez, July 2, 1993.
6. Interview with Martinez.
7. Interview with Raymond Abreu, March 14, 1998.
8. Interview with Hector Rodriguez.
9. Interview with Tomas Silverio, March 14, 1998.
10. Ibid.
11. Ibid.
12. Ibid.
13. Howard J. Wiarda and Michael J. Kryzanek, *The Dominican Republic: A Caribbean Crucible* (Boulder, CO: Westview Press, 1982), p. 134.

14. Klein, p. 12.
15. Wiarda and Kryzanek, p. xvii.
16. Jan Knippers Black, *The Dominican Republic: Politics and Development in an Unsovereign State* (Boston: Allen and Unwin, 1986), p. 17.
17. Wiarda and Kryzanek, p. 29.
18. Ibid, p. 29.
19. Rob Ruck, *The Tropic of Baseball: Baseball in the Dominican Republic* (New York: Carroll & Graf, 1991), p. 22.
20. Ibid., p. 24.
21. Ibid., p. 27.
22. Ibid., p. 30.
23. Ibid., p. 42.
24. Black, p. 32.
25. Klein, p. 13.
26. Wiarda and Kryzanek, p. 17.
27. Black, p. 58.
28. Klein, p. 9.
29. Black, p. 58.
30. Interview with Hector Rodriguez.
31. Interview with Silverio.
32. Ibid.
33. Interview with Plaza.
34. Ibid.
35. Interview with Abreu.
36. Interview with Plaza.
37. Interview with Silverio.
38. Interview with Martinez.
39. Interview with Silverio.

CHAPTER FIVE

1. *The Baseball Encyclopedia: The Complete and Definitive Record of Major League Baseball*, 9th edition (New York: Macmillan, 1993), p. 749.
2. Jules Tygiel, "Black Ball," in *Total Baseball* (New York: Warner Books, 1989), p. 550.
3. Samuel O. Regalado, *Viva Baseball: Latin Major Leaguers and Their Special Hunger* (The University of Illinois Press, 1998), p. 10.
4. *The Baseball Encyclopedia*, p. 749.
5. Ibid.
6. Peter C. Bjarkman, *Baseball with a Latin Beat* (McFarland & Company Inc., 1994), p. 120.
7. Ibid., p. 198.
8. Regalado, p. 28.
9. Cockroft, p. 13.
10. Peterson, pp. 311 and 323.
11. Michael M. Oleksak and Mary Adams Oleksak, *Beisbol: Latin Americans and the Grand Old Game* (Indianapolis, IN: Masters Press, 1991), p. 27.
12. Ibid., p. 27.
13. Donn Rogosin, *Invisible Men: Life in Baseball's Negro Leagues* (New York: Atheneum, 1985), p. 159.
14. Bob Addie, *Sports Writer* (Sparta, NJ: Accent Publishing, 1980), p. 176.

15. Bjarkman, p. 203.
16. Ibid., p. 201.
17. John Krich, *El Beisbol: Travels Through the Pan-American Pastime* (New York: The Atlantic Monthly Press, 1989), p. 157.
18. Interview with Juan Gonzalez, May 12, 1993.
19. Cockroft, p. 14.
20. Jules Tygiel, *Baseball's Great Experiment: Jackie Robinson and His Legacy* (New York: Oxford University Press, 1983), p. 25.
21. Bjarkman, p. 386.
22. Oleksak and Oleksak, p. 45.
23. Collie Small, "Baseball's Improbable Imports," in *The Saturday Evening Post*, August 2, 1952, p. 28.
24. Ibid.
25. Regalado, p. 29.
26. National Baseball Library, file on Adolfo Luque, dated January 21, 1923.
27. Peter C. Bjarkman, "First Hispanic Star? Dolf Luque, Of Course," in *Baseball Research Journal* 19, 1990, pp. 28–32.
28. John B. Holway, *Blackball Stars: Negro League Pioneers* (New York: Carroll & Graf Publishers/Richard Gallen, 1992), p. 59.
29. Peterson, p. 212.
30. Ibid.
31. Oleksak and Oleksak, p. 22.
32. Peterson, p. 243.
33. Oleksak and Oleksak, p. 34.
34. Peterson, p. 245.
35. Oleksak and Oleksak, p. 23.
36. Holway, p. 125.
37. Interview with Vic Power, June 24, 1993.
38. Interview with Orlando Cepeda, April 9, 1993.
39. Orlando Cepeda with Bob Markus, *High and Inside: Orlando Cepeda's Story* (South Bend, IN: Icarus Press, 1983), p. 17.
40. Bjarkman, p. 148.
41. Ibid.
42. Tygiel, p. 56.

CHAPTER SIX

1. Larry Moffi and Jonathan Kronstadt, *Crossing the Line: Black Major Leaguers, 1947–1959* (Iowa City: University of Iowa Press, 1994), p. 42.
2. Ibid., p. 43.
3. Minnie Minoso with Herb Fagen, *Just Call Me Minnie: My Six Decades in Baseball* (Champaign, IL: Sagamore Publishing, 1994).
4. Interview with Minnie Minoso, June 12, 1993.
5. Interview with Chico Carrasquel, June 12, 1993.
6. Ibid.
7. Ibid.
8. Ibid.
9. John C. Hoffman, "Baseball's New 'Mr. Shortstop,' " *Colliers*, April 28, 1951, p. 82.
10. Ibid.
11. Interview with Carrasquel.
12. Ibid.

13. Ibid.
14. Interview with Vic Power, June 24, 1993.
15. Dan Daniel, "Weiss Refuses to Curtail TV at the Stadium," *New York World Telegram and Sun*, July 18, 1952.
16. Interview with Power.
17. Dan Daniel in the *New York World Telegram and Sun*, April 16, 1954.
18. Interview with Power.
19. Interview with Jose Pagan, June 24, 1993.
20. Interview with Alou.
21. Interview with Alou.
22. Interview with Pagan.
23. Robert H. Boyle, "Time of Trial for Alvin Dark," *Sports Illustrated*, July 6, 1964, p. 26.
24. Cepeda, p. 36.
25. Interview with Alou.
26. Interview with Jim Ray Hart, June 18, 1993.
27. Interview with Alou.
28. Ron Fimrite, "The Heart of a Giant," *Sports Illustrated* "Classic," Fall 1991, p. 59.
29. Interview with Pagan.
30. Interview with Alou.
31. "A Giant Issue," *Newsweek*, August 17, 1964, p. 54.
32. Ibid.
33. Interview with Tony Oliva, June 10, 1993.
34. Interview with Luis Mayoral, October 9, 1996.
35. Jimmy Cannon in the *New York Post*, March 16, 1972.
36. Jerome Holtzman, *Chicago Sun-Times*, October 15, 1971.
37. Interview with Oliva.
38. Ibid.
39. Ibid.
40. Jerry Izenberg in the *Binghamton Press*, 1973.
41. Bill Madden, "Collecting Memories," *The Sporting News*, May 28, 1984, p. 11.
42. *USA Today*, July 7, 1995.

CHAPTER SEVEN

1. Interview with J. P. Naumes, March 21, 1998.
2. Greg Stiles, "Young Shortstop Ticket for A's," *Medford Mail Tribune*, June 14, 1995, p. B1.
3. Oakland Athletics 1996 Media Guide.
4. Ibid.
5. Stiles, Ibid.
6. Interview with Martinez.
7. Source: Naumes Inc. Website.
8. Interview with Bobbi Naumes, March 21, 1998.
9. Ibid.
10. Ibid.
11. Greg Stiles, "In Minors, New Bat Gets Mixed Views," *Medford Mail Tribune*, June 27, 1995, p. B1.
12. Greg Stiles, "A's Exec Pays Visit to Miles," *Medford Mail Tribune*, July 7, 1998, p. B1.
13. *Tribune*, July 7, 1998.

14. Alan Schwarz, "Teams Often Get Zonked by International Signing," *Baseball America*, March 2–15, 1998, p. 9.
15. Interview with Dan Kilgras, March 6, 1998.
16. Interview with Jill Ramirez, March 25, 1998.
17. Interview with Ramirez.
18. Interview with J. P. Naumes.
19. Interview with Ron Plaza, March 20, 1998.
20. Interview with Jose Paulino, March 5, 1996.
21. Interview with Paulino.
22. Interview with Jeison Arias, March 6, 1996.
23. Interview with Mario Encarnacion, February 29, 1996.
24. Ibid.
25. Ibid.
26. Interview with Porfiria Gonzalez-Alvarez, February 29, 1996.
27. Interview with Juan Dilone, March 8, 1996.
28. Interview with Arturo Paulino, March 9, 1996.
29. Source: City of Modesto.
30. Interview with Alderson.
31. Interview with Dan Marchy, March 23, 1998.
32. Source: City of Ceres.
33. Ron Agostini, "Tejada Tears It Up for Li'l A's: Modesto Has a Jewel in Teen-age Shortstop from Dominican," *Modesto Bee*, May 21, 1996, p. C1.
34. Kristie Ackert, "Modesto's Tejada Out 4–6 Weeks," *Modesto Bee*, July 23, 1996, p. C2.

CHAPTER EIGHT

1. Interview with Murray.
2. Interview with Ron Plaza, March 15, 1996.
3. Interview with Miguel Rodriguez, September 20, 1996.
4. Interview with Clemente Sosa, September 2, 1996.
5. Interview with Jose Santana, September 2, 1996.
6. Interview with Santana.
7. Ramona Hernanez and Francisco Rivera-Batiz, *Dominican New Yorkers: A Socioeconomic Profile*, City University of New York; Columbia University, 1997.
8. Interview with Santana.
9. James Traub, *The New Republic*, January 27, 1997, p. 12.
10. Interview with Jorge Moreno, August 31, 1996.
11. "Major League Beisbol," *ESPN Outside the Lines*, aired July 22, 1997.
12. Interview with Victor Martinez, September 9, 1996.
13. Ibid.
14. Interview with Moises Perez, September 5, 1996.
15. Interview with Tony McDonald, August 31, 1996.
16. Interview with Ron Clark, September 23, 1996.
17. Interview with McDonald.
18. Interview with Balderson.
19. Interview with Rafael Avila, September 20, 1996.

CHAPTER NINE

1. Interview with Martinez.
2. Interview with Felipe Alou, July 27, 1993.
3. Steve Kettman, "Spring Training Notebook," *San Francisco Chronicle*, March 6, 1997, p. D7.
4. Robert Kunada, "A's Notebook," *San Jose Mercury News*, March 17, 1997, p. 3D.
5. Pedro Gomez, "A's Display Faith After 5–4 Victory," *Sacramento Bee*, August 1, 1996, p. D3.
6. Source: City of Huntsville.
7. Interview with Mike Quade, July 18, 1997.
8. Source: Major League Baseball.
9. Frank Blackman, "Cactus League Beat," *San Francisco Examiner*, March 20, 1998, p. D7.

INDEX